THE CONSTITUTION UNDER PRESSURE

A Time for Change

THE CONSTITUTION UNDER PRESSURE

A Time for Change

MARCIA LYNN WHICKER,
RUTH ANN STRICKLAND, AND
RAYMOND A. MOORE

PRAEGER

New York
Westport, Connecticut
London

Library of Congress Cataloging-in-Publication Data

Whicker, Marcia Lynn.
    The constitution under pressure.

    Bibliography: p.
    Includes index.
    1. United States—Constitutional law.   2. United
States—Constitutional law—Amendments.   3. Law and
politics.   I. Strickland, Ruth Ann.   II. Moore, Raymond A.
III. Title.
KF4550.W47   1987   342.73′029   87-13178
ISBN 0-275-92703-2 (alk. paper) 347.30229
ISBN 0-275-92704-0 (pbk. : alk. paper)

Library of Congress Catalog Card Number: 87-13178
ISBN: 0-275-92703-2
ISBN: 0-275-92704-0 (pbk.)

First published in 1987.

Praeger Publishers, One Madison Avenue, New York, NY 10010
A division of Greenwood Press, Inc.

Printed in the United States of America

The paper used in this book complies with the
Permanent Paper Standard issued by the National
Information Standards Organization (Z39.48-1984).

10 9 8 7 6 5 4 3 2 1

Contents

Chapter Seven

Chapter Eight

Tables

Acknowledgments

Until August of 1986 when Marcia Whicker moved to Virginia Commonwealth University, all three of the co-authors were associated with the Department of Government and International Studies at the University of South Carolina. There they worked in close collaboration with each other and with departmental colleagues. Especially helpful were M. Glenn Abernathy who contributed greatly to our understanding of the Supreme Court and judicial reform, and our two Chairs, Earl Black and William Mishler, who allowed us generous access to computers, word processors, printers, and most of all our competent and cooperative secretarial staff. Sandra Hall and Barbara Anderson were always helpful in meeting our requests and Harriet Bradham, Becky Deaton, Lori Joye, Sophia Kennedy and Emma Jean Kokesh were always willing and efficient in carrying out those requests.

Miles Richards, a graduate student of history at the university, helped draft our historical chapter, and Ruth Gottlieb Moore proof-read and edited the entire manuscript twice over with diligence and skill. We are most thankful to all for their considerable help and guidance.

The authors would also like to express their thanks to those who over the years have helped shape their ideas on politics and the Constitution. Marcia Whicker would especially like to pay tribute to Tom Cronin for stimulating a life-long interest in U.S. politics and government, and to Malcolm Jewell for providing a panoramic intellectual understanding of legislatures.

Ruth Ann Strickland is indebted to her family, Tom, Shirley and Larry Strickland, for supporting her throughout her undergraduate and graduate endeavors and for encouraging her to succeed.

Raymond Moore would like to acknowledge long-standing intellectual debts to William T. R. Fox and David Truman who first excited his interest in foreign policy and U. S. politics at Columbia University during the golden years of the old department of Public Law and Government in the decade after World War II.

Introduction

We are living in a time of bicentennial celebrations. The first was the 1976 bicentennial tribute to the signing of the Declaration of Independence. We celebrated with tall ships, massive displays of fireworks and a recommitment to the spirit of independence. In 1987 came the celebration of the Constitutional Convention of 1787. 1989 marks the two hundredth birthday of the ratification of the Constitution by the states and 1991 is the anniversary of the adoption of the Bill of Rights.

To help celebrate these auspicious occasions, numerous plans have been developed and undertakings launched across the country, including, at the presidential level, a commission to commemorate these historic events. The chief justice of the U.S. Supreme Court, Warren Burger, even resigned his judicial appointment to chair this commission. Activities surrounding the bicentennial celebrations have ranged from the intellectual and analytical to the symbolic. Learned bodies have addressed the question of how well the Constitution has withstood the test of time. Mock constitutional conventions have been held with modern students playing the parts of the constitutional framers. The Statue of Liberty, amidst great fanfare, was refurbished and given an impressive birthday party.

The prestigious Committee on the Constitutional System, headed by Nancy Landon Kassebaum, Lloyd N. Cutler and C. Douglas Dillon, undertook an assessment of the Constitution and how well it works. A group of over two hundred prominent citizens discussed the problems of modern governance and evaluated various proposed reforms. Some of their proposals called for changes in party rules for nominating candidates, some for federal statutes to funnel campaign finances through the parties and others for draft constitutional amendments designed to synchronize the terms of national elected officials, including congressmen, senators and the president.

Never has the time been more propitious to examine the basic fundamental structures of U.S. government. If we no longer wish to water the tree of liberty with the blood of martyrs every twenty years, as Thomas Jefferson once suggested, then surely we should undertake a thorough, meticulous and thoughtful reexamination of our constitutional system. Although the Constitution has been amended twenty-six times, most of the amendments have not altered the fundamental structure of government, but rather have expanded individual civil liberties. Of the seven constitutional amendments which clearly altered the structure of government, most refined relatively minor imperfections rather than implementing massive institutional change. Essentially, the system of separation of powers, checks and balances, and federalism developed by the framers remains intact.

Now is the time for the nation to see the totality of the Constitution and its impact in the context of the modern era. Can it govern as well in an era of microchips, supersonic transport, satellites, intercontinental ballistic missiles, robots, artificial intelligence and life sustaining medical support systems as it did in an era of small farms, yeomanry, horse-drawn plows and buggies, cheap land, seemingly endless frontiers and slave labor? The challenges of the modern day have globalized problems and impinged upon the narrow rights of national sovereignty. The question we are left with is this: if the Constitution has served us passingly well for two hundred years, will it do so for another two hundred? If the answer is no, in totality or in part, what changes should we adopt?

This book explores the role that the Constitution has played in shaping government and political representation in the United States. The forces which influenced the development of the Constitution are examined, as well as major trends in its interpretation. The process of amending the Constitution is analyzed, as are the major reforms suggested to cope with modern pressures. In tribute to the iconoclastic spirit of the original Revolution, revolutionary reforms as well as more traditional proposals to restructure political parties and to move toward a parliamentary system are analyzed. Original, innovative and unique proposals for functional as well as geographic representation are considered.

Chapter One

Constitutional Conflicts: The 1787 Convention

BRITISH MISRULE IN THE COLONIAL UNITED STATES

Conflict, not consensus, surrounded the separation of the United States from England and the founding of its Constitution. Perhaps the biggest conflict arose over whether the United States would become a separate country at all. While many colonists (called Revolutionaries or Patriots) favored the break with the mother country, the Royalists or Tories, who were often members of the colonial elite, did not. The forces which led to the Revolution in 1776 were complex.

Contributing to dissent over English rule was a shift in attitudes held by the elite in the British Empire toward the colonies. Until the late 1700s, mercantilism had been the predominant economic policy employed under British colonial rule. Under mercantilism, the colonies were used as markets and sources of raw materials. Political control was mainly used to achieve those economic objectives. The British Navigation Acts, passed between 1660 and 1696, embodied the prevailing philosophy of mercantilism and included three main principles: all trade with plantations in the colonies must be in English ships or colonial ships manned by English or colonial crews; certain designated commodities, such as tobacco, sugar, indigo, rice, cotton and naval supplies, could only be shipped to England; and colonies could only receive imports from Britain.

In the late 1770s, British economic policy shifted toward a policy of imperialism. Imperialism involved greater political and financial control over the colonies and increased use of British military power to impose greater taxation and economic regulation. The shift toward imperialism adversely affected the interests of most colonists, including lawyers, merchants and landowners. Perceiving economic ruin for themselves if the policies of imperialism were sustained, many colonists began a long-standing debate with the British over the nature of the Empire's constitutional system and the severity of tax and trade regulations. Although the elite merchants and landowners originally attacked British rule, they eventually shifted their support from the Patriots to the British. (There were a few notable exceptions, however, particularly in Virginia.)

Another source of dissent with British rule stemmed from early experience with colonial political institutions. Each colony had an assembly in which at least one chamber was elected. These legislatures provided the colonists with a taste of self-governance, a taste the early colonial elite found wholly to their liking. Colonial assemblies were frequently quite active and managed their own affairs, occasionally restrained by royal instructions. Their activity and independence sometimes led colonial governors, appointed by the English crown, to complain of their headstrong nature and inclination to ignore official edicts. Many of the founders of the United States and its early leaders honed their leadership skills in pre-revolutionary political roles. Notable among these were Thomas Jefferson, Samuel Adams, John Adams, James Madison and Roger Sherman.

Contributing to the sense of self-efficacy of the colonists and their willingness to assert self-governance through their elected assemblies was the haphazard nature of the British administration of colonial affairs. The primary interests of the British in the United States had always been economic rather than political. This contributed to the inattentiveness of British officials to colonial political interests. No one agency or institution within British government was responsible for governing the U.S. colonies; rather, rule was dispersed across six institutions—the Secretary of State for the Southern Department, the Privy Council, the Treasury and Customs Office, the Board of Trade, the Admiralty and the Parliament. Not until the eve of the Revolution did Britain recognize the flaws in this decentralized administrative structure.

The British secretary of state appointed colonial governors. British secretaries of state were usually competent but typically were poorly informed about colonial affairs. While they theoretically retained control of the actions of colonial governors, in reality they gave very little attention to the governors' activities after they were appointed, confining their interests mainly to military affairs, foreign policy and piracy.

The Board of Trade handled affairs relating to commerce and trade. This body was theoretically advisory in nature but was more involved in colonial governance than any of the other British agencies. Its duties were many. It instructed colonial governors on all domestic questions. While it had no formal power to remove governors, it was instrumental in deposing governors that did not adhere to instructions from the board. The board had the power to disallow legislation passed by colonial legislatures and did so over 400 times between 1696 and the beginning of the U.S. Revolution. It was often sluggish in the performance of this duty, sometimes disallowing colonial laws years after they went into effect. While this control remained one of the few checks that the British retained over colonial government, its application—especially its seemingly arbitrary nature—contributed to colonial dissatisfaction with British rule. Some argue that this function of legislative disallowance exercised by the British Board of Trade set a precedent for the later exercise of judicial review by the U.S. Supreme Court.

The Privy Council reviewed colonial court cases and also disallowed colonial laws. It was assisted by the Board of Trade which advised it on disputed questions of fact or policy. The Treasury and Customs Commissioners in the British government collected colonial taxes and enforced navigation laws. The High Court of Admiralty created vice admiralty courts within the colonies which ruled in marine and trade disputes. The rulings of these courts formed the body of U.S. admiralty law which was later adopted by federal courts under the Constitution.

The British Parliament passed acts that controlled the economic life of the colonies. Among these were the Woolens Act of 1699, the Hat Act of 1733 and the Iron Act of 1750. In other acts, the British Parliament set up an intercolonial post office, fixed the value of foreign coins in the colonies and forbade the production of paper money by the colonies. In 1764 Parliament passed the Sugar Act which taxed a variety of imports into the colonies, including sugar, indigo, wine, calico, linen and coffee. This act represented a shift on the part of Parliament from using colonial taxes for regulating trade to using them as a source of British revenue.

While the colonies were still reacting to the Sugar Act, Parliament passed another revenue measure in the Stamp Act of 1765. Its economic and commercial ramifications in the colonies were so great that colonists began to question the powers of Parliament. As a protest against British taxes in general some Boston citizens dumped tea into the Boston Harbor. The tea they threw overboard was being imported by the East India Company and was subject to new taxes. Parliament retaliated by passing a series of acts implementing a punitive trade policy and military rule. Among these were the Boston Port Act and the Quartering Acts of 1774.

British administration of the U.S. colonies was haphazard, inattentive and decentralized. This ultimately contributed to the growth of colonial discontent with British rule. The British attempted to strictly regiment colonial economic life but did not accompany the regimentation with planning, political strategizing or diplomacy. When the British did recognize that they had been excessive in ignoring colonial demands, particularly in the areas of taxation and commerce, the concessions that were made were not implemented in a manner that restored good will among the colonists toward the British. This lack of diplomacy and coordination precipitated increased protest among the colonists until the battle of Lexington on April 19, 1775. With "a shot that was heard around the world," the U.S. Revolution began.

THE ABORTED CONSTITUTION

During the Revolution, the country was governed by provincial congresses and the Continental Congress. These were ad hoc revolutionary bodies. The Continental Congress encouraged the formation of state governments and the adoption of state constitutions. Between 1776 and 1780 all but two of the former colonies adopted new state constitutions. In the remaining two, Rhode Island and Connecticut, the old colonial charters were accepted as viable forms of government and lasted into the next century. States differed as to whether or not constitutional conventions were to be called to adopt the new state constitutions. In three states, South Carolina, Virginia and New Jersey, the state legislatures drafted their respective constitutions without asking for any new authority from the population. In the other states, including New York, North Carolina, Delaware, Maryland, Pennsylvania and Georgia, elections were held for new state congresses which drafted the new state constitutions as well as attending to legislative matters. None of these states submitted their new constitutions to their citizens for popular approval. An exception to this legislative adoption for new state constitutions occurred in Massachusetts where the provincial congress formulated a constitution and submitted it to the people. The citizens rejected the first draft. The provincial congress then formulated a second draft which did win popular support.

Many of these state constitutions had a bill of rights protecting individual freedoms from government oppression. Outstanding among these was the Virginia Bill of Rights which contained the doctrine of natural rights, the right to revolution and the contract theory of the state. Religious freedoms received some protection as well. All of the new state constitutions extended equal political rights to Protestant groups. Some went further and extended political rights to all Christians, including Catholics. The constitutions of New York, New Jersey, Pennsylvania, Virginia and the Carolinas prohibited compulsory support of any church. In addition to their bills of rights many of the new state constitutions incorporated the principle of separation of powers. In comparison to colonial government the new state constitutions were somewhat more democratic than the charters they succeeded (Kelly and Harbison 1976; McLaughlin 1935).

By 1775 Ben Franklin, among others, recognized the need for a government to coordinate activities among the former colonies. Franklin submitted a document called the Articles of Confederation and Perpetual Union to the Continental Congress. In 1777 a compromise version was adopted by Congress. The compromise established a confederacy which provided for the independence of each state. Ratification was needed by every state to make the articles binding. Final state ratification occurred in March 1781. The primary effect of the Articles of Confederation was to legalize an ad hoc form of government that had developed before 1781.

Under the articles Congress retained a broad range of powers, including war powers, oversight of foreign affairs, authority to decide territorial disputes among the states, to coin money and to establish a post office. Each state received one vote on legislative issues. Across the following years a few modest successes occurred under the governmental structure established by the Articles of Confederation. Foremost among these was the fact that the states were able to expand their territories during this period. However, in those few areas where the Congress did receive authority to act from the articles, passing legislation proved difficult because it required the affirmative vote of nine out of thirteen of the confederate states.

More important than the powers Congress received were the powers that the articles denied Congress. Among these were the powers to levy taxes and to regulate commerce. Several weaknesses resulted. The Confederation spent much of its short life in financial chaos. Since the Congress had no authority to levy taxes, it had no authority by which to eradicate the large public war debt. Attempts to create a national bank failed. The Bank of North America was created in 1781 but was soon rechartered in the state of Pennsylvania when its status under the confederacy was questioned. Since the Continental Congress was incapable of regulating commerce, it was not able to construct a coherent national economic policy. Trade and commerce wars between the states went unhampered by intervention from the confederate government.

Nor did the articles provide for a clearly defined national executive. What executive power did exist was held by a series of congressionally-appointed committees designed to deal with various problems, such as the Committee on Finance and the Committee on Foreign Affairs. Often the duties and functions of the various committees overlapped, creating confusion. Under this highly decentralized system, no one person could be held accountable for government policy or actions. The multiplicity of committees made the development of policy difficult and the coordination of those policies that did emerge almost impossible.

Also missing from the Articles of Confederation were provisions for a federal judiciary. The judicial power to settle interstate disputes was vested in the Confederate Congress. During the Confederacy period Congress settled six such disputes, including a case between Connecticut and Pennsylvania over claims to what is presently western Pennsylvania. Congress was given the authority to establish informal ad hoc courts to assist it in the settlement of interstate disputes. The decisions of the ad hoc courts carried the force of law just like an act of Congress. Congress could establish similar courts to deal with private controversies involving disputes over land grants from two or more different states. The articles also gave Congress the power to set up courts to try high seas crimes including piracy and felonies at sea.

Under the articles, states fulfilled many government functions. This decentralized method of service delivery was often unsatisfactory, however. States frequently proved irresponsible in enforcing confederate law. Congressional laws were interpreted by the state courts, and in some cases state courts refused to recognize any laws that did not originate within their own jurisdictions.

The period of the Confederacy was one of trial and tribulation. The decentralized structure of the new government proved inadequate in dealing with the financial pressures and social unrest created by the Revolution, nor was it particularly successful in abating interstate jealousies. The industrial and commercial confusion of the times contributed to the general chaos. From the beginning, one constant and central problem was how to raise revenues for the elimination of Revolutionary War debts and for the continuation of government operations. Interest on foreign and domestic debts incurred by the new Congress was reaching staggering levels. Paper monies issued by the various states contributed to the financial confusion.

George Washington, among others, lamented the social unrest of the times and feared that he and his cohorts might live to see another revolution. The fears of the propertied elite were further fueled in 1786 by an outbreak of domestic violence in Massachusetts. In an incident led by Daniel Shays called Shays' Rebellion, a group of farmers rebelled against the prosecution of debt cases in that state. These farmers armed and disrupted court proceedings to prevent foreclosure on their mortgages. They also tried to force the passage of inflationary legislation in the state assembly. The rebellion died when the farmers were killed from a cannon barrage levied at them by state authorities. Although Shays' Rebellion was short-lived, it sent a message to the political leadership that the machinery of government needed to be strengthened. As a result, seven states appointed delegates to attend a convention in

Philadelphia in 1787, and a new era of U.S. constitutional government began.

THE DELEGATES TO THE 1787 CONVENTION

Seventy-five delegates were appointed but only fifty-five of them attended the 1787 Convention. Of those fifty-five, a dozen dominated the proceedings. Those delegates who did not attend gave a variety of reasons for their absence. Eleven of the twenty disapproved of the convention and considered it rigged from the start. The remaining delegates offered various excuses: some were ill, others could not afford the trip, and some had urgent conflicting personal business. One reluctant delegate was George Washington, who cited bad health and disarray in his personal finances as excuses for not attending. His compatriot, James Madison, persuaded Washington to attend anyway, and Washington became the presiding officer of the convention. Although he took little direct part in the proceedings, he did serve as a moderator of conflict.

Several prominent figures in politics at the time did not attend the 1787 Convention. They included Thomas Jefferson, Aaron Burr and John Adams. Thomas Jefferson was not a major proponent of the new Constitution. He had served as the revolutionary governor of Virginia, was a member of the Continental Congress and had been foreign minister to France. He later became the first secretary of state of the United States, vice president and subsequently president, serving two terms. His attitude toward the Constitution was one of ambivalence. Jefferson was displeased with the omission of a Bill of Rights or the fact that officials, especially presidents, could succeed themselves without rotation. Nor did Jefferson believe that the founders could possibly devise a Constitution which would forever meet the nation's needs, and he thought that the independence of the courts was dangerous.

Aaron Burr was a pessimist who predicted that the Constitution would collapse within fifty years. During the framing of the Constitution, Burr was politically inactive. He did not oppose the creation of the new Constitution, although he had grave doubts about its functional capabilities. These doubts, however, did not prevent him from holding office under its framework. Later, Burr became a U.S. senator in 1791 and served two terms in the New York state legislature. In 1800 he was elected vice president. Burr was later accused of treason when he led an armed expedition down the upper Ohio River and Mississippi toward New Orleans. Jefferson and others feared that he wished to sever the Southwest from the rest of the country. Burr was captured in the wilderness and brought to trial in Virginia under Chief Justice John Marshall in one of the most sensational trials of the century. He was found not guilty but his role in U.S. politics was over.

John Adams was another prominent politician of the day who did not attend the 1787 Convention. A leading revolutionary of the time, he was the U.S. minister to London during the gathering in Philadelphia and therefore could not be present. He nonetheless provided a detailed critique of the new Constitution in private correspondence with several prominent delegates. He feared that government would in effect become a game of leapfrog played by factions that leaped over each other's backs every decade. Adams thought that the president's lack of power over Congress would produce instability. Like Jefferson and Burr, however, his doubts about the new government and its Constitution did not prevent him from holding high office under its framework. Adams was the first vice president and the second president of the United States.

Another prominent figure who was to subsequently write five Federalist Papers in support of Constitutional ratification was John Jay. He was a member of the New York delegation but did not attend the convention. Jay was older than Alexander Hamilton and James Madison, the other two contributors to the Federalist Papers. At the time of the 1787 Constitutional Convention and the subsequent fight over ratification, he was a distinguished and prosperous lawyer in New York. He also had an outstanding record of public service. He had written the New York Constitution of 1777 which served as a source of ideas for the 1787 Convention and helped negotiate the Treaty of 1783 which brought final independence to the United States. Jay also served as secretary of foreign affairs under the aborted confederate government.

The delegates who did attend the 1787 Convention were predominantly lawyers and politicians. Of the fifty-five, thirty-three were lawyers. The past political credentials of the delegates were impressive: forty-four were present or past members of Congress; forty-six had held political office in their home states; seven were either present or former state governors; and five were high state judges. Many of the delegates further developed their political careers after the 1787 Convention, establishing even more impressive political credentials. No less than twenty-seven became members of Congress. Two were future presidents, one a future vice president, one a Speaker of the House of Representatives, four were future U.S. district judges, and five subsequently served as justices of the U.S. Supreme Court.

The list of distinguished delegates is long. In addition to George Washington, two of the most notable were James Madison and Alexander Hamilton. Madison has come to be recognized as a brilliant political thinker who provided leadership and made some of the greatest contributions to Constitutional concepts and philosophy. Madison is sometimes called the Father of the Constitution. He was the floor leader and one of the most effective delegates. He could and did speak with eloquence, skill and cogency. Historians were later indebted to the detailed notes that Madison took during the Constitutional Convention to develop a fuller understanding of its operations and outcomes.

Unlike most of the other delegates, Madison did not own a great deal of property. Nor was he a lawyer. Rather, he was a philosopher and an expert on government. Madison had been elected to the Orange County, Virginia, Revolutionary Committee at age twenty-three. Subsequently he was elected a member of the Virginia convention which requested that the Continental Congress declare independence from Britain. He also served on the Virginia Council of State, the Annapolis Convention of 1786 and the U.S. House of Representatives. Madison served as Jefferson's secretary of state and later became the fourth president of the United States.

As a youth Madison was educated by his preacher father. He later attended the College of New Jersey, a Presbyterian college which later became Princeton University. When he left college he continued to study in the areas of theology and public law. Throughout his life Madison was a diligent reader who studied so much that some felt he had damaged his health with his overzealous intellectual inquiries. Despite this criticism from his less intellectual peers, Madison died in 1836 at age eighty-five, the last survivor of the 1787 delegates.

His opposite in style and talent was Alexander Hamilton. Born in the West Indies, Hamilton was illegitimate and was abandoned by his father at the age of twelve. His mother had died while he was young. He had to fend for himself, working for merchants in the West Indies ports. He proved to be such a quick study that a preacher raised funds for Hamilton to travel to the continental United States to complete his education. Hamilton enrolled in Kings College, which later became Columbia University, but dropped out after a year to engage in revolutionary activities. In addition to making fiery speeches, he produced two major pamphlets on the need for revolution. His subsequent marriage to a young heiress from the Schuyler family of New York transformed Hamilton from a young radical to a spokesperson for propertied interests. Unlike Madison, the quintessential political thinker, Hamilton was rumored to be a master partisan politician, yet he failed to exercise influence in the Constitutional Convention proportionate to his national reputation. The main reason was that Hamilton's views supporting centralized government were out of line with the sentiments of a majority of the delegates. As one of three members of the New York delegation, he was consistently outvoted by the other two members, John Lansing and Robert Yates. Often regarded by his contemporaries as impetuous, Hamilton died an untimely death in a duel with Aaron Burr.

Ben Franklin, also a Constitutional Convention delegate, exhibited such a broad range of talents that some have described him as a Renaissance man. He was known worldwide as a statesman and a scientist. Throughout his life he had been a diplomat, a publisher and the editor of a collection of homilies known as *Poor Richard's Almanac.* In addition, he had flirted with international business leaders as well as with numerous women. Franklin had been a member of the Second Colonial Congress at Albany, New York, as early as 1754. At that time, he suggested a centralized union of the colonies but his prescient ideas proved premature. During the time of the Constitutional Convention, Franklin was, perhaps, past his prime. At age eighty-two he still remained active, but had lost some of his earlier mental sharpness. His rambling speeches were felt to miss the point of discussion and to contain little of immediate practical value. Franklin died at eighty-five in 1790, three years after the Convention.

James Wilson was also a delegate from Pennsylvania. A legal theorist, he became a strong supporter of an effective national government founded on a popular electoral base. It was Wilson who suggested the electoral college when he saw that the Convention was unwilling to embrace his ideas for direct popular rule. After the Convention, Wilson lectured in law at the University of Pennsylvania until Washington appointed him associate justice to the U.S. Supreme Court.

Numerous other delegates deserve mention. Roger Sherman, a delegate from Connecticut, had been a shoemaker and a lawyer. He served one of the longest tenures in the Continental Congress and later opposed the Bill of Rights, arguing that any government which wished to violate the civil liberties of its citizens would do so anyway. George Mason, a delegate from Virginia, was an outstanding liberal of the eighteenth century. A good friend of Thomas Jefferson, Mason authored the Virginia Declaration of Rights in 1776. He refused to sign the final version of the Constitution on the grounds that it was too aristocratic. Edmund Randolph of Virginia was the author of one of the major proposals before the convention: the Virginia Plan, which required representation based on population and was biased in favor of the large states.

Luther Martin of Maryland was a champion of states' rights and state sovereignty and espoused anti-majoritarian views during the convention. Fortunately for his opponents and unfortunately for all of the delegates who had to suffer through his speeches, which sometimes lasted for hours, his public speaking was disjointed and rambling. Although later he performed brilliantly in the trial of Aaron Burr, drunkenness subsequently caused the demise of his career.

A New Jersey delegate, William Patterson, proposed the New Jersey plan which favored small states by requiring two national representatives per state regardless of state population. Elbridge Gerry of Massachusetts, like many of his colleagues, feared popular control of governmental machinery but inconsistently refused to sign the final Constitutional draft because he felt it was too aristocratic. Gerry was a masterful and manipulative politician who lent his name to the term "gerrymandering," the drawing of legislative boundaries to maximize partisan election potential.

One South Carolina delegate was Charles Pinckney. He came from a well-established southern family and was only twenty-nine at the time of the convention. He championed the cause of counting slaves for representation, a position clearly advantageous to the South. He also argued that no constitutional limitation should be placed on imports. Pinckney spoke frequently at the convention, including several speeches against the Bill of Rights, but most of his ideas had little impact. By contrast, John Rutledge headed the South Carolina delegation and was an effective and established politician. He had headed the revolutionary party in South Carolina, had helped draft that state's constitution in 1776 and had served as governor. Rutledge supported effective national government, but also spent much time defending established southern interests by arguing for representation based on wealth.

Now glorified in history books and made to appear bigger than life with the passage of time, these delegates to the 1787 Convention possessed a cornucopia of talents, skills, views, philosophies and passions. The delegates differed on much, yet from these differences they managed to rise above parochial concerns to fashion a new Constitution for a new nation. It represented a bold new concept of self-governance rarely tried in the history of the world. The document they created embodied great compromises between conflictual factions, nor were opponents and neutrals to many of the final compromises subsequently penalized, for opponents and proponents both held high office in the fledgling country. Even proponents of the final compromises left the Convention somewhat disgruntled—hopeful in their hearts that the Constitution would provide a successful framework for governing the newly independent, heterogeneous and sometimes unruly states, yet fearful that it would not.

THE RULES OF THE 1787 CONVENTION

The 1787 Convention was in session for four months, from May 14 to September 11. As is the case in any legislative proceeding, the rules of 1787 had some impact on the final outcome. When the delegates arrived in Philadelphia in May of 1787 they first discussed the rules that would govern the convention proceedings. The most important rule on which they agreed was the procedure by which voting would occur. The convention decided to use the same voting procedure as that employed by the U.S. Congress. The thirteen states had one vote each, regardless of the size of the state. The several members from each state delegation voted among themselves to determine how their state vote would be cast.

The delegates from the larger states, particularly Pennsylvania, were dissatisfied with this procedure since smaller states had the same voting power as larger states. The Virginia delegates stifled attempts to abolish unit voting. While Virginia was a large state, its delegates were fearful that attempts to change the voting system to one based on state population would release unbridled conflict and would undermine the entire convention before it began. The Virginians privately (and futilely) hoped that small states would give up their voting prerogatives in the interest of effective governing.

A second major rule which affected posterity as well as the convention and its delegates was a rule of secrecy. Although there was some dissent, the rule of secrecy was readily adopted by the delegates who argued that it would increase their candor and foster more informed and impassioned debate. This rule meant that the convention proceedings would not be published. While an official journal was kept, no one could make copies of the journal without official permission of the entire delegation. Remarkably, this rule was rigidly observed, not only by the delegates themselves, but also by the press and the public. Most of the delegates refused to divulge convention debates and activities even to their best friends. Some historians feel that this secrecy enabled the convention to flourish and write the new Constitution as it had set out to do. Anti-nationalists felt that the delegate selection process was biased against them in favor of the nationalists, and the secrecy rule reinforced their alienation. The anti-nationalists felt that the secrecy rule was designed to keep them in the dark, preventing them from acting against the convention while it met.

The delegates also agreed upon rules of decorum to govern activities during convention proceedings. Delegates were not to whisper, read or pass messages while one of their peers was speaking. As interesting as the rules that the delegates adopted, however, were the rules they failed to adopt. The delegates rejected a rule which would have allowed any member of the convention to demand a recorded roll call vote. This allowed the delegates to change their minds on issues as often and as freely as they wished. They could feel secure in the knowledge that their positions on issues and shifts in those positions would be secure, not only from posterity, but from immediate scrutiny as well.

THE CONFLICT BETWEEN BIG AND SMALL STATES

The opening battle after the rules were adopted focused on the basis for representation in the new national legislature. Two opposing plans were presented—the Virginia Plan which favored big states, and the New Jersey Plan which favored small states. The Virginia Plan was sponsored by Edmund Randolph, a delegate from that state. It called for a bicameral national legislature to replace the ineffective unicameral legislature which existed under the Articles of Confederation. A lower house would be elected directly by the people. Representation in this branch would be based on population. Nominations for the upper house would be submitted by the various state legislatures. Final election of the upper house would occur within the lower house. The Virginia Plan also called for significant expansion of the powers of the national legislature over those currently held by the Continental Congress. Among these powers would be the supremacy of national law over any state law.

The most difficult and controversial part of the Virginia Plan was that which made both houses of the new Congress proportionate to the population of each state. Under the Virginia Plan, the heavily populated and richer states would have been able to dominate the smaller states. This proposal, in particular, produced conflict. Coalitions among states were formed to oppose this resolution. Particularly opposed were Maryland, Connecticut, Delaware, New York and New Jersey. Opposing coalitions, however, were not based strictly on population, since the least populous states were Georgia, Rhode Island, Delaware and New Hampshire. Interestingly, one of the opposing states, New York, was moderately sized (see table 1-1).

Competing with the Virginia Plan was the New Jersey Plan which was offered by William Patterson, a New Jersey delegate. This plan was merely a modification of the Articles of Confederation and left intact much of the structure of the confederacy as well as the sovereignty of each state. Under the New Jersey Plan, Congress would acquire additional powers such as raising additional revenues by levying import duties, collecting stamp taxes, regulating commerce and forcing delinquent states to honor requisitions. All treaties and acts of Congress under the New Jersey Plan would have become the supreme law of the states and would have been enforceable in state courts. Some delegates noted that while the Virginia Plan sought to replace the confederacy of the Articles of Confederation with a strong national government, the New Jersey Plan was an extension of the confederacy. Proponents, later acknowledging that it was too little too late, were united only in their opposition to large state nationalism.

Table 1-1
1790 Population of the Thirteen Original States

STATE	1790 CENSUS *
Large States:	
Virginia	747,000
Massachusetts (incl. Maine)	474,000
Pennsylvania	434,000
North Carolina	393,000
Moderate Sized States:	
New York	340,000
Maryland	319,000
South Carolina	249,000
Connecticut	237,000
Small States:	
New Jersey	184,000
New Hampshire	141,000
Georgia	82,000
Rhode Island	68,000
Delaware	59,000

* Data from the U.S. Census, rounded to the nearest 1,000

In a Committee of the Whole, the New Jersey Plan was voted down seven to three. Its only supporters in the final vote were New York, New Jersey and Delaware. Opposed were Massachusetts, Connecticut, Pennsylvania, Virginia, North Carolina, South Carolina and Georgia. Yet many of the states which opposed the New Jersey Plan were also opposed to the Virginia Plan. Although the Virginia Plan was reported to the floor, considerable opposition existed to it there.

On June 29th the convention agreed that the lower house should be based on population, leaving unsettled the question of the basis of representation in the upper house. On July 2nd a vote was taken on the question of whether representation in the upper house should be proportional to population. Those espousing the interests of the small states managed to deadlock the vote five to five. A committee of eleven delegates was appointed to find a compromise. These eleven delegates were either moderates or supporters of state sovereignty.

The Connecticut delegation played a prominent role in fashioning what was eventually to be known as the Great Compromise or the Connecticut Compromise. Roger Sherman of Connecticut, although not on the committee, seems to have been the first to suggest that the upper house allow each state to have an equal vote, regardless of population.

On July 5th the committee reported a proposal which called for representation according to population in the lower house of the new Congress and an equal vote for each state in the upper house. In an attempt to appease the large states, the committee recommended that revenue bills should originate in the lower house where representation was based on population. The committee also recommended that the ratio of representatives to population in the lower house be one representative per forty thousand inhabitants, resulting in sixty-five seats among the thirteen states. Madison unsuccessfully tried to double the number of representatives.

On July 11th the convention decided on a number of issues related to representation. It was decided that the census would be the basis for determining population and for reapportioning the lower house seats, and that a slave would count as the equivalent of three-fifths of a citizen for the purpose of representation. Finally, on July 16th, a vote was taken on the Great Compromise, which proposed equal representation in the Senate and proportionate representation in the House. The compromise succeeded by a narrow margin of five to four. Voting for it were Connecticut, New Jersey, Delaware, Maryland and North Carolina. Opposed were Pennsylvania, Virginia, South Carolina and Georgia. Massachusetts was divided. The swing vote was North Carolina whose delegation switched to support the compromise at the last moment.

The implications of the Connecticut Compromise for the nature of representation in the new country were significant. The Connecticut Compromise resulted in the House of Representatives being elected on the basis of population while states were given an equal vote in the Senate. This compromise has lasted across two centuries. Among major democratic nations around the world, the United States remains unique in having such a powerful upper house where the basis for representation is skewed against proportionate representation. Thus history drives destiny.

OTHER CONFLICTS DEALING WITH REPRESENTATION

That the new government would be a representative one was not a question at the convention. The founders rejected pure or simple democracy where people make direct decisions. The size and population of the nation made direct democracy infeasible. Yet more than pragmatic concerns about technical limitations fed the delegates' distrust of direct popular control. Many were fearful that direct democracy would result in disorder and confusion as crafty orators and demagogues would cause citizens to forsake their independent judgements. By contrast, representative government would offer two benefits. It would allow the existence of a national government over a much larger territory and population than would otherwise be possible. It would also give citizens some expression in public outcomes but would cause their views to be refined through the medium of delegates chosen for their wisdom and ability to discern the best interests of the country. In short, representative structure would provide regulation of otherwise unfettered public expression.

Several issues concerning representation, in addition to the controversy over the representative basis for the upper house, had to be resolved by the 1787 Convention. The first was how many houses or chambers the new Congress would have. The pattern of two house legislatures had already been established in colonial assemblies at the time of the Convention. In the pre-revolutionary period, the upper house typically represented royal authority, while the lower house represented colonial interests. A major purpose of this colonial structure was to balance aristocratic and popular interests. A similar motive prompted the 1787 delegates to propose a two-house national assembly. A second purpose of the bicameral legislature was to limit the passage of new legislation, hopefully screening out ill-formed or ill-advised statutes.

The decision that the basis for representation in the upper house would be equal in power for each state did not, however, resolve the issue of who would select upper house representatives. The delegates resolved this issue by granting the power to elect members of the upper chamber of the national assembly to the respective state legislatures. Proponents argued that given the popular election of state legislatures, it was improbable that they, in turn, would select national senators who were incompatible with the majority popular views; however, state legislative selection did place a buffer between the citizens and their national senators, biasing the upper house toward elite interests. This system of selection remained in place for over 120 years.

How long should representatives serve in the new national assembly? The delegates wanted the representatives to be accountable, but were afraid that too much accountability would undermine rational debate and deliberation. Six-year terms for the Senate were adopted by the Convention to partially free the members of the upper house from constant popular pressure. Two-year terms were adopted for the House of Representatives, however, to keep lower chamber members close to the will of the people.

Perhaps the most controversial issue surrounding representation, other than the conflicts between large and small states over the basis of Senate representation, was the question of the population base to be used for determining the number of representatives from each state to serve in the lower chamber. Some delegates from the South wanted to count all slaves in the population base for representation. Northerners responded angrily. On what criteria, they asked, could such an action be justified? Would slaves then become citizens? If not, would they continue to be property? Could property be a legitimate basis for distributing representatives in the lower house?

A delegate from North Carolina, William R. Davie, insisted that a slave should at least count for three-fifths of a citizen in the computations for representation. Davie contended that unless his demands were met, North Carolina would never join the union. Another delegate, Gouvernor Morris of Pennsylvania, responded that taxation and representation should be based on the same computation. Morris's suggestion was accepted as a compromise. Three-fifths of the total slave population would be counted for both representation and taxation. The implications of this compromise for representation were immediate and clear. The implications for taxation were less clear. Did the three-fifths requirement apply to direct or indirect taxes, or to both? As the resolution was phrased, it referred to direct taxes. Most of the taxation of that period, however, was indirect, including taxes on imports and excise taxes.

Related to the question of how slaves would count for representation was a bitter conflict between northern and southern delegates over the importation of slaves. If the importation of slaves continued, those states who imported more would gain increased representation in the lower house as a result. Some southern delegates, especially Charles Pinckney and John Rutledge of South Carolina, adamantly demanded the right to continue to bring slaves into the country. Some northern delegates, especially Gouvernor Morris, bitterly opposed it. However, opposition to the importation of slaves and even to slavery itself also existed among some southern delegates. George Mason from Virginia and Luther Martin from Maryland were among those who gave impassioned speeches to the convention delegates against the evils of slavery.

Most of the New England delegates, including Roger Sherman and Oliver Ellsworth of Connecticut and Rufus King of Pennsylvania, were also opposed to continuation of the slave trade but were unwilling to disrupt the convention over the issue. Their reluctance helped to produce yet another compromise. The convention ultimately decided to tax rather than prohibit slave importation. A head tax of ten dollars was placed on each slave brought into the country. The possibility of ending slave importation after 1808 was written into the Constitution to appease anti-slavery sentiment.

CONFLICT OVER THE STRUCTURE
OF THE EXECUTIVE BRANCH

The great crisis of the 1787 Convention was over the structure of the national legislature. However, the delegates devoted even more time to problems associated with the structure of the executive branch, splitting into two camps on the issue of the national executive. One coalition, consisting of Roger Sherman, John Dickinson and Luther Martin, advocated a weak executive who would be chosen by and accountable to the national legislature. The views of the coalition supporting legislative supremacy were popular at the time.

Another coalition consisted of James Wilson, James Madison, Gouverneur Morris and Alexander Hamilton. This group preferred a powerful, independent executive chosen by direct popular vote. The emphasis on a strong, independent executive was inspired by and compatible with the doctrine of separation of powers, while the emphasis on legislative supremacy was incompatible. These two competing views clashed when the Committee of the Whole deliberated the Virginia Plan, which included a provision for an executive elected by Congress.

The strong sentiments against popular control espoused by many delegates during the debate over the Virginia Plan prompted James Wilson to propose the compromise solution of the electoral college. Under the electoral college each state legislature could dictate how electors would be selected within their own state, leaving open the possibility of selection by direct popular vote. Each elector, in turn, would vote for two national executive candidates. The candidate with the largest number of votes would become president if the leading candidate received a majority of votes. If the leading candidate did not receive a majority, the House would elect the president. The candidate with the second largest vote would become the vice-president.

Several principles were embodied in the adoption of a national president elected by an electoral college. House election in the absence of a simple majority was a direct concession to the advocates of legislative supremacy. Within a few years after the 1787 Convention, however, nearly all the states had passed laws requiring selection of electors by direct popular vote. In most instances, electors were reduced to figureheads. The principle of popular election of the national executive was eventually, if not initially, realized. The electoral college also represented a victory for the doctrine of separation of powers. If legislative ascendancy had prevailed, the president would have been an appendage of the Congress, and the United States would most likely have evolved into a parliamentary form of government. The Constitutional emphasis on separation of powers implemented by an independent president thwarted such an evolution.

One point of controversy raised by the Virginia Plan was whether or not the chief executive would be eligible for reelection. Under the original Virginia Plan, the president was ineligible for a second term. In floor debate after the Virginia Plan was introduced, delegates expressed fear that a national president, selected originally by Congress as the Virginia Plan specified and not eligible for reelection, would pander excessively to the parochial interests of Congress. Once an independent national executive was adopted, the issue of whether or not the president could be reelected receded in importance since an independent executive would be less likely to speak for any specific parochial interests. The Convention did not adopt a restriction on the number of terms a president could serve.

CONFLICT OVER THE STRUCTURE AND POWER OF THE FEDERAL JUDICIARY

Some agreement existed among the delegates on the establishment of a national Supreme Court as a court with final jurisdiction. However, disagreement surrounded most other aspects of the federal judiciary, including the method of selecting judges. The compromise adopted for the organization of the national executive also included a plan for the organization of the national judiciary. Initially, the Virginia Plan specified that judges would be elected by the legislative branch. Countering this proposal was a plan by the Federalists calling for the appointment of Supreme Court justices by the executive branch. Both camps wanted an independent judiciary, but disagreed over the appropriate appointment method and structure to assure independence. Most delegates were apparently influenced more by judicial practices within their home states than by theoretical arguments, and supported the compromise solution of nomination of Supreme Court justices by the president and approval by the Senate.

Additional debate surrounded the issue of lower courts. Two of the delegates, Rutledge of South Carolina and Sherman of Connecticut, were opposed to the establishment of a new set of courts. Rutledge favored creating only an additional Supreme Court. Sherman felt that a new set of courts would prove expensive and redundant with already existing state courts.

James Madison and James Wilson, among others, wanted additional lower federal courts to alleviate the number of appeals to the Supreme Court. Madison contended that an effective judiciary was as important to the political health of the new nation as an effective executive. However, the Committee of the Whole voted against the establishment of lower federal courts. Madison and Wilson did succeed in persuading the delegates to grant authority to the national legislature to establish lower federal courts as needed. Some delegates, including Butler from South Carolina, feared the states would revolt at even this modest encroachment of their judicial power. Such a revolt, however, did not materialize.

What was to be the power of the new Supreme Court? Madison and Wilson asked that the delegates debate whether or not the judiciary should be involved in the revision of laws. Madison believed that the power of the executive would be too limited if the judiciary assumed such a preeminent role. Madison argued that both should be involved in the revision of laws, and that checks and balances could be best maintained if the executive branch shared this power with the judicial branch.

Many of the delegates objected to this shared power in the belief that it would subvert the principle of separation of powers. Madison countered that the reason for separation of powers was to provide checks and balances, and that checks and balances in this instance could be better served by sharing the power of revision of laws. By a vote of eight to three, Madison was defeated in his attempt to persuade the Convention to make legal revision a power to be constitutionally shared between the executive and judicial branches. Ultimately the Constitution was mute on this point. Revolution of the issue awaited the assertion of the power of judicial review by the Supreme Court years later.

THE POLITICS OF RATIFICATION

The Constitutional Convention of 1787 adjourned on September 17. Some of the delegates to the convention anticipated lukewarm reception of the new Constitution by the Congress. Nevertheless, ten days later, an unenthusiastic Congress submitted the Constitution to the states. The various state legislatures had to set convention dates and issue calls for the election of delegates to consider the ratification of the proposed Constitution. In all the states except Rhode Island, opponents were unsuccessful in their efforts to delay or permanently postpone the calling of ratification conventions. Delegates in the twelve states convened to debate whether or not to adopt the new Constitution.

The ratification struggle lasted from September 1787 through July 1788. Federalists supported the new Constitution; Anti-Federalists did not. Anti-Federalists spanned all the geographic regions and the various social classes. Often opponents on an issue sided together in their opposition to the new Constitution which was constructed from an intricate fabric of compromises. Many South Carolina plantation owners opposed the Constitution for not providing full safeguards for slavery, while Pennsylvania Quakers and others opposed the stipulation that Congress could not restrict slavery for twenty years. North Carolina Baptists wanted a stronger statement of religious freedom, while Connecticut Congregationalists wanted a stronger statement of religious belief in God. Some delegates were concerned about the distance of the new capital from much of the population.

Eventually, Anti-Federalists did coalesce to make some common arguments against the Federalists. The Anti-Federalists contended that the Federalists were trying to adopt a system so new and novel that it even lacked a name. The Anti-Federalists charged that the Federalists had no mandate to write a new Constitution and that the 1787 delegates had acted in secrecy and contrary to both the law and the spirit of the Articles of Confederation. Additionally, they argued, the Constitution would move the country down the road of monarchy and aristocratic rule in repudiation of the 1776 Revolution.

Some Anti-Federalists argued that the Constitution was anti-republican because of the establishment of a separate and powerful executive. In contrast, other Anti-Federalists contended that the legislature was too strong. The necessary and proper clause of the proposed Constitution stated that Congress had the power "to make all laws which shall be necessary and proper" for executing the enumerated powers of the federal government. Critics of a strong national legislature felt this clause vested too much power in the Congress.

The greatest criticism and outrage, however, was reserved for the consolidation of power in a national government. National supremacy would cause the states to decline and ultimately to die, it was argued. The new Constitution included a national supremacy clause which stated that the Constitution and U.S. law were the supreme law of the land and that state officials were bound to uphold it. Further concern was expressed over the new powers of taxation granted to the national government. Opponents of centralization feared that the national government would use its powers of taxation to drain resources from the states, making them ineffective.

Supporters of the Constitution wrote the Federalist Papers under the pseudonym of Publius to argue for ratification of the new Constitution. Inspired by Alexander Hamilton, the leader of the ratification forces, the other main authors were James Madison and John Jay. Totaling eighty-five in number, the Federalist Papers appeared in the New York press between October 1787 and July 1788. Hamilton wrote fifty of the papers, Madison wrote thirty and Jay wrote five. In addition to presenting partisan arguments for Constitutional ratification, many of the Federalist Papers predicted future behavior under the proposed government.

The authors of the Federalist Papers pursued two possibly conflictual objectives. On the one hand, they sought to reassure and win the support of the hesitant Anti-Federalists. In order to do this, the Federalists had to depict the power of the proposed national government as subdued and unlikely to infringe on the sovereignty of the states. Madison, in particular, emphasized that Congress was limited by the enumerated powers in the Constitution. In addition, possibly tyrannical or unwise legislation would be subject to an arduous process of checks and balances whereby bills would be inspected by the two houses of Congress, the President and the courts before becoming law.

On the other hand, Hamilton, Jay and Madison pursued the objective of justifying national ascendancy. This sometimes conflicted with their goal to woo the support of the Anti-Federalists. In Federalist Paper No. 44, for example, Madison argued that Congress should have the authority to interpret the "necessary and proper" clause to formulate laws for constitutional ends not specifically stated in the Constitution. They advocated appeals from state courts to federal courts as necessary for a consistent interpretation of the Constitution and for national unity. In Federalist Paper No. 81, Hamilton contended that the Supreme Court should be allowed to declare acts of Congress void, further enhancing the power of the national judiciary.

Perhaps the most famous of all the Federalist Papers was Number 10, authored by Madison. This article summarized many of the finest points of the proposed Constitution. Written partially to assuage the fears of the Anti-Federalists, the Paper examined the likely sources and consequences of factions in the newborn government. Conflictual interests created factions which could undermine the foundations of democracy. Factions were formed when a number of citizens united and acted on common impulses or passions in a manner adverse to the interests of other citizens and the community at large. The harmful effects of factions could be cured either by removing their causes or by controlling the consequences. Madison advocated the constitutional system of checks and balances and elaborate representation with overlapping terms as solutions to potential harm by factions.

One of the major debates over ratification concerned the absence of a bill of rights. This issue had been discussed briefly at the Philadelphia Convention when George Mason introduced a resolution to form a committee which would draw up a bill of rights. Roger Sherman stated that a bill of rights would be redundant with existing bills of rights already in state constitutions and was unnecessary. The issue did not die but reemerged during the ratification fight as the Anti-Federalists used the absence of a bill of rights to attack the proposed Constitution. Opponents of the Constitution argued that without a bill of rights there were no protections for civil liberties.

In response, the Federalists argued that it was unnecessary to attach further limitations to the power of Congress since limitations were already enumerated in the Constitution. Other nationalists, such as Wilson, claimed that it was not only unnecessary but unrealistic to expect an enumeration of all the rights of the people in the Constitution, as everything not listed would be assumed to have been intentionally omitted from protections.

The absence of a bill of rights actually became a bargaining chip for the Federalists during the ratification struggle. Federalists promised that once the new constitution was ratified, a bill of rights would be adopted by amendment. In a few of the state ratification conventions, such as those in New York, Massachusetts and Virginia, this last minute understanding about the bill of rights contributed to victory for the Federalists.

Many of the state conventions proposed amendments which they thought should be contained in the Bill of Rights. These proposed amendments provided the foundation for the final version of the Bill of Rights adopted in 1789. Debate occurred over the proposed amendments in both houses of Congress. During this process, additions, changes and eliminations were made. One unadopted proposal would have allowed citizens to instruct their congressional representatives how to vote on specific issues. The Federalists argued that such a strong delegational approach to representation would undermine the deliberative nature of Congress. Their arguments were sufficiently persuasive to defeat this change. Among other rejected proposals were suggestions to exempt conscientious objectors from military draft and to limit state police power.

After considerable debate, the proposed Bill of Rights included ten amendments (see table 1-2). It was to become the cornerstone for the protection of citizens from undue government intrusion into their private affairs. Two amendments in the Bill of Rights explicitly protected general individual freedoms. Ultimately to become the most famous amendment, the First Amendment identified and protected individual civil liberties. Among these were the rights to freedom of speech, religion, a free press, and the rights to assemble and to petition the government. This amendment also prohibited the establishment of a government-sanctioned religion. The Ninth Amendment stated that failure to enumerate protections for certain individual civil liberties in the Constitution did not mean that citizens were denied those rights.

Three amendments restricted the use of national government force against individuals and prevented the government from stripping individuals of weapons. The Second Amendment established the right to bear arms and recognized the necessity of a militia to maintain a free state. Quartering of soldiers in private homes without consent was forbidden in the Third Amendment. The Fourth Amendment prohibited unreasonable searches and seizures of citizens, and the issuing of warrants without probable cause.

Four amendments clarified police powers and court procedures for criminal cases. The Fifth Amendment required a grand jury indictment for capital crimes, prohibited self-incrimination and double jeopardy, and protected due process of law. The Sixth Amendment upheld

Table 1-2
The Bill of Rights

AMENDMENTS PROTECTING CIVIL LIBERTIES

    First
Protected freedom of religion, speech, press; guaranteed rights to assemble and petition the government; prohibited the establishment of a government sanctioned religion

    Ninth
Protected non-enumerated citizen rights

AMENDMENTS RESTRICTING THE USE OF NATIONAL GOVERNMENT FORCE

    Second
Right to bear arms; the necessity of a militia for state security

    Third
No quartering of soldiers without consent

    Fourth
No unreasonable searches and seizures; no warrants without probable cause

AMENDMENTS CLARIFYING POLICE POWERS AND COURT PROCEDURES

    Fifth
Required grand jury trials for capital crimes; protected against self-incrimination and double jeopardy; assured due process of law; just compensation required for taking of private property for public use

    Sixth
Right to a speedy and just public trial by an impartial jury; rights to be informed of the accusation, to confront witnesses, and to have counsel

    Seventh
Right to jury trial in common law cases

    Eighth
No excessive bail or fines; no cruel and unusual punishment

AMENDMENT CLARIFYING STATE AND FEDERAL POWERS

    Tenth
Reserved non-delegated powers for the states

---

the right to a speedy trial by an impartial jury, the right to be informed of any charges, and the right to confront witnesses and to have the assistance of counsel. Trial by jury in common-law cases was required in the Seventh Amendment. Cruel and unusual punishment and excessive fines and bails were prohibited in the Eighth Amendment.

The last amendment in the Bill of Rights clarified the distribution of powers between the states and the national government. The Tenth

Amendment reserved nonenumerated powers for the states. Controversy surrounded the wording of this Amendment, as it reserved for the states any powers not explicitly delegated to the national government, as long as those powers were not explicitly prohibited to the states. However, states' rights proponents wanted an even stronger statement of state sovereignty which would prohibit the federal government from exercising any power not explicitly delegated to it. Madison and others opposed this states' rights position and were able to block this move, arguing that to prohibit the national government from exercising any implied powers would limit its effectiveness. This Madisonian victory ultimately had a significant impact on the evolution of the delegation of powers between the national and state governments across the next two hundred years.

With the understanding that the proposed Bill of Rights would soon follow, the proposed U.S. Constitution was submitted to the states for ratification. Since opinion prevailed that the newly-proposed national charter was more generous to the less populous states, these states were among the first to ratify the Constitution. Smaller states which granted approval in 1787 or early 1788 were Delaware, New Jersey, Georgia and Connecticut (see table 1-3).

Table 1-3
State Ratification of the U.S. Constitution

STATE	DATE RATIFIED	MARGIN OF APPROVAL/DISAPPROVAL
Delaware	December 7, 1787	30 – 0
Pennsylvania	December 12, 1787	46 – 23
New Jersey	December 18, 1787	38 – 0
Georgia	January 2, 1788	26 – 0
Connecticut	January 9, 1788	128 – 40
Massachusetts	February 6, 1788	187 – 168
New Hampshire	February 20, 1788	30 – 77 *
Rhode Island	March 24, 1788	237 – 2708 **
Maryland	April 28, 1788	63 – 11
South Carolina	May 12, 1788	149 – 73
New Hampshire	June 21, 1788	57 – 47
Virginia	June 25, 1788	89 – 79
New York	July 26, 1788	30 – 27
North Carolina	November 21, 1788	194 – 77
Rhode Island	May 29, 1790	34 – 32

*   Indicates Convention Adjourned Amid Strong Opposition
** Indicates Rejection In A Popular Plebiscite

Source: Ferdinand Lundberg. 1980. Cracks in the Constitution.
        Secaucus, N.J.: Lyle Stuart, Inc.

Pennsylvania approved the Constitution early, but not without conflict. The Anti-Federalists there attempted to defeat ratification by not
attending the state assembly and preventing a legislative quorum. When
a quorum failed to materialize on the first day, the assembly voted to
have the ratification vote without a quorum. This proved unnecessary,
however, when citizens took the issue into their own hands. During the
next day's meeting when the vote was to occur, a mob seized two Anti-
Federalists, dragged them into the assembly hall and held them in their
seats by force. A legislative quorum and a big victory for the Federalists
resulted.

In Maryland, Luther Martin tried an unsuccessful filibuster of the
ratification vote. Despite his efforts to delay, Maryland ratified in April
of 1788, and South Carolina followed in May. In Massachusetts, New
York and New Hampshire, the Constitution was ratified by narrow
margins only after hard-fought battles. By late July 1788, only North
Carolina and Rhode Island had failed to ratify the Constitution. Each
later reversed an earlier negative vote, ensuring the unity of the thirteen states.

The Bill of Rights was submitted to all the states by September 1789.
Vermont had been admitted to statehood, bringing to fourteen the
number of states to consider ratification of the proposed Bill of Rights.
Under the new Constitution, once initiated by Congress with a two-
thirds vote in each house, constitutional amendments had to be ratified
by three-fourths of the states. Incorporation of the Bill of Rights into
the Constitution required approval by eleven states. Between 1789 and
1791, the Bill of Rights received this approval and was adopted. Three
states—Massachusetts, Connecticut and Georgia—failed to ratify the Bill
of Rights.

With the ratification of the Constitution in 1788 and the adoption of
the Bill of Rights in 1789, the United States embarked on a democratic
journey unprecedented in the world. The Declaration of Independence in 1776 had boldly proclaimed the right of self-government, and
the right to life, liberty and the pursuit of happiness. The Constitution
and the Bill of Rights provided the compass and navigational charts for
the journey, developing a sense of direction and general guidelines for
the newly formed government. The Constitution also would serve as
an anchor in troubled times when anti-democratic pressures threatened
to undermine the Revolution of 1776.

REFERENCES

Beck, James M. 1924. *The Constitution of the United States: Yesterday, Today—and
    Tomorrow?* New York: George H. Doran Co.
Eidelberg, Paul. 1968. *The Philosophy of the American Constitution: A Reinterpreta-
    tion of the Intentions of the Founding Fathers.* New York: Free Press.

Graham, George J. Jr., and Scarlett G. Graham. 1984. *Founding Principles of American Government: Two Hundred Years of Democracy on Trial.* Chatham, N.J.: Chatham House Publishers, Inc.

Hamilton, Alexander, James Madison, and John Jay. 1961. *The Federalist Papers.* Introd. Clinton Rossiter. New York: The New American Library.

Holcombe, Arthur N. 1950. *Our More Perfect Union: From Eighteenth Century Principles to Twentieth Century Practice.* Cambridge, Mass.: Harvard University Press.

Kelly, Alfred H., and Winfred A. Harbison. 1976. *The American Constitution: Its Origin and Development.* 5th ed. New York: W. W. Norton & Co.

Lundberg, Ferdinand. 1980. *Cracks in the Constitution.* Secaucus, N.J.: Lyle Stuart, Inc.

McLaughlin, Andrew C. 1935. *A Constitutional History of the United States.* New York: Appleton-Century-Crofts Inc.

Rossiter, Clinton. 1968. *1787: The Grand Convention.* New York: Signet Classics.

Rutland, Robert Allen. 1983. *The Ordeal of the Constitution: The Anti-Federalists and the Ratification Struggle of 1787–1788.* Boston: Northeastern University Press.

Southerland, Arthur E. 1965. *Constitutionalism in America: Origin and Evolution of Its Fundamental Ideas.* New York: Blaisdell Publishing Co.

Swisher, Carl Brent. 1954. *American Constitutional Development.* 2nd ed. Cambridge, Mass.: Houghton-Mifflin Co.

Van Doren, Carl. 1948. *The Great Rehearsal: The Story of the Making and Ratifying of the Constitution of the United States.* New York: Viking Press.

Wills, Gary. 1982. *Explaining America: The Federalist.* New York: Penguin Books.

Chapter Two

Liberalism and Capitalism: The Pillars of U.S. Constitutionalism

U.S. POLITICAL IDEAS

While armies advance on their stomachs, nations crawl forward through history on their ideas. The political ideas of a nation define its existence. Abstract yet real, ideas determine the range of the possible for decision-makers and citizens. Political ideas may represent the best of a nation's spirit, setting standards and goals and defining what is desirable for society. Yet ideas may limit as well as uplift. To examine a nation's ideas is to peer into its soul.

Often political ideas may conflict with one another at some level, so that nations may simultaneously adhere to incompatible values. Among possibly conflicting ideas in American government are majority rule versus minority rights, freedom versus equality and individualism versus collective action. Basic American values include liberty, private property rights, achievement and merit. Yet a sometimes contradictory set of American values emphasizes abolishing discrimination, community well-being, helping the underdog, generosity and fairness. The most fundamental of American values incorporated in the U.S. Constitution are derived more from the first set than from the second. Among these fundamental values are individualism, property, contracts and law, freedom and equality, and democracy.

Individualism

The lone hero disappearing into the setting sun epitomizes the great attachment to individualism which has characterized the United States since colonial days. In few other countries in the world is individualism so deeply rooted. Heroic cultural figures of this genre, ranging from the lone crusader fighting "city hall" to the solitary entrepreneurial businessman succeeding against all odds (as in the Horatio Alger myth), reinforce the appeal of individualism. The early pioneers of the western United States endured hardships and possible death, often in a solitary and lonely existence. Their individualism and stamina were praised in ballads then and today. The favorite U.S. hero for decades was the cowboy, who faced inhospitable elements and hostile rustlers, often living off the land during the long and dangerous cattle drives which covered hundreds of miles between Texas and the Kansas cow-towns during the 1870s. The epitome of rugged individualism, the cowboy relied only on his horse, his lasso and his gun.

Myths of leaders focus on their individual strengths, pitted against a sometimes unsympathetic external world. Abe Lincoln walked five miles to return a modest amount of money that he overcharged an unsuspecting customer. As a child (according to myth but not necessarily history) George Washington bravely told the truth and accepted individual responsibility for chopping down a cherry tree on his father's plantation.

Other prominent Americans, especially wartime leaders, have also been praised for individual heroic actions. Jim Bowie and Davy Crockett were immortalized for their heroic but futile stand against thousands of Santa Anna's troops during the Texas rebellion against Mexican rule. Theodore Roosevelt's leadership of the charge up San Juan Hill is vividly remembered from the Spanish-American War. General George Patton was praised for his daring and his dogged pursuit of the Germans during World War II. General Douglas MacArthur acquired great popular appeal when he pursued communists up the Korean peninsula after the brilliant landing at Inchon, returning to a ticker tape parade in New York despite his removal by Truman.

Nor have acts of individual determination mythologized in popular culture been limited to the arena of war. Inventors of practical innovations that have improved the quality of life have also received prominent places in a U.S. mythology which glorifies individualism and risk-taking. Benjamin Franklin daringly tied a key to a kite and flew the kite during a thunderstorm to verify his speculations about the nature of electricity. Thomas Edison became a hero for his long and lonely pursuit of many modern technological innovations, including the electric light bulb and the generator. Henry Ford invented a new process of mass-producing cars which ultimately spread to the production of other consumer goods, opening the door to twentieth-century industrialization and mass consumption aimed at the general populace.

Even today, images of rugged individualism continue to have great popular appeal. Surgeons who do heart transplants, defying odds and holding life and death in their hands, receive great public acclaim. Trial lawyers—from earlier attorneys like Daniel Webster and Clarence Darrow to fictionalized characters like Perry Mason to modern types like F. Lee Bailey—undertake unpopular causes in the face of great risk and potentially great gain. Of modern presidents, Ronald Reagan, more than any other, has emphasized the values of individualism, tradition and self-help. His presidential popularity ratings have been among the highest of this century.

Many positive outcomes from the emphasis on individualism have accrued across two hundred years. Settled by immigrants often fleeing oppressive governments, class structures, religions and societies, many newcomers to the United States clung strongly to the belief that through hard work, perseverance and education, they could overcome most if not all obstacles. This spirit, called the "Protestant ethic," facilitated upward mobility among many newcomers. Individualism has also contributed greatly to innovation and practical improvements in technological processes. With an emphasis on meritorious individual achievement and recognition, the best and the brightest presumably do rise to the top of social and political institutions, unfettered by cultural barriers or by notions of egalitarianism.

Individualism also has a negative aspect, however. In increasingly complex and technological societies, an extreme emphasis on individualism at the expense of collective action may no longer be appropriate. What was desirable and daring on the open frontier becomes disruptive and disturbing in closely knit, technologically interdependent organizations. An extreme emphasis on individual responsibility and control undermines reasoned examination of societal barriers to progress, including discrimination in all forms. While individualism rewards the best and the brightest, it leaves behind the depressed and the downtrodden. As society changes, notions of individualism may ultimately be forced to adapt. Rugged individualism may be transposed into rational individualism where people must work within large bureaucracies and persuade others in order to achieve their goals.

Private Property

Private property is a cornerstone of American values and commerce and is considered an inalienable right. The emphasis on private property rights results from the strong concern with individualism. Early U.S. settlers viewed control over the ownership and use of property, particularly land, as crucial to self-support and self-sufficiency. The acquisition of property has always been viewed as a desirable goal.

Legal origins for protection of private property were derived from

English common law, which is a complex set of codes for protecting and conveying property rights. Closely coupled with the economic system of capitalism, private property was a concept readily embraced by the early settlers.

Thomas Jefferson was among the early founders who linked property ownership to citizenship, arguing that land ownership was the only way to assure sufficient individual independence for free and thoughtful political inquiry. For him the sturdy yeoman farmers were the backbone of the Republic. Jefferson further argued that a landless peasant population would lose its independence, be subject to overwhelming economic pressures and be manipulable in the realm of public affairs.

Alexander Hamilton also viewed property ownership as an important prerequisite to citizenship, but contended that ownership of stocks, bonds and other forms of investment securities was more crucial than ownership of land. Foreshadowing the eventual urban economy, Hamilton felt that these types of properties were important to stimulate industrialization and trade and to make the United States a great power. Despite disagreements over which types of properties were most critical, the founders agreed that the ownership of private property was necessary for effective citizenship.

Like Jefferson and Hamilton, James Madison also thought that property ownership played a critical role in citizenship. In Federalist Paper No. 10, Madison embraced a Lockean philosophy stating that acquisitiveness was a desirable virtue. Locke wrote of "life, liberty and property," but made acquisitiveness respectable by arguing that it was necessary for promoting economic growth. Madison also saw problems with differential acquisitive passions, however. He feared the harmful effects of factions upon democracy and believed that the most common and durable source of factions was the unequal distribution of property. The battle between factions for dominance was the new republic's greatest danger according to Madison.

Under British rule, the U.S. colonies had required property ownership as a prerequisite to voting. This practice was continued by the states after the adoption of the new Constitution. Under the Constitution, the power to require property ownership was delegated to the states. Originally, state legislatures required property ownership as a prerequisite for the right to vote. Between 1815 and 1865 a spirit of democratization swept through the country, resulting in the abandonment of many formal restrictions on participation. During this period, the majority of states in the union held constitutional conventions and adopted new state constitutions, and most states dropped property ownership and tax paying requirements.

Today the norm of private property ownership is not questioned, but the nature of what is defined as property is. From the viewpoint of the founders, private property was a means to an end: economic self-sufficiency so that citizens could participate freely in public affairs. When the country was first founded, the ownership of physical property, especially land, was sufficient to assure economic independence in an agrarian society. In today's highly mobile service economy, the meaning of property has been expanded to include rights to income such as pensions and government benefits, which are often more crucial than access to land for assuring economic independence. The battle over the definition and distribution of these new property rights has yet to be fully resolved.

Contracts and Law

Firmly embedded in U.S. values is a faith in contracts and law. These beliefs date back to the colonial period when many citizens adhered to the idea that government powers should be controlled by some form of contract. A corollary to this was the belief that the controlling contract should be outside the reach of people in power, including legislatures and popular majorities. The limitations should be based on the natural rights of individuals. The Constitution was to be the manifestation of such a basic contract. Implied in the contract theory of government is the idea that the people must give their consent to be governed.

Belief in contracts and law as a method of governing has been likened to a civil religion in the United States. Overlapping values have been woven into the cloth of which this civil religion is composed. Among these values are faith in the future of the United States, and in contracts, constitutions, natural law, higher law and individualism. Law provides a set of seemingly neutral rules by which individuals striving to achieve the implementation of these and other values can be regulated. Law not only regulates great concerns like school desegregation or whether women should be excluded from the draft, but also practical problems of everyday living such as buying and selling or defining traffic violations.

A system of law performs several useful functions. One function served is to maintain order in society; therefore law is a way to exercise social control. Other institutions in the United States derive their legitimacy partly because they are governed by laws. Some societies control their populations through excessive use of force. In U.S. society, where there are many religions, ethnic groups, and belief systems, force is a last resort due to the emphasis on the rule of law.

Another function of the legal system is to promote and enforce moral standards in society. Sometimes legality equals morality, but not always. One example of a divergence between legality and morality is self-defense. Most moral codes denounce killing another human, yet most legal codes permit it under life-threatening conditions. Divergence between morality and legality also occurs when laws are unjust. Laws that promote arbitrary inequality such as those promoting racial segregation or unequal treatment of women in the workplace are examples. When people engage in civil disobedience, they claim that a certain law or set of laws conflicts with a higher law, such as the Constitution, or with their individual consciences.

Laws are a source of rules of conduct. These rules of conduct outline what is permitted and what is forbidden. These limits on behavior provide basic guidelines for a variety of circumstances. For example, a person is allowed to browse in a department store without buying anything, or the person may enter the store with the intent to purchase something, find nothing suitable, and then leave. However, a person may not shoplift or tamper with the goods.

In addition to providing rules of conduct, laws provide a way to settle disputes peaceably. Conflict is a condition of everyday human life. Throughout most of history, violence has been the final arbiter of conflict. Even in modern times, wars are used to settle international disagreements. In the United States, citizens can use the law to settle disputes with individuals or organizations. U.S. citizens even have the right to challenge government bureaucracies and authorities over issues ranging from traffic tickets to the death penalty.

Finally, laws meet economic and social needs in societies. Laws which govern property and contracts facilitate exchange and production processes in U.S. society, providing economic liquidity and a basis for commercial transactions. Other laws provide for the smooth operation of the social system. These include family law and much of civil law, such as torts and personal injury statutes. Laws do not always cover all the needs of the economy and the society effectively, but at least some framework exists which attempts to serve them.

While performing all these functions, laws themselves are rarely, if ever, neutral. When laws or the Constitution are interpreted by judges, lawyers or the Supreme Court, important value choices are made. Most people base their judgements of the fairness or neutrality of a law at least partially on the impact the law has on their personal well-being. Disputes over how laws affect individual interests contribute to controversy surrounding the role of lawyers and the legal system itself.

The emphasis on law in the United States heightens the importance and power of lawyers vis-à-vis other professions. A society that emphasizes and values law is a society that employs many lawyers. When contracts constitute the basis for daily interactions, interpreters of law and contracts—namely lawyers—become numerous and collectively powerful. Facilitation and adjudication become vital roles which depend largely on the acquisition of legal skills. The branch of government where legal skills and interpretations dominate—the courts—becomes more prominent. In the United States the large number of lawyers and their prominent role within society has contributed to, if not caused, the rise of administrative law in the bureaucracy and the importance of common law.

Freedom and Equality

Fundamental to American values are the twin, and sometimes conflicting, beliefs in freedom and equality. To some, freedom is the absence of restraint. This "negative" notion of freedom emerged in the eighteenth century. Politically, "negative" freedom implies freedom from government interference with individual personal liberties and economic activities. Classical liberalism and Adam Smith's *Wealth of Nations* especially prized the idea that government should adopt a laissez faire attitude regarding economics. Listing prohibitions on government activity to protect individual liberties, bills of rights in both the United States and state constitutions embody this notion of freedom.

Others define freedom as the ability to act and to achieve goals, arguing that the absence of restraints is a necessary but not sufficient condition for action. This "positive" concept of freedom views government as a tool to help individuals realize their potential and to improve their social and economic status. Emerging in the twentieth century, the ideal of "positive" freedom has been embraced by modern liberals who believe that government should be used to benefit individuals.

Each of the alternative definitions of freedom implies individual choice. Implicit in the concept of freedom is an auxiliary concept of free will. Only when people have free will do they have the capacity to discriminate between alternatives. One way to expand freedom is not merely to assume that individuals have the ability to discriminate between choices, but in addition to enhance their range of choices through creation, innovation and invention.

Constraints on innovation and creation can occur through peer pressure, social conformity and pressures from the prevailing power structure, as well as formal government restraints. Government may experience tendencies to limit innovation, since the freedom to innovate is the freedom to do the unexpected, and that may threaten social order and even represent a direct political challenge.

Ideas of equality are similarly diverse. In the United States, political equality has evolved into the concept of equally weighted votes under the rule of one person, one vote. This view of political equality does not acknowledge the unequal political influence that wealthy people can and do exert in the electoral process. Legal equality implies equal treatment under the law for people in the same class or category. Equality of opportunity involves providing equal chances for advancement within a merit system. More recently, equal opportunity has also implied the elimination of inappropriate barriers, such as racial and religious discrimination, which inhibit social and economic advancement.

Even more basic is the notion of moral equality asserted by Thomas Jefferson in the Declaration of Independence. In his proclamation that "all men are created equal," Jefferson seemed to be arguing that all people were moral equals at a fundamental human level, rather than claiming that people were equal in political, social or economic power, or had equal talents.

An inherent conflict between freedom and equality includes the tension between majority rule and minority rights. Majority rule reflects a commitment to political equality, while minority rights represents the value of political freedom. When these two ideas coexist, there is a possibility that the majority will restrict the freedom of the minority unnecessarily. Interestingly, John C. Calhoun used this argument to defend Southern sectional rights before the Civil War. Another such conflict occurs between economic freedom and economic equality. Enforcing equality removes freedoms from those who would like the freedom to acquire as much property and wealth as possible under capitalist constraints.

A third conflict between freedom and equality occurs in the clash between social freedom and economic equality. Those who perceive this conflict to be inherent argue that only strict rules and enforcement could cause an economic leveling of society, and that the presence of strict rules would encourage conformity to the point of stifling innovation and social freedom.

Democracy

Democracy was valued at the birth of the nation, but most of the constitutional developers considered themselves "republicans" and had deep reservations about this form of government. The concept of democracy implies public participation and control over what governments do. Yet in the early years, most thought democracy also had undesirable characteristics. To opponents and skeptics, democracy represented "rule by the rabble," bordering on "mob rule." The founders of the nation, however, chose a less extreme and more positive view of democracy. They designed a representative democracy which modified some of the excesses of direct democracy.

The authors of the Constitution modified direct democracy, where citizens have a direct impact on substantive decision making, into a representative or republican form of government. By 1900, however, democratic norms became so strong that several devices of direct democracy emerged at the state and local level, especially in the western states. Two more widely used direct democracy devices were the referendum and the initiative. These reforms were the hallmarks of the Progressive Reformers.

The referendum is more conservative than the initiative. Under a referendum system, voters can veto legislation which has already been passed by the legislature. This procedure is conservative because it adds another decision making layer to the system, increasing the probability that policies will stagnate or stall. Citizens are given only the power of veto, not of initiation.

Under the citizens' initiative system, citizens may directly initiate a petition as well as participate in passing it. With a direct initiative, a person or group has to submit a proposed law to the secretary of state. Supporters of the initiative must then secure the required number of signatures to get the initiative onto the ballot. Under an indirect initiative, citizens must still initiate the proposal, unlike a referendum. Supporters submit the proposed change to the state legislature. For bills passed by the state legislature, the proposal becomes law with no further action. If the legislature fails to act, citizens may approve or disapprove the proposal at the next general election.

A third device, the recall, does not give citizens the power to vote directly upon substantive legislation. It does increase citizen power, however, by allowing citizens to elect representatives or to remove them from office. The recall requires a petition, typically signed by twenty-five percent of the voters in the last election. A recall petition usually requires more signatures than either a referendum or an initiative. If the petition drive is successful, a recall election is held. Officials may be removed by majority vote. Deposed officials do not have to be proven incompetent but merely perceived as frustrating popular preferences.

Free elections are crucial to democracy. In modern times several essential characteristics must exist if free elections are to occur. Elections must be held at regularly scheduled intervals within prescribed time periods. Officials cannot unilaterally decide to postpone elections, and citizens must be presented with a meaningful choice between at least two candidates for each office to be filled. Freedom to form political parties and nominate candidates must also be maintained, so that no major group in the population is denied participation. Freedom of discussion must be available both for candidates and for citizens. Universal adult suffrage is also a characteristic of free elections, as is equal weighting of votes. Voters must have the right to register their electoral preferences without repercussions or interference. Secret balloting facilitates this type of freedom. Finally, votes must be accurately counted and recorded.

CLASSIC LIBERAL THOUGHT

Many of the basic concepts of classical liberalism are the same as the values cherished within U.S. culture. Classical liberalism places emphasis foremost upon the individual. Classic liberal thought has roots in antiquity. Both the Stoics and the Epicureans valued individuals above all social considerations. Flowering in the eighteenth century, liberalism began as a challenge to absolutism and monarchy. It continued to exhibit great appeal through the mid-nineteenth century, and eventually became a comprehensive theory of individual rights to challenge and limit absolute political power.

Liberalism particularly appealed to the rising new classes, especially the merchant and industrialist classes which were accumulating new forms of capitalistic wealth. It also appealed to some peasants resisting the landed aristocracy. To others, bourgeois liberalism was equated with the new capitalistic order. The working class was generally interested in greater freedom and equality. Liberalism was opposed by the monarchy, the landed aristocracy and the Church.

Some scholars view liberalism as an intellectual outgrowth of the development of the scientific method. In the preceding medieval and feudal periods, people had looked to God to provide heavenly help for earthly problems. Many people led wretched lives and the promise of divine intervention and deliverance was important to maintaining social order. Discoveries throughout the seventeenth and eighteenth centuries by scientific pioneers such as Isaac Newton, Copernicus, Galileo and Bacon, improved the quality of life and caused people to wonder "if technological problems can be solved through human reasoning, could not social and political problems be addressed in the same manner?" The growing faith in human reason contributed to the growth of a liberalism which was optimistic about the ability of people to analyze and solve their own problems.

Often credited as the founder of classical liberalism, John Locke was an English philosopher who lived from 1632 to 1704. In a well-known book, *Two Treatises on Government*, Locke developed a contract theory of the state. He argued that the state was the custodian of the natural rights of life, liberty and property. He believed that human beings were moral, competent and intelligent, and had a right to consent to being governed. Should the government fail to uphold its role as the protector of natural rights, citizens could appropriately withdraw their consent to be governed, and could rebel. Locke's ideas about natural rights helped shape the U.S. Declaration of Independence. Thomas Jefferson wrote of "inalienable rights" endowed by the Creator and stated that all men were created equal. Jefferson was so confident of the Lockean notions that he asserted that these rights were "self-evident" truths.

The absence of governmental restraint was Locke's definition of freedom. Coupled with this idea of freedom was the concept of limited government. Lockean liberals reasoned that since the role of government is to protect the God-given rights of man, its functions are inherently limited. Jefferson crystallized the concept with his dictum "that government is best which governs least."

Another variant of classic thought, utilitarian liberalism, was espoused by John Stuart Mill. Unlike Locke, Mill feared equality, predicting it would have a detrimental leveling effect upon society. He felt that mass public education would provide a vehicle for the state to impose its opinions on students. Despite this fear, Mill did favor egalitarianism in many settings, arguing that social inequality was just only when the preservation of social utility (the general public well-being) demanded it. Mill continued to show more concern about the trade-offs between individual rights and societal interests than did many other classical liberal thinkers.

Mill rejected the Lockean notion of natural rights, but in his work defended both private property and liberty. He saw the acquisition of property as the chief pleasure in life. Mill believed that the government which created the greatest potential for the acquisition and accumulation of property was the best form of government. However, in his book *On Liberty* he defended the individual natural right of personal liberty. Mill was an avid proponent of free speech and personal liberty, viewing these as crucial to the maintenance of a democratic society. He believed that debate is necessary for democracy to flourish; consequently, democratic institutions would be nourished by a competition of ideas.

LIBERAL IDEAS IN THE CONSTITUTION

The U.S. Constitution has many elements of classical liberal thought of the eighteenth century, yet it is also a conservative document. Several basic principles constituted the core of political liberalism: individual consent, constitutionalism, representation and representative government, limited government and individual liberties. The Declaration of Independence argued for the principle of individual consent and plainly stated the grounds for colonial separation from England. The list of grievances in the Declaration against the King of England is long, and Jefferson criticized him for the lack of representative government on such crucial fronts as the administration of justice and the economic system of mercantilism. The Constitution focused on the remaining core principles of political liberalism.

Constitutionalism

The very creation of the Constitution by the 1787 Convention, as well as prior reliance on state constitutions, reflected the principle of constitutionalism. This principle states that a constitution is necessary to provide guidance to government. A constitution should spell out the powers of government and the rules of procedure to be used in governing. The United States Constitution embodies the principle of constitutionalism so well that it has often been used as a role model by foreign states.

Under this principle, constitutions should specify eligibility requirements for government officials and procedures for how they should acquire power, as well as definitions of the scope of that power. Constitutions should not specify rules of conduct for individual daily behavior—these are strictures that are better placed in statutory law. Since constitutions are more difficult to modify, the rules of governance should be long-lasting, enduring and anchored in "constitutional cement." By contrast, technology and economic conditions may alter norms for individual behavior. Rules of conduct governing individual behavior are more temporary and are determined by prevailing conditions. They should be placed in more easily modified codes of law.

The U.S. Constitution is primarily concerned with defining procedures of government and limits on government power. The first three articles of the U.S. Constitution establish and define the powers of the three branches of the national government (see table 2-1). Article I describes legislative powers. Article II enumerates executive powers. Judicial powers are defined in Article III. The nature of interstate relations, including the admission of states to the union, interstate extradition privileges and immunities, and full faith and credit recognition of the laws of a state by other states, are described in Article IV.

The last three articles deal directly with the Constitution itself. How

Table 2-1
Major Sections of the U.S. Constitution

Article I.	Legislative Powers
Article II.	Executive Powers
Article III.	Judicial Powers
Article IV.	Interstate Relations
Article V.	Amendments to the Constitution
Article VI.	Constitutional and National Supremacy
Article VII.	Ratification of the Constitution
Bill of Rights	Protections for Civil Liberties

the Constitution may be amended is defined in Article V. Article VI firmly states the principle of constitutionalism, declaring that the Constitution and laws made under its authority are the supreme law of the land, and that obedience by every state is required. Article VII also addresses the principle of constitutionalism by setting nine as the number of states needed to ratify the 1787 Constitution. Perhaps the most famous part of the Constitution is the Bill of Rights (or first ten amendments) which also embodies a principle of constitutionalism by identifying limits on the powers of government.

Representation

The founders of the Constitution agreed from the outset on the principle of representative government, perceiving it as a method to end the seemingly arbitrary decisions experienced under British rule. Nevertheless, many were fearful of rule by mobs or malicious factions that would undermine the public interest, the collective good and the status of the elite propertied classes. The confluence of these conflicting ideas was a modified representative structure embodying the principle of representation, but falling short of either universal suffrage or the equality of a one-person one-vote criterion.

Within the Constitution the founders constructed a representative national legislature in Article I. The House was representative; the Senate was elected, but was less representative. Representation in the lower house was proportionate to population, incorporating the principle of one-person one-vote. States were given equal representation in the upper house, regardless of state population. This was a violation of the one-person one-vote principle.

While the lower house was directly elected, members of the upper house were elected by their respective state legislatures. However, state legislatures had to be representative. Article V, Section 4 of the Constitution stipulated that state legislatures were to be republican in form. The Constitution mandated that the national government assure the representativeness of state legislatures.

In many ways, the House of Representatives was analogous to the House of Commons and the Senate to the House of Lords. The Senate was removed from popular elections, had higher membership requirements, longer terms and possessed advise and consent powers on appointments and treaties.

Limited Government and Individual Liberties

There are two types of limits on government power in the U.S. Constitution. The first type constrains and defines the powers of each level of government vis-à-vis the other level. In Article I, Section 8, the Constitution spells out the powers of Congress. The powers of state governments are not directly enumerated, but limits on the powers of both the national and state governments are specified. Article I, Section 9 enumerates the powers denied to Congress. Section 10 of the Article enumerates the powers denied to the states (see table 2-2).

A second type of limit on government restricts direct government actions against citizens. This type of protection for civil liberties is embedded in the Bill of Rights. With the exception of the Tenth Amendment, which reserves nondelegated powers for the states, the entire Bill of Rights enumerates restrictions upon government actions against individuals. The heart of the Bill of Rights and the heart of classical political liberalism can be considered one and the same.

Table 2-2
Article I Limits on Government Power

SECTION 9.   FEDERAL LIMITS

No prohibitions upon immigration to the states prior to 1808
No suspension of writ of habeas corpus
No ex post facto laws
No bills of attainder
No taxes on interstate commerce
No preferential treatment of ports in different states
No federal treasury expenditures without appropriations
No granting of titles of nobility

SECTION 10.   STATE LIMITS

No state may enter into a treaty or alliance with a foreign country
No granting of letters of marque and reprisal
No coining of money by states
No bills of attainder
No ex post facto laws
No violation of contract obligations
No granting of titles of nobility

Congressional consent is required for:
Import or export taxes
Duty on shipping tonnage
Keeping troops or war ships in peacetime
Interstate agreements or compacts
Agreements with foreign powers
Engaging in war, unless invaded

CLASSIC CAPITALIST THOUGHT

The ideological twin of political liberalism is the economic theory of capitalism: both serve as philosophical legs for the body of the U.S. Constitution. Just as John Locke was one of the main theorists of political liberalism, Adam Smith was among the principal formulators of capitalistic theory. His great treatise enunciating market movements through the laws of supply and demand was *An Inquiry into the Nature and Causes of the Wealth of Nations*. This book was published in 1776, the same year as the U.S. Revolution. Since 1749 Smith had devoted much of his adult life to developing this monumental work. Between 1749 and 1776, his thinking grew from the contents of a few unrefined lectures to a synthesized and sophisticated theory of free markets and how they work. Much of his theory was shaped during intense conversations with his London friends, Dr. Samuel Johnson, Edmund Burke, Humphrey Davy, Edward Gibbon and Oliver Goldsmith.

Individualism was the foundation for free market capitalism just as it was for political liberalism. Smith assumed that each individual was the best judge of his or her own interests. Given freedom, people would rationally pursue their own self-interests. This argument concerning the pursuit of self-interest was not new. Previous philosophies and world views, including some religious teachings, also assumed that individuals would pursue their own self-interests if given free rein. The radical departure in Smith's thinking was his assessment of the implications of self-interested pursuit for societal well-being. Previous ideologies, especially prevailing views within Christianity, interpreted the pursuit of self-interest as deleterious to the social whole, and maintained that such impulses should be denied. Smith argued that the unfettered pursuit of self-interest was beneficial to society as a whole, and should be encouraged.

How is economic wealth maximized and general prosperity encouraged to flourish from individual pursuit of gain? An "invisible hand" in the marketplace—namely prices and profits—guides consumers and producers sensitive to economic cues. In capitalistic theory, both consumers and producers operate under marginalism, making decisions on the basis of the last unit purchased or produced. Consumers, sensitive to price and opportunity costs, will continue to buy a product until the satisfaction from the last unit purchased is comparable to the price of the last unit. Producers, attuned to revenues and prices, will continue to produce an item until the marginal profit from the last unit produced equals the marginal addition to revenues gained from its sale.

When both consumers and producers make marginal decisions, laws of supply and demand govern the total amount produced and the price of items sold. Demand and supply curves may be plotted, reflecting relationships between the price of a product and the quantity produced and purchased. Demand curves reflect an inverse or negative relationship between price and quantity purchased. As the price rises, the quantity demanded declines. Supply curves reflect a positive or direct relationship between price and quantity produced. As price rises, the quantity produced increases. At the intersection of these two curves is the equilibrium or optimal price and quantity, given consumer preferences and producer costs.

Smith saw markets as an efficient mechanism for allocating economic resources. Markets could allocate resources to satisfy consumer preferences more efficiently than centralized command systems, including the mercantile system that free enterprise replaced. Underlying Smith's theoretical conclusion that unrestrained individual pursuit of gain would result in the greatest economic growth were several crucial assumptions.

First, Smith, as did classical and neoclassical economists who followed him, assumed that all people were maximizers of wealth and were responsive foremost to economic cues. Individuals were assumed to maximize wages and other forms of compensation. Corporations were assumed to maximize profits.

A second critical assumption was that markets were competitive. In competitive markets, both consumers and purchasers were so small that no single consumer or producer could affect either the quantity produced or the price of a product. Smith saw individual workers as atomized, and not as united by unions or labor organizations. Similarly, corporations and producers were isolated from each other, not members of trade associations, cartels or collusive arrangements.

A third assumption was the absence of barriers to the flow of goods and workers. Corporations had unrestricted entry into new production fields. Workers could move freely from one geographic location to another as well as from one occupation and industry to another. Information to facilitate rational decisions for maximizing profits and wages also flowed freely, unhampered by restrictions.

Just as political liberalism favored the individual through the doctrine of natural rights, Adam Smith's theory favored the individual consumer. In free markets, prices cannot be fixed, and production levels cannot be set. Competition is supposed to obviate the possibility of cartels and monopolies. In capitalist theory, entrepreneurs also have much liberty and are unrestrained by government regulation. They may hire and fire workers as their production needs demand, and they may determine wage levels and prices. Laissez-faire or noninterference by the government in the marketplace was to be accompanied by free trade abroad.

Proponents of capitalism advanced several arguments. In addition to maximizing total wealth and growth, the forces which drive the free enterprise engine reflect human nature. Unlike central planning, capitalism promotes individual freedom. Proponents such as Thomas Paine and Joseph Priestly approved highly of the marriage of capitalism and democracy in the fledgling United States, arguing that both were necessary to preserve individual liberty.

Many challenges exist today to free market capitalism, yet despite dramatic cumulative changes in the nature of technology, production, corporate structures and markets over the last two hundred years, neoclassical economists of the twentieth century continue to echo many of the arguments supporting capitalism first advanced by Adam Smith. Milton Friedman remains a prominent spokesperson for the neoclassical view, contending that state intervention in the economy will destroy moral and political freedom of individuals and will cause an inefficient allocation of economic resources.

Critics of classical and neoclassical capitalist theory contend that changes in the economy have made most of its crucial assumptions outdated or irrelevant. Both corporations and individuals often meet basic requirements with respect to economic gain, rather than maximizing opportunities. Management and stockholders are now two separate and distinct classes with sometimes conflicting goals for the corporation. Technology has raised fixed costs of production and, along with fixed costs, barriers to market entry in capital-intensive fields.

Most major industries also lack free, competitive markets and instead are oligopolistic, dominated by a few producers. In monopolistic markets, such as defense, the government is the only purchaser. Neither are workers mobile with access to perfect information and unfettered by social and personal ties. Regardless of the current stresses and strains on free enterprise, however, the economic landscape of the Constitutional founders was definitely capitalistic.

CAPITALISM AND THE CONSTITUTION

The U.S. Constitution does not endorse capitalism directly, but capitalistic values permeate much of its text. Debate has sometimes focused on the role of private property, a fundamental building block of capitalism, in the creation of the Constitution. In a now famous 1913 analysis, *An Economic Interpretation of the Constitution,* Charles Beard questions the motives and values of its founders. Beard had argued earlier that the Constitution was an anti-democratic reaction against majority rule.

In his 1913 book, Beard continued his criticism of the motives of the founders by arguing that the Constitution was designed to strengthen and protect the propertied classes. His thesis holds that a strong national government was created to protect the economic holdings of the delegates from usurpation by popularly controlled state legislatures. The clash of economic interests within the 1787 Convention was between merchants, slaveholders and manufacturers—a debate between "haves" and other "haves," not between "haves" and "have nots."

Beard contends that the background of the delegates supports his argument. Some of the delegates were land speculators who wished to exploit western land holdings. Others were wealthy lawyers, planters and merchants. Many had substantial Confederation bond holdings, including some delegates who were bond speculators. Under Article VI of the 1787 Constitution, all debts incurred by the confederacy were honored at face value, allowing bond speculators to make great profits. Some reaped financial gains in the millions of dollars.

Beard offers other evidence as well to back his thesis that the Constitution was designed by a self-interested propertied elite to protect their own holdings. Article I, Section 8 deals with commerce powers. This section gives the propertied class the power to make decisions over its own trade and commerce. Beard also argues that provisions giving the national government control over money and credit and guaranteeing the national debt were beneficial to the creditor class.

Other critics of the economic motives of the Constitution were even harsher. Parenti (1980) argued that protection of property lay behind the creation of a national militia. According to Parenti, the founders did not believe that the states were capable of resisting popular uprisings by the propertyless classes. They created an army militia and a system of forts as much to protect against internal insurrection as against foreign invasion. Even Adam Smith, the founder of capitalist theory, noted the ability of the propertied classes to use government to protect their wealth. He observed in *The Wealth of Nations* that "civil authority, so far as it is instituted for the security of property, is in reality instituted for the defense of the rich against the poor, or of those who have some property against those who have none at all" (1952, 309).

Brown (1956), a "consensus" historian, has criticized Beard's analysis on the grounds that Beard was arbitrarily selective, using quotes out of context, particularly in the case of *The Federalist Papers*. Brown questions the presence of a propertyless class. He contends that even the poor were interested in preserving private property rights. According to Brown, the founders appealed primarily to a desire for national unity and protection against invasion. Many cross-cutting cleavages on a variety of issues and background characteristics other than property and wealth influenced the convention, including religious pluralism and attachments to competing political ideals. Political differences, not economic differences, were the main source of conflict within the convention. Lastly, Brown contends that the founders were too smart to think they could deceive the majority with a plan designed to protect their own wealth.

Regardless of the original motives of the founders, the Constitution has served capitalism well across the intervening two hundred years. Private property rights have unquestionably been maintained. However, the structure of capitalism has changed in the two centuries since the Constitution was ratified as the nation has undergone a long-term trend from decentralization to greater centralization.

Ironically, the first impulses toward centralization were in the private sector, as robber barons and other corporate magnates devised cartels, interlocking directorates and other restraints to reduce competition and manage markets. In the Sherman Act of 1890 and the Clayton Act of 1914, the government responded with antitrust legislation to prevent impediments to competition. Over time, natural monopolies, market failures and an increased demand for public goods accelerated government intervention in the markets.

The Keynesian Revolution of the 1930s, which was the intellectual basis of much of Roosevelt's New Deal, increased government intervention in the economy even further. Lord Keynes, the great British economist, argued that a decline in aggregate demand contributed to, if it did not cause, the deflation of the Great Depression. The problem was insufficient money in the economy to stimulate production and increase employment. The Keynesian solution was greater government spending, financed by deficits if necessary, to prime the economy. Franklin Delano Roosevelt called it "priming the pump." Tax cuts would also help prime a deflated economy. Conversely, in times of inflation, when aggregate demand was too high with too many dollars used to purchase too few goods, Keynes called for a reduction in government spending and tax increases.

Construed by some as a radical challenge to free enterprise, Galbraith (1956) has argued to the contrary that at heart the Keynesian Revolution was conservative. Both its intent and its impact were to shore up a faltering capitalistic system that otherwise would have collapsed into chaos and possibly socialism. The business-oriented Supreme Court of the 1930s, the so-called "Nine Old Men," initially challenged Roosevelt's New Deal programs as a constitutional violation of substantive due process. Under great pressure, "a switch in time [Justice Owen Roberts] saved nine," and the Court reconsidered and allowed New Deal programs to reinvigorate the ailing American capitalist system.

REFERENCES

Baradat, Leon P. 1979. *Political Ideologies.* Englewood Cliffs, N.J.: Prentice-Hall, Inc.

Beard, Charles. 1913. *An Economic Interpretation of the Constitution of the United States.* New York: Macmillan.

Brown, Robert E. 1956. *Charles Beard and the Constitution: A Critical Analysis of an Economic Interpretation of the Constitution*. Princeton, N.J.: Princeton University Press.

Burns, James MacGregor, J. W. Peltason, and Thomas E. Cronin. 1985. *Government by the People*. 12th alt. ed. Englewood Cliffs, N.J.: Prentice-Hall, Inc.

Friedman, Milton. 1962. *Capitalism and Freedom*. Chicago, Ill.: University of Chicago Press.

————, and Rose Friedman. 1980. *Free to Choose*. New York: Harcourt Brace Jovanovich.

Galbraith, John Kenneth. 1956. *American Capitalism: The Concept of Countervailing Power*. Boston: Houghton Mifflin.

Hagopian, Mark N. 1985. *Ideals and Ideologies of Modern Politics*. New York: Longman, Inc.

Herson, Lawrence J. R. 1984. *The Politics of Ideas: Political Theory and American Public Policy*. Homewood, Ill.: Dorsey Press.

Kreml, William P. 1985. *A Model of Politics*. New York: Macmillan Publishing Co.

McCoy, Charles Allan. 1982. *Contemporary ISMs: A Political Economy Perspective*. New York: Franklin Watts.

Macridis, Roy C. 1983. *Contemporary Political Ideologies: Movements and Regimes*. 2nd ed. Boston: Little, Brown & Co.

Medcalf, Linda J., and Kenneth M. Dolbeae. 1985. *Neopolitics: American Political Ideas in the 1980s*. New York: Random House.

Parenti, Michael. 1980. "The Constitution as an Elitist Document." In *How Democratic Is the Constitution?* Robert A. Goldwin and William A. Schambra, eds. Washington, D.C.: American Enterprise Institute.

Putnam, Robert D. 1982. *Governing*. 3rd ed. New York: Holt, Rinehart and Winston.

Sederberg, Peter C. 1977. *Interpreting Politics: An Introduction to Political Science*. San Francisco, Calif.: Chandler and Sharp.

Smith, Adam. 1952. *An Inquiry into the Nature and Causes of the Wealth of Nations*. Chicago, Ill.: Encyclopaedia Britannica, Inc.

Stone, Alan, and Richard P. Barke. 1985. *Governing The American Republic: Economics, Law, and Policies*. New York: St. Martin's Press.

Tinder, Glenn. 1979. *Political Thinking: The Perennial Questions*. 3rd ed. Boston: Little, Brown & Co.

Chapter Three

Federalism in Theory and Practice: The Growth of Federal Power

FEDERALISM WITHIN THE CONSTITUTION

There was no substantial debate at the 1787 Convention about the type of governmental system to set in place. The unequivocal answer was a federalist system. Federalism was selected almost by default. Since many of the colonists had fled the oppression of the unitary British system, a strongly centralized unitary system was not considered a viable option, nor was a confederacy seriously considered in 1787. This system had been tried under the Articles of Confederation and had been found lacking, unable to give sufficient guidance to keep the fledgling ship of state on course.

As a constitutional form of government, federalism is the system in the middle—conceptually sandwiched between a more decentralized confederate system and a more centralized unitary system. How do these three systems differ? Both confederacies and federalist systems have two constitutionally defined types of government—a national government on the one hand and subnational or state governments on the other hand. Confederacy and federalism differ in the powers allocated to these two constitutionally distinguished types of governments. Under a confederacy, only the state or subnational government has the power to regulate individual behavior. The powers of the central or national government are defined by the states and are subject to state approval. The central government is comparatively weak and has no constitutional right to regulate the behavior of individuals.

In federalist systems, both national and subnational governments have constitutionally defined powers. Both typically have the power to regulate individual behavior and to make laws. Each level or type of government has a complete set of legislative, executive and judicial institutions. An alteration in the constitutional powers of either type of government typically requires the approval of both types through the constitutional amendment process.

Unitary systems have just one type of government—a national or central government. Subnational divisions of the central government are created to increase administrative efficiency, but these subnational divisions do not have the status or authority since they are not constitutionally defined. Modification of the subnational units typically requires only the approval of the appropriate decision-making body—often the national legislature, but sometimes administrative officials—in the central government. Individual behavior is regulated by laws passed by the central government.

THE ADVANTAGES OF A FEDERAL SYSTEM

Supporters of federalism argue that it offers many advantages, including the following:

(1) Federalism presumably brings government closer to the people by creating constitutionally defined state governments which cannot be arbitrarily abolished or rendered powerless by a capricious national government. State governments cover a smaller geographic territory than does the broader and bigger central government. Because of their proximity, state governments can more easily "feel the pulse" of public opinion. The smaller size of state governments also makes state officials more easily accessible to the average citizen than federal officials. Citizens can more readily express their preferences and vocalize their problems to geographically close state officials than to the distant officials of the central government.

(2) A federal system provides multiple points of access for citizens, increasing the probability that citizens will be able to effectively express their concerns to attentive officials. Federal systems have many avenues of entree. Two levels of government have more access points than does a single central government. Additionally, each level has a complete set of government institutions. Citizens who fail to achieve satisfactory resolution of an issue or problem in one branch of state government may turn either to other branches of the same government or to institutions at the federal level. For example, civil rights activists who failed to achieve racial equality at the state level in the South turned to federal courts.

Similarly, after blockage by officials of desired actions at the federal level, citizens may still turn to state officials for help. In the 1970s proponents of capital punishment were frustrated with a 1972 U.S. Supreme Court ruling in the case of *Furman v. Georgia* that most state capital punishment laws were unconstitutional. In the following years proponents used state legislatures to rewrite capital punishment laws that would pass constitutional muster, thus achieving their goal.

(3) A federalist structure of government is a structure replete with checks and balances which Madison, among others, felt would enhance individual liberty and prevent the central government from encroaching on citizen civil rights. Multiple governments reduce the probability that one political party or faction can capture the entire governmental machinery and act arbitrarily and capriciously. Opposition parties which never acquire official power by achieving electoral success have a difficult time surviving. A federalist system, more than a centralized unitary system, provides the opportunity for electoral success for opposition parties and therefore reduces the chance of single party hegemony or, even worse, tyranny.

(4) The "laboratory thesis" in support of federalism contends that subnational governments are good places to experiment with unproven government policies before adopting the policies at the national level. Many examples of initial state trials of policies eventually embraced at the national level include allowing women to vote, the adoption of minimum wage laws and the passage of air pollution control programs.

(5) Not only does a federal structure allow different policies to be adopted in various parts of the country, federalism proponents contend that policy diversity is desirable and even necessary to meet differing local needs. The country is not uniform, argue federalism supporters. Hence, government policies also should not be uniform. The application of rigid national standards which obfuscate local culture and needs is more likely in a unitary system.

THE DISADVANTAGES OF A FEDERAL SYSTEM

According to critics, federalism is plagued with several limitations and disadvantages:

(1) Diversity in state laws creates chaos, unfairness and inequities. Fines and criminal penalties vary radically from state to state. For example, in the mid-1980s average felony convictions resulted in prison sentences ranging from thirteen months in South Dakota to fifty-eight months in Massachusetts. A conviction of shoplifting in the mid-1980s typically resulted in probation in Albuquerque, New Mexico and three months imprisonment in Charlotte, North Carolina. States also apply differing standards for the application of capital punishment, with some states not applying the death penalty. States also vary in how the death penalty is applied to various age groups. In some states youth as young as ten who commit capital offenses may be executed, while in other

states only those eighteen or older at the time of the crime's commission can be executed.

(2) Federalism may result in excessive decentralization and duplication of services provided by the various levels of government. Both federal and state governments are involved in and sometimes overlap in the areas of education, transportation, parks and recreation, crime prevention, worker and consumer safety regulations, financial regulation and corrections. Scholars of federalism often refer to a "marble cake" rather than a "layer cake" arrangement of government functions. Critics charge that much of the service duplication in federalism is needless and wasteful.

(3) Even when federal and state governments coordinate to provide a common program rather than duplicate efforts, filtering services through multiple layers diminishes accountability and causes slow and wasteful delivery. Most typically in joint federal-state programs, authorization of legislation and program financing are provided at the federal level, while administration and implementation occur at the state level. Critics argue that separating the responsibility for raising funds for a program from the responsibility for administering the program undercuts its responsiveness to citizens. State officials who can spend without raising taxes undercut their accountability.

(4) Wealthier states have greater resources to deliver a higher level of services more effectively. By decentralizing some financing of government services to the state and local level, federalism fails to correct these inequalities in resources and wealth. In fiscal year 1983, per capita state and local tax collections varied from a high of $4,908 for Alaska to a low of $769 for Mississippi, giving Alaska 6.38 times greater per capita revenue to provide services.

The national per capita average for state and local tax collections in 1983 was $1,214. The regional averages for New England ($1,337), the Midatlantic ($1,544), the Far West ($1,321) and the Great Lakes ($1,213) were at or exceeded the national average, while the per capita tax collections for the Plains states ($1,153), the Southeast ($928), the Southwest ($1,050), and the Rocky Mountain states ($1,173) were below the national average. The Midatlantic, the wealthiest region, has average per capita tax revenues 1.66 times greater than the Southeast, the poorest region. Critics contend that federalism does not rectify these significant discrepancies in the resources available for government services.

(5) Federalism also fails to correct inequities among the service levels provided by states, making national standards difficult to develop and administer. Similar differences are observed in per capita state and local direct general expenditures. In 1983, state and local per capita expenditures varied across the states from a high of $8,662 in Alaska to

a low of $1,372 in Arkansas. A similar pattern for regional per capita state and local expenditures holds for tax revenues. In 1983, the national average was $1,982. New England ($2,021), the Midatlantic ($2,305), the Rocky Mountain states ($2,052), and the Far West ($2,211) exceeded this average, while the Great Lakes ($1,936), the Plains states ($1,936), and the Southeast ($1,646) fell below it. The state with the highest per capita expenditures spent 6.31 times more than the state with the lowest per capita expenditures, while the highest region exceeded the lowest region by 1.4 times.

EXPRESS, IMPLIED, INHERENT, RESERVE AND CONCURRENT POWERS

The Constitution distinguishes between several types of powers. Express powers are specifically delegated to the national government, primarily in the first three articles which define legislative, executive and judicial powers. Among the powers delegated to the national government which deal with international relations are making treaties, declaring war, regulating commerce with foreign nations, establishing rules of naturalization, providing for an army and a navy, and defining and punishing piracy and crimes committed at sea. Delegated powers which are primarily concerned with domestic affairs include coining money, levying and collecting taxes, borrowing money on government credit, repaying government debts, controlling patents, establishing post offices and post roads, governing the District of Columbia, establishing federal courts and their jurisdictions and developing uniform rules on bankruptcies (see table 3-1).

Additionally, the Constitution delegates implied powers which may be reasonably inferred from the express powers to Congress. Implied powers are based on the "necessary and proper" clause of Article I, Section 8, which gives Congress the power "to make all Laws which shall be necessary and proper for carrying into Execution the foregoing powers, and all other powers vested . . . in the Government of the United States." The Case of *United States v. Curtiss-Wright Corp.* (1936) established that the national government also has inherent powers in foreign affairs—powers that do not depend on specific grants of authority. Inherent powers given the national government the same authority in dealing with other nations that it would have if it were a unitary government.

Reserve powers are those not specifically mentioned by the Constitution and thus left to the states. The Tenth Amendment establishes this principle by stating "powers not delegated to the United States by the Constitution, nor prohibited by it to the states, are reserved to the states respectively, or to the people." Included among reserve powers

Table 3-1
Constitutional Powers of the National Government

POWERS PRIMARILY CONCERNED WITH INTERNATIONAL RELATIONS

Declaring war
Making treaties with foreign nations
Defining and punishing piracy and crimes committed at sea
Establishing rules of naturalization
Providing for an army and navy
Regulating commerce with foreign nations

POWERS PRIMARILY CONCERNED WITH DOMESTIC AFFAIRS

Coining money
Borrowing money on government credit
Regulating interstate commerce
Levying and collecting taxes
Repaying government debts
Controlling patents
Establishing post offices and post roads
Governing the District of Columbia
Establishing federal courts and their jurisdictions
Establishing uniform rules on bankruptcies

are police authority, control of elections, and regulation for public health, safety, education and morals. Some powers—called concurrent powers—are shared by the national and state governments. These include taxation and spending.

Some actions are denied either to the national or the state governments, or to both. States may not make treaties with foreign governments, grant letters of marque and reprisal authorizing individuals to engage in piracy, coin money, issue bills of credit or use anything but official currency to repay debts. Nor may states pass bills of attainder convicting individuals of crimes by statute rather than through the courts or pass ex post facto laws which retroactively declare an action a crime when it was not a crime at the time it was committed. The Constitution also prohibits states from passing laws which impair obligations of contracts and from granting titles of nobility. The Fourteenth Amendment prohibits states from violating due process of law and equal protection under the law or from abridging the privileges and immunities of citizens.

The Constitution specifies that some state actions require the approval of Congress, including state taxing of imports, exports and foreign ships; maintaining troops except for the national guard; entering into compacts with other states or foreign nations; and engaging in war unless invaded or in imminent danger of attack.

Powers constitutionally denied to the national government include suspension of the writ of habeas corpus (which requires jailers to explain to a judge why they are holding a prisoner in custody) unless rebellion or public safety call for suspension. The national government is also prohibited from passing bills of attainder and ex post facto laws or granting titles of nobility. The national government may not discriminate in favor of the ports of any one state over others. Through the Bill of Rights the federal government is also prohibited from violating individual civil liberties. Originally the Bill of Rights applied only to the federal government, but over time many provisions within it have been interpreted by the Supreme Court to apply to states as well (see table 3-2).

STAGES OF INTERGOVERNMENTAL RELATIONSHIPS

Over the two centuries since the adoption and ratification of the 1787 Convention, the powers of both the national and the state governments have increased as the scope of government has expanded. When comparing the growth of the two levels of government during this time period, the power of the federal government has increased more than the power of the states. Federal powers have slowly, incrementally and inexorably expanded vis-à-vis the states although periods of retrenchment have occurred at various points where the Supreme Court has given some advantage to the states.

Scholars of intergovernmental relations do not agree on the exact number and nature of stages in federal-state relations. Deil Wright (1982) proposes six phases of intergovernmental relations. These include: (1) conflict: 1930s and before; (2) cooperation between the 1930s and 1950s; (3) concentration between the 1940s and 1960s; (4) creative federalism in the 1950s and 1960s; (5) competition in the 1960s and 1970s; (6) calculative federalism in the 1970s and 1980s. These periods of federalism are not mutually exclusive and often overlap at various points in time.

Conflict Between 1790 and the 1930s

The first period identified by Wright reflected attempts by government officials at all levels to identify the proper spheres of influence and appropriate boundaries between the powers of the different governments. Relationships were antagonistic. A landmark case during this time period was *McCulloch v. Maryland* which established national supremacy by sustaining the power of the national government to establish a national bank and by denying Maryland the right to tax that bank. This case opened a battleground between officials of various jurisdictions over who could tax what. This period has often been called "layer cake" federalism due to efforts to describe exclusive spheres for national, state and local governments.

Table 3-2
Powers Denied by the Constitution

POWERS DENIED TO THE STATES

Making treaties with foreign governments

Granting letters of marque and reprisal

Coining money

Issuing bills of credit

Repaying debt with unofficial currency

POWERS DENIED TO THE STATES WITHOUT THE CONSENT OF CONGRESS

Taxing imports, exports, and foreign ships

Keeping troops or ships in peacetime except for the National Guard

Entering into compacts with other states or foreign nations

Engaging in war unless invaded or in imminent danger of attack

POWERS DENIED TO THE NATIONAL GOVERNMENT

Suspension of the writ of habeas corpus

Favoring the ports of one state over those of another state

Violating a limited number of civil liberties protected in the Bill
of Rights not yet applied to state governments by court interpretation

POWERS DENIED TO ALL GOVERNMENTS

Granting titles of nobility

Passing bills of attainder

Passing ex post facto laws

Violation of most civil liberties protected in the Bill of Rights

---

Cooperation between the 1930s and the 1950s

During the period of cooperation from the 1930s through the 1950s, the uppermost concern of the nation was how to alleviate economic distress and international threats to security. Incentives for collaboration were strengthened. Cooperation occurred in the areas of national planning, tax credits and formula-based grants-in-aid. Thus the prime mechanism for cooperation was based on fiscal ties. This period has been described as one of "marble cake" federalism because of the shared functions by the federal and state governments.

Concentration from the 1940s through the 1960s

Throughout the Truman, Eisenhower and Kennedy administrations, federal-state relations became more concentrated. The use of grant-in-aid programs was expanded and nearly doubled since the depression era. The motive force behind the concentration, spread and increased use of categorical grant programs was the need of government to respond to the needs of the middle class and to suburbanization. This stage of intergovernmental relations has sometimes been called the "watertap" phase, reflecting the increased flow of federal monies to state and local governments.

Creative Federalism in the 1950s and 1960s

The "creative" phase in the 1950s and 1960s grew out of and overlapped with its earlier phases of cooperative and concentrated periods. Three mechanisms were prevalent in government programs during this period, largely as a result of federal efforts to disseminate them to states: program planning, project grants and popular participation. Described as the "flowering" period, federal innovations proliferated to other levels of government. Federal grants grew in number, scope and size.

Picket Fence Federalism in the 1960s and 1970s

The "picket fence" phase of federal-state relations in the 1960s and 1970s was characterized by competition and reactionary sentiments, especially at the state level, toward the creative phase and its innovations. States demanded and received special and general revenue-sharing which gave states broader discretionary power than the more narrowly defined and specific categorical grants had done. Competition during this phase was more moderate than that of the "layer cake" phase because officials had developed realistic notions of the interdependence of the different levels of government and realized that a return to a sharp division of power was impossible.

Calculative Federalism in the 1970s and 1980s

The last stage, the "calculative" phase of the 1970s and 1980s, is noted for the problems of accountability, bankruptcy of local governments and loss of public confidence. This phase is dominated by three per-spectives: fungibility, gamesmanship and overload. States began to see federal aid as fungible or able to be shifted from one program area to another. States also began to apply concepts of gamesmanship to at-tempts to modify federal formulas to their advantage. Political overload occurred in the sense that modern government was overwhelmed by its new responsibilities of caring for and regulating the broad, new areas of economic activity and providing expanded protection of civil liber-ties.

David Walker (1981) of the U.S. Advisory Commission on Intergov-ernmental Relations has delineated four historical periods in federal-state relations: (1) the pre-civil war period between 1789 and 1860, (2) the post-civil war period leading up to the Great Depression, between 1861 and 1930, (3) the Roosevelt era, through the administration of Eisenhower from 1930 to 1960; (4) the current era which began with the election of John F. Kennedy as president, from 1960 to the present.

Early Dual Federalism between 1789 and 1860

Walker describes the pre-civil war period between 1789 and 1860 as one of "dual" federalism. Although *McCulloch v. Maryland* in 1819 clearly sanctioned national supremacy, during this period the U.S. Supreme Court also recognized that certain commerce-related activities fell un-der the states' police power and were not to be regulated by the na-tional government. The Court developed the idea that states could reg-ulate commerce and navigation in the absence of Congressional legislation. The Court also upheld state bankruptcy laws and ruled that the Bill of Rights did not apply to state actions. In the period from 1835 to 1863 under the Taney Court, some scholars believe that Su-preme Court decisions were so favorable to states' rights that they con-stituted a threat to the national supremacy clause. Others have count-ered this view by arguing that the Taney Court was not an extreme champion of states' rights, but rather developed the doctrine of "selec-tive exclusiveness" which provided states a limited, concurrent state power over commerce. Overall, the era of dual federalism was an era of two separate spheres of power with minimal overlap between national and state powers.

Mature Dual Federalism between 1861 and 1930

The second era, between 1861 and 1930, was an extension of dual federalism. Mature dual federalism lasted approximately seventy years. Its dominant political theme was the perfection of the free economy. The need for increased services resulted in a shift in the predominant source of financing for the national government from tariff and sales receipts from the western properties to the income tax. States also began a slow shift to the income tax during this period.

The Civil War had destroyed the doctrine of nullification which stated that each state had the right to interpose or nullify an action of Congress and the right to secede from the union. This doctrine was officially rejected by the U.S. Supreme Court in *Texas v. White* (1869), a decision which also partially laid out dual federal theory, recognizing the Constitution as supreme law at the national level, yet also holding that there should be no loss of separate and independent autonomy to the states.

After the Civil War, the Thirteenth, Fourteenth and Fifteenth Amendments were imposed on the southern states by the Congress. The U.S. Supreme Court, however, eventually stopped drastic constitutional change in the area of civil rights and voting. The cumulative effect was to leave civil and voting rights issues to the discretion of the states until the 1950s and 1960s.

Intergovernmental fiscal transfers rose significantly during the last thirty years of this era, constituting a dramatic break from the early period of dual federalism. At first, federal assistance was modest, as demonstrated by the Morrill Act of 1862 which opened public lands to states for establishing agricultural colleges. This act was later supplemented by the Hatch Act of 1887 which provided funding for agricultural colleges in the form of cash grants.

By 1920, six more cash grant programs were enacted, such as assistance to state marine schools, state and private forestry cooperation, highway construction, vocational education, vocational rehabilitation and agricultural extension services. By 1930, fifteen federal grant programs wee operating, although highway assistance predominated. Especially at the end of the era the rise of industrialization contributed to the weakening of dual federalism as the national government became stronger constitutionally, judicially and fiscally as well as through regulation of the states by adding strings to intergovernmental grants.

Cooperative Federalism between 1930 and 1960

Cooperative federalism lasted from 1930 to 1960. Its seeds had been sown in the era of mature dual federalism. Unlike Hoover, Roosevelt rejected states' rights views and initiated sweeping economic reforms by adopting a broad interpretation of the federal commerce power. At first the U.S. Supreme Court struck down his New Deal proposals but by 1937, under the threat of a court-packing scheme, the Supreme Court reversed itself and upheld measures such as the Social Security Act, the National Labor Relations Act and the Farm Mortgage Act, all of 1935.

The post-1937 Supreme Court permanently enlarged the scope of federal power so that areas of authority which had earlier been left to the states or the private sector were upheld by the Court to fall within congressional prerogative. The New Deal established many new areas of federal policy such as the sale of securities, flood control, agricultural production and marketing, public utility operations and labor-management relations. Since national government authority far outweighed state authority, especially in regulatory activities, dual federalism became a dead doctrine.

Across the cooperative era the federal share of domestic outlays grew, jumping seventeen percent in 1929 to forty-eight percent in 1959. In comparison, the state share of domestic outlays remained fairly constant, hovering around twenty-three percent throughout the period. The rise in grants-in-aid across these three decades was also significant. It increased over thirty-two times, growing from $192 million in 1933 to $6.3 billion in 1959. State aid to localities during the same time increased over tenfold, from $801 million in 1932 to $8.1 billion in 1958.

Creative Federalism and Its Variants Since 1960

Creative federalism, the last major era in federal-state relations, occurred between 1960 and the present and has had several substages. The first major variation to emerge was President Lyndon Johnson's creative federalism. Johnson expanded the concept of cooperative federalism into a partnership principle, including cities, counties, school districts, nonprofit organizations, as well as states. With increased direct federal linkages to substate units and local governments, much more complicated patterns of intergovernmental relations arose. The emphasis on intergovernmental relations shifted from nonurban areas to urban areas where the major concentrations of population occurred. There was not only a massive expansion of categorical grants but also increased usage of project grants. There was little debate over whether or not the federal government should administer these new programs, since unlike the New Deal, federal involvement was considered appropriate.

New federalism came to fruition under President Richard Nixon and reacted to creative federalism in the sense of being anti-centralization, anti-categorical grant and anti-administration. During this era the evolution of more power to recipient units was a popular idea. General revenue-sharing became the mechanism for decentralizing power. With the election of Jimmy Carter to the presidency, a heavy urban focus in urbanization and centralization returned, as well as interest in a variety of governmental programs. Federalism during this period was marked by confusion and the absence of a consistent ideological perspective.

When Ronald Reagan was elected to the White House in 1980, he engaged in the largest effort in recent times to dismantle the labyrinthic system of intergovernmental grants and to decentralize federal power. Reagan's "New Federalism" proposals were introduced shortly after he assumed the presidency and included a provision for the national government to exchange programs with the states, taking responsibility for Medicaid from them while giving them responsibility for Food Stamps and Aid to Families with Dependent Children. Although blocked politically, this exchange would have federalized responsibility for governmental health programs and returned responsibility for welfare programs to the states.

Reagan's New Federalism also called for the federal government to return to the states 120 categorical grants, along with adequate revenue sources to fund those programs the states wished to continue. The Omnibus Budget Reconciliation Act of 1981 created nine block grants which replaced seventy-seven categorical grants and gave greater discretion to the states. The grant system was further reduced through outright elimination of sixty-two programs. Federal regulations stressed state flexibility and accountability. Funds for many intergovernmental programs were cut. A presidential task force on regulatory relief, headed by Vice-President George Bush, revised and deleted numerous government regulations on the basis of cost-benefit analysis. Not until 1982 did Reagan decide to simplify what he called the jungle of grants-in-aid and restructure the intergovernmental grant systems. The federal government was also to reduce the scope and pervasiveness of cross-cutting cleavages, requirements unrelated to the substance of a grant but applied to a variety of federal aid programs.

By 1983 New Federalism had been relegated to the political back burner since Reagan's proposal to convert thirty-four categorical grants to four mega-grants received little local support (Richter 1986, 83–85). The Reagan era represented a reaction to increased power at the federal level and an attempt to devolve power to the states. Reagan achieved some of these goals but not all, since their objectives often clashed with those of powerful constituencies and interest groups and the proclivities of Congress to retain categorical grants to deliver pork barrel benefits. Despite the popularity of Reagan and his capture of the conservative mood of the country, the factors that initially pushed the federal government to greater involvement in the private economy and to being the senior partner in federal-state relations remain. If history repeats itself and long-term trends continue, the Reagan revolution of devolution may be short-lived.

THE U.S. SUPREME COURT AND
INTERGOVERNMENTAL RELATIONS

The U.S. Supreme Court has played a key role in shaping the nature of intergovernmental relations and, since the era of dual federalism, in contributing to the growth of federal power. The case of *Marbury v. Madison* (1803) was significant in establishing an independent federal judiciary. This case established the principle of judicial review by affirming the right of the Court to declare acts of Congress unconstitutional. National government was further strengthened in *McCulloch v. Maryland* (1819).

The Court and the Interstate Commerce Clause

Five years later in the case of *Gibbons v. Ogden* (1824), the Court addressed the implications of the interstate commerce clause by defining commerce, setting the scope of congressional regulation over commerce and determining whether the Constitution should be construed strictly or broadly. This decision held that congressional regulatory power over commerce was complete, but it failed to address the issue of the extent to which states could also regulate interstate commerce.

After the Civil War, the Supreme Court continued to bolster national supremacy in the case of *Texas v. White* (1869). By the 1880s, state impotency in controlling the arrogance of the robber barons and captains of industry in the early phases of industrialization became apparent, leaving to Congress the task of dealing with the negative aspects of the U.S. industrial revolution. Congress passed the Interstate Commerce Act of 1887 giving the Interstate Commerce Commission (ICC) the power to hear complaints, oversee records and accounts of railroads, hold hearings and issue cease and desist orders against any interstate carrier violating commission regulations and rates.

The Supreme Court in its efforts to bolster the philosophy and practice of laissez-faire economics ruled against parts of the statutory authority granted to the ICC. The Court struck down the ability of the ICC to compel testimony and to make a final determination of private rights in the case of *Interstate Commerce Commission v. Brimson* (1894), severely handicapping the effectiveness of the ICC. Due to this ruling, control over interstate commerce became a constitutional no-man's-land where the powers of federal and state governments were vaguely defined.

The Court reacted similarly to the Sherman Antitrust Act of 1890 which legislated that private restraints on interstate or foreign trade were illegal. When the federal government brought suit against the American Sugar Refining Company to dismantle its near monopolistic holdings, the Court ruled against the government in the case of *United States v. E. C. Knight Co.* (1895). The federal government had claimed that the monopoly was a restraint of interstate trade and resulted in unnaturally high prices, but the Court, relying on a narrow definition of commerce, held that "commerce succeeds to manufacture and is not a part of it." The Court admitted that the sugar trust was a monopoly restraining the manufacture of sugar, but declared that this was not a part of interstate commerce.

Use of the Commerce Power
to Enhance National Police Power

The absence of a police clause in the Constitution led to problems in defining national and state police authority in a variety of areas. One of the early cases dealing with this issue involved congressional policing of gambling. Congress passed an 1895 act which made interstate shipment of lottery tickets illegal. In *Champion v. Ames* (1903), the Court rejected the arguments that Congress could not use its commerce power to prohibit any activity entirely and that the lottery tickets in and of themselves had no real value and therefore were not included under interstate commerce. This case paved the way for increasing use of the commerce power as a federal policing mechanism.

The police power of the national Congress was further enhanced by the Court in *McGray v. United States* (1904) in which the Court rejected the position that Congress could only tax for the purpose of raising revenues. In this case, use of federal tax authority to limit the sale of artificially colored oleomargarine was upheld. The Court's ruling gave Congress incentives to further expand its police powers by passing the Pure Food and Drug Act, the White Slave Trade Act and the Meat Inspection Act (Colella 1986).

By the early twentieth century, important precedents had been set giving the national government the power to tax and spend, regulate the economy and police state and corporate activities. By the end of the Great Depression, the American federal system was transformed to one in which the national government played an even greater role. This transformation was not uniformly smooth however. In *Schechter Poultry Corporation v. the United States* (1935), the Court struck down the National Industrial Recovery Act of 1933. In *Carter v. Carter Coal Co.* (1936), the Court invalidated the industry-specific national recovery agencies. In *United States v. Butler* (1936), the Agricultural Adjustment Act of 1933 was ruled unconstitutional.

Perhaps shaken by the unsuccessful but very bold Roosevelt court-packing plan of 1937 which sought to add an additional justice to the Court for every sitting justice who had not retired within six months of his seventieth birthday (a total of six justices for Roosevelt), the Supreme Court began to rule more favorably for national power and New Deal legislation. It upheld the National Labor Relations Act in *National Labor Relations Board v. Jones and Laughlin Steel Corporation* (1937). In the 1937 cases of *Steward Machine Co. v. Davis* and *Helvering, Welch, and Edison Electric Illuminating Co. v. Davis*, the Court upheld the constitutionality of the 1935 Social Security Act. The Court also upheld the 1938 Fair Labor Standards Act in a 1941 case, *United States v. Darby Lumber Co.* The Agricultural Adjustment Act was finally upheld in *Wickard v. Filburn* (1942), which closed judicial scrutiny of the New Deal.

Regulation of State and Local Government

Through the congressional power to regulate commerce and the application of the Bill of Rights to the states through the Fourteenth Amendment, the federal government has continued to expand its authority and power. The possibility of conflict between the federal and state governments due to overlapping jurisdictions has increased as the scope of issues considered at all levels of government has been enlarged. Under the national supremacy clause, Congress can preempt the power of the states, although in some instances states may preempt the federal government in administering regulation of a policy area if their laws are at least as stringent as national standards. Several recent laws, including the Clean Air Act and the Federal Water Pollution Control Act, include such partial preemption mechanisms. The Court has upheld the concept of partial preemption.

More recent cases have focused on the ability of Congress to regulate the internal affairs of state and local governments. In the suprise ruling of *National League of Cities v. Usery* (1976), the Court upheld state preemption of federal power to regulate working conditions for state and local government employees. This case questioned the validity of 1974 amendments to the 1938 Fair Labor Standards Act extending minimum wage and maximum hour standards to most state and local employees. Regressing to earlier interpretations of the commerce clause and the Tenth Amendment, Justice Rehnquist, in a narrow five to four decision, argued that Congress could not use its power to regulate commerce to govern the integral functions of states.

In *Equal Employment Opportunity Commission v. Wyoming* (1983), the Court retreated slightly from its earlier position in *National League of Cities v. Usery.* The 1974 Amendments to the Age Discrimination in Employment Act (ADEA) expanded the definition of "employer" to include state and local governments. Consequently age discrimination by state and local governments became illegal. The Supreme Court ruled that this particular congressional use of the commerce clause to regulate states was constitutionally valid because the state failed to show that the ADEA would hinder its ability to govern its own internal operations.

THE GROWTH OF FEDERAL POWER
IN THE TWENTIETH CENTURY

In addition to U.S. Supreme Court cases, several other factors have contributed to the growth of federal power in the twentieth century. Among them are long-term economic growth, an elastic federal tax structure, Keynesian economics, federal ability to deficit spend, rising expectations of federal problem-solving responsibilities, fragmentation of subnational jurisdictions and heightened importance of national security. Other factors are a greater emphasis on interpersonal equity, negative spillovers of locally based technologies and social problems, and rigid, inflexible state constitutions.

Long-term Economic Growth

One contributory factor to the expansion of federal power has been long-term economic growth. U.S. national income has grown steadily in the twentieth century except during the Great Depression years. This growth in national income has been accompanied by a corresponding growth in technology and productive capacity. Public expenditures in most countries are income elastic, growing faster than national income. Further, public goods and services are often regarded as luxuries, affordable only when income increases and basic survival needs have been met. The expansion of technology also accelerates the need for public goods (Musgrave and Musgrave 1984, 136). With the strong historical bias in the United States against large government and ideological preference for private sector economic activity, economic growth and an "expanding pie" have been particularly important to the growth of the federal government in the United States.

The Adoption of a Progressive Federal Income Tax

A second factor contributing to expanded federal power was the adoption of the federal income tax with the ratification of the Sixteenth Amendment in 1913. Equally as significant as its adoption was its progressive rate structure (Pechman 1977, 54–122). Under progressive taxation, high-income citizens pay a greater percentage of their total income in taxes than do low-income individuals. Taking the largest tax bite out of those personal incomes which are growing with the greatest absolute dollar increments makes the tax elastic. Elastic taxes produce tax revenues which grow at a faster rate than the actual tax base. In short, the federal government became the rich Uncle Sam in comparison to state and local governments as federal revenues were increasing at a faster rate than revenues produced by the more regressive state and local tax systems. Inflation in the 1970s and 1980s accelerated the growth in federal revenues by pushing citizens into higher marginal tax brackets, even without an accompanying increase in purchasing power.

Keynesian Economics

Keynesian economics provided an additional impetus to expanding the power of the federal government. Keynes articulated a need for governmental intervention in the market place to modulate boom-and-bust business cycles. Keynes specified how governments should mitigate wild cycle fluctuations. In periods of economic slumps, such as recessions and depressions, the solution of pump priming required a cut in taxes and an increase in government spending. Through tax cuts and increased government expenditures, additional dollars would flow into the private sector, stimulating production and reducing unemployment via the multiplier effect. Periods of economic inflation required the reverse fiscal remedy of raising taxes and cutting spending.

The political reality of Keynesian economics was that remedies for rectifying recessions and depressions were popular with presidents and Congress, while the palliatives for preventing inflation and price escalation were politically unpopular. Despite the uneven application of Keynesian philosophy in the arena of U.S. partisan politics it resulted in a significant expansion of federal power to include macro-level fiscal regulation to promote the goals of economic stability.

Federal Ability to Deficit Spend

Another dimension of expanded federal power is the ability of the national government to engage in deficit financing and planned budget deficits. Keynes did not condone deficit spending but rather advocated broadening the time frame for balancing the federal budget from an annual focus to one coinciding with the business cycle. Keynes fully expected years of budget surplus to counterbalance years of budget deficits although, in reality, politics prevented the accumulation of surpluses. Keynes was followed by a school of thinkers who justified these political actions by arguing that deficit spending, unbalanced by surplus years, could continue indefinitely without additional negative effects beyond a rise in interest rates as money markets tightened. As long as the national debt was held internally and citizens were constantly willing to roll it over, no great harm was done.

Although Congress does operate under a national debt ceiling, Congress also statutorily controls the ceiling and resets it at a higher level when accumulated debt is in danger of exceeding the statutory limit. By contrast, state and local governments are usually prohibited by their own state constitutions or by statute from using deficit financing for operating expenditures and are restricted to using debt to finance capital projects and improvements. This greater financial flexibility has enhanced the power of the national government relative to that of the states.

Rising Expectations of Federal Problem-solving Abilities

The role of the federal government has also been increased due to rising expectations from citizens that the national government should assume social responsibilities previously addressed by other social institutions such as the family, the church and the political party. Changing social patterns and the breakdown of the extended family (and in many instances the nuclear family) have strengthened the federal government as a major supporter of millions of people who previously received support and protection elsewhere. Changing market structures and economic conditions have also forced farmers and small businessmen to rely more on federal support. Because television and mass media coverage have increased the visibility of the presidency, increased public expectations of presidential problem-solving abilities have become more pronounced. However, expectations of Congress and the bureaucracy have not lagged far behind.

Negative Spillovers of Locally Based Technologies and Social Problems

Many problems handled locally have caused negative spillover effects requiring federal intervention. If one local government mishandles a problem such as waste disposal, other communities may suffer from the irresponsible handling of waste by the first locality. Other environmental issues, such as water management or air purity, have heightened the role of the federal government and its regulations in these areas. Environmental issues are illustrative but by no means inclusive of policy areas where spillover effects transcend subnational political boundaries. Crime, education, welfare, consumer issues, civil rights, and health and transportation, among other policy areas, may also be included on the list of issues where spillover effects pose a concern. New technologies, in addition to increasing social interdependencies, have provided further incentives for augmenting federal power.

Greater Emphasis upon Interpersonal Equity

Greater concern for equity is another contributing factor to federal expansion and growth. Beginning with the creation of the social security system, the Tennessee Valley Authority and public works jobs in the 1930s, Americans in the twentieth century have been willing to give some attention and money to improve the plight of the poor, the disabled and the handicapped (Galbraith 1958, 72–77). The emphasis on interpersonal equity in the United States has been much less pronounced than in Western Europe and has always been offset by traditional concerns for personal freedoms, profits, investment capital and the free enterprise system.

Still, the growing emphasis on equity has created escalating federal expenditures on a constellation of federal programs including Medicare, Medicaid, Aid to Families with Dependent Children, Food Stamps and subsidized housing. Despite such social programs, the gap between the rich and the poor continues to grow. The inability or unwillingness of the private sector to absorb much of the population into the work force assures continuing federal involvement in alleviating inequity.

Fragmentation of Subnational Jurisdictions

Fragmentation of local governments further accelerates federal involvement into traditionally nonfederal policy areas. The range in geographic areas and populations of various states is great, yet states have continued to serve as the basic political unit in American life. As population centers and their concomitant problems sprawl across subnational boundaries, the federal government has become involved in the financing and coordination of a greater number of functions which were previously the exclusive domain of states and their localities. Examples of these functions include education, transportation, environmental protection and housing.

Despite federal attempts to centralize and coordinate planning for subnational service delivery, local governments in particular have opposed consolidation of urban governments. In those instances where population centers cross state lines, standard metropolitan area-based governments would require state boundary alterations, an unlikely occurrence given the constitutional independence of states. Wealthier suburban units do not wish to join with center cities since doing so would increase the likelihood that suburban residents would have to at least partially support the larger populations of indigents, elderly and minorities that live in core cities. Nor do local officials presiding over current governments wish to have their positions and offices abolished.

The combined effect of often excessive subnational fragmentation and local resistance to consolidation has been the increase of the federal coordinating and financing role for public services.

National Security

The federal government has always had the primary responsibility for national security and national defense, but the Cold War and its aftereffects have made these functions more important and have expanded federal power. Traditionally during wars presidents have used national emergency and wartime powers to expand federal control over resources and the private economy. After World War II the perceived threat of communist takeover also encouraged the maintenance and continued expansion of federal domestic police power. Information in some federal bureaucracies was often classified for national security reasons. Citizen membership in perceived subversive organizations was closely monitored. In darker moments, citizens were placed in quasi-concentration camps due to their nationality.

The doctrine of deterrence and the accompanying arms race fueled an expanding defense sector in the economy which responded to market cues from the federal government. Across time, perceptions of missile gaps have contributed to further growth in defense expenditures and to the development of new weapons systems. National security and defense have been the justification for initial federal expansion into a variety of areas previously dominated by the states, including highway building and public education, both at the elementary and secondary and at the college levels.

Rigid and Inflexible State Constitutions

Many states have rigid and inflexible constitutions which have handicapped them in solving state and local problems. State constitutions are often longer, wordier, and less clear than the national Constitution and may favor special interest groups. Constitutional scholars argue that the best constitutions emphasize governmental processes—who holds the power and what the scope of that power is to be—rather than specific policies which impinge directly on the daily lives of citizens. Specific policies are more dependent on technology and social patterns and may need to be modified more frequently to accommodate changing norms. By contrast, effective constitutions frame the basic processes of government. Many state constitutions have violated this wisdom under pressure from interest groups to include policies favorable to them, resulting in a document that is difficult and costly to change.

CAN FEDERALISM SURVIVE
IN THE TWENTY-FIRST CENTURY?

Despite the long-term increase in federal power, states in recent years, especially under the Reagan administration, have enjoyed a resurgence and reflowering. Factors which have enhanced state resurgence include lack of public confidence in and distrust of the federal government after many Great Society programs were overpromised and oversold, state government reform, increased state lobbying, increased two-party competition in some states where one party previously dominated, and cutbacks in federal grants (Bowman and Kearney 1986, 10–18). These factors may affect whether or not federalism will survive in its current form or be transformed to an appreciably different structure.

Ideological differences between liberals and conservatives often affect which level of government is viewed as appropriate to finance and administer domestic, social and regulatory policy. Liberals generally favor more centralized national financing and administration while conservatives favor devolution of responsibility for domestic functions from the federal level to state and local units.

Liberals prefer national policy making for a variety of reasons. The opportunities for redistribution, a goal favored by liberals, are greater at the federal level than at subnational levels. At the national level, because of the considerably larger geographic region covered, there are wider ranges of income and greater economic heterogeneity, making possible more extensive redistribution. The possibilities for redistribution are lessened under state tax systems where sale taxes place a greater portion of the burden of financing government services on low-income individuals and families. By contrast, until the mid-1980s, the federal tax structure was at least nominally progressive. Hence at the federal level, redistribution occurred not only through expenditures but also through the tax structure. The federal government also had the potential for setting minimum national standards for social benefit programs, a power precluded from the individual states.

Conservatives have historically favored a return of power to the states. Although powerful at the national level, business and producer interests have historically been even more powerful at the state level. When confronted with the possibility of federal regulation and policy development, powerful industries such as the insurance industry have actively fought to retain a system of state regulation and control. In the 1950s and 1960s, opponents of civil rights for blacks and other minorities argued for states' rights, since minority rights could be more easily abridged and denied at the state level. Fearful of "foreign" ideas, conservatives have resisted federal intervention in education and have consistently favored local control of public schools. When federal intervention occurred, despite conservative efforts to the contrary, many conservatives abandoned the public schools and enrolled their children in private schools.

Given the clash of perceptions of liberals and conservatives over the appropriate roles for federal and state governments and given the opposing directions in which they push government when assuming power, can federalism survive the constant buffeting by opposing philosophies, and progress into the twenty-first century? Across the past two centuries the U.S. Constitution has proved sufficiently flexible to accommodate a tremendous growth in federal power as changing environmental conditions have increased the need for centralized policy development and coordination. Perhaps it can continue to be sufficiently flexible to accommodate another century of inevitably and inexorably altered federal-state relations. However, as trends toward greater nationalization continue, jointly administered federal-state programs often prove cumbersome and awkward, revealing possible structural weaknesses in a federal system which must survive in an increasingly competitive international political arena and global economy. This debate over the survival of federalism is not trivial and its resolution will affect the quality of life in the United States for future as well as current generations.

Growth of government is likely to occur at both the state and federal levels. Resurgence of the states may continue since the number of people and services for them will multiply, yet there are potential depressions of this predicted state resurgence. Included among possible depression factors are cutbacks in federal aid, economic warfare among states in interstate commerce, rising political corruption at the state level, and the control or lack thereof of natural resources.

Of these twin trends of government growth, the expanding federal government is likely to outstrip the resurging states. There is a need for national leadership both domestically and internationally. In the areas of crime, drug trafficking, urban decay, and international debt and trade, firm, decisive national leadership must provide the guidance needed to meet and solve these problems. Looking toward the twenty-first century, states will not be capable of providing guidance at this level. Thus, the trend of devolution and decentralization currently espoused by the Reagan administration may be a temporary retrenchment of federal government power. Local governments clearly affect quality of life whereas states increasingly appear to be an artificial administrative device, unable to set national trends or effectively address national problems. Consequently, future political leaders will envision the need to rely more on national government-centered policy development, planning and implementation.

REFERENCES

Beer, Samuel H., Edward M. Kennedy, Helen F. Ladd, Norman Y. Mineta, Charles Royer, and Lester M. Salamon. 1982. *Federalism: Making the System Work.* Washington, D.C.: Center for National Policy.

Bowman, Ann O'M., and Richard C. Kearney. 1986. *The Resurgence of the States.* Englewood Cliffs, N.J.: Prentice-Hall, Inc.

Colella, Cynthia Cates. 1986. "The United States Supreme Court and Intergovernmental Relations." In *American Intergovernmental Relations Today: Perspectives and Controversies.* Robert Jay Dilger, ed. Englewood Cliffs, N.J.: Prentice-Hall, Inc.

Dilger, Robert Jay, ed. 1986. *American Intergovernmental Relations Today: Perspectives and Controversies.* Englewood Cliffs, N.J.: Prentice-Hall, Inc.

Elazar, Daniel J. 1984. *American Federalism: A View from the States.* 3rd ed. New York: Harper and Row.

Galbraith, John Kenneth. 1958. *The Affluent Society.* New York: The New American Library.

Glendening, Parris, and Mavis Mann Reeves. 1977. *Pragmatic Federalism: An Intergovernmental View of American Government.* Pacific Palisades, Calif.: Palisades Publishers.

Hawkins, Robert B., Jr., ed. 1982. *American Federalism: A New Partnership for the Republic.* San Francisco: Institute for Contemporary Studies.

Jeffreys-Jones, Rhodri, and Bruce Collins. 1983. *The Growth of Federal Power in American History.* Edinburgh: Scottish Academic Press.

Jones, Charles O., and Robert D. Thomas, eds. 1976. *Public Policy Making in a Federal System.* Beverly Hills, Calif.: Sage Publications.

Kincaid, John, ed. 1982. *Political Culture, Public Policy, and the American States.* Philadelphia: Institute for the Study of Human Issues.

Musgrave, Richard B., and Peggy B. Musgrave. 1984. *Public Finance in Theory and Practice.* 4th ed. New York: McGraw-Hill.

Pechman, Joseph A. 1977. *Federal Tax Policy.* 3rd ed. Washington, D.C.: Brookings Institution.

Richter, Albert J. 1986. "The President and Intergovernmental Relations." *American Intergovernmental Relations Today: Perspectives and Controversies.* Robert Jay Dilger, ed. Englewood Cliffs, N.J.: Prentice-Hall, Inc.

Schechter, Stephen L., ed. 1983. *Publius: Annual Review of American Federalism: 1981.* Lanham, Md.: University Press of America.

Walker, David B. 1981. *Toward a Functioning of Federalism.* Cambridge, Mass.: Winthrop Publishers, Inc.

Wildavsky, Aaron, ed. 1967. *American Federalism in Perspective.* Boston: Little, Brown and Co.

Wright, Deil S. 1982. *Understanding Intergovernmental Relations.* 2nd ed. Monterey, Calif.: Brooks-Cole Publishing Co.

Chapter Four

Interpreting the Constitution: The Role of the Courts

Historically the Constitution has retained its flexibility because interpretations of its meaning have changed. Choosing between two or more sets of competing values, the Supreme Court has played a major role in maintaining this flexibility. This chapter will discuss major trends in Court interpretation of constitutional issues, including trends toward greater judicial review and activism, the role of the Court in civil rights and the Court's support for individual liberties through its use of the Fourteenth Amendment to incorporate the Bill of Rights and apply it to the states.

The proclivity toward judicial activism began in the early years with the Supreme Court's assertion of the right of judicial review. In *Marbury v. Madison* (1803), the Supreme Court established a precedent for subsequent Supreme Court declarations of the unconstitutionality of congressional acts. Later the Court continued its judicial activism by making policy in the areas of civil rights for blacks and the poor, reapportionment of state legislatures on the basis of the one-person one-vote principle, court-ordered busing and prison reform. Typically, eras of judicial restraint and strict constructionism have alternated with periods of judicial activism and broad constructionism. This chapter will explore this cycle and its implications.

A second significant trend has been the extension of civil rights to the previously powerless. This extension occurred through numerous cases, some of which expanded the meaning of the Fourteenth Amendment. While the Fourteenth Amendment provisions of due process and equal protection under the law clearly applied to the states, the Bill of Rights protections did not. Beginning with *Gitlow v. New York* (1925), a series of decisions began to incorporate into the due process and equal protection clauses of the Fourteenth Amendment many of the protections in the Bill of Rights. The implications for civil liberties have been enormous. This chapter will discuss each of these trends.

THE STRUCTURE OF THE COURTS
AND THE CONSTITUTION

Article III of the U.S. Constitution established federal courts and their authority. Relatively short, with only three sections, Article III was subsequently modified by the Eleventh Amendment which states that the judicial power of the U.S. shall not extend to any suit commenced or prosecuted against one of the states by citizens of another state or of any foreign state. The Constitution specifically established the U.S. Supreme Court and delegated to Congress the powers to set up necessary inferior courts. In the Judiciary Act of 1789, Congress established federal district courts and U.S. courts of appeals. By the mid-1980s, there were ninety-four federal district courts and thirteen U.S. courts of appeal. These three different types of courts are often called constitutional courts since they deal with matters involving the Constitution, in comparison to legislative courts, such as the federal tax court or military courts, which administer a particular body of law.

Jurisdictions of Federal Constitutional Courts

Each of the three constitutional federal courts has separate jurisdictions. Original jurisdiction means that a court is the first to hear a case as compared to appellate jurisdiction where a court reviews a decision of a lower court. The U.S. Supreme Court has original jurisdiction in controversies arising between the United States and a state, or between two or more states. It also has original jurisdiction over cases involving foreign ambassadors or other foreign ministers or counsels, in cases involving the actions of a state against citizens of another state, or against aliens or a foreign country. The Supreme Court has appellate jurisdiction from all lower federal constitutional courts as well as most federal legislative and territorial courts and the highest state courts when a substantial federal issue is involved (Abraham 1983, 14–15) (see table 4-1).

Cases heard in federal district courts may be appealed to one of the U.S. circuit courts of appeals. Unlike lower courts, the U.S. courts of appeals have only appellate jurisdication, and therefore may only consider cases first tried at the district level. In addition to appellate jurisdiction from U.S. district courts, the circuit courts have appellate jurisdiction from U.S. territorial courts, U.S. Tax Court, U.S. Claims Court,

Table 4-1
Jurisdictions of the Major Federal Constitutional Courts

THE U.S. SUPREME COURT

Original Jurisdiction:

 Between the United States and a state
 Between two or more states
 Controversies involving foreign ambassadors, foreign public
  counsels or ministers
 Action brought by a state against citizens of another state
 Action brought by a state against aliens
 Action brought by a state against a foreign country

Appellate Jurisdiction:

 All cases from lower federal constitutional courts
 Most but not all cases from federal legislative and
  territorial courts
 Cases from the highest state courts when a substantial federal
  question is involved

U.S. CIRCUIT COURTS OF APPEALS

Appellate Jurisdiction:

 Cases from U.S. district courts
 Cases from U.S. territorial courts
 Cases from the U.S. Tax Court
 Cases from the U.S. Claims Court
 Some cases from District of Columbia courts
 Cases from the U.S. Court of International Trade
 Cases from U.S. independent regulatory commissions
 Cases from certain federal administrative agencies and
  departments

U.S. DISTRICT COURTS

Original Jurisdiction:

 All crimes against the United States
 All civil actions arising under the Constitution, laws, or
  treaties of the United States with value over $10,000
 Cases involving citizens of different states valued over $10,000
 Cases involving U.S. citizens and aliens with value over $10,000
 Admiralty, maritime and prize cases
 Reviewing and enforcing actions of certain federal administrative
  agencies and departments
 All such other cases prescribed by Congress in law

---

some District of Columbia courts, U.S. independent regulatory commissions, U.S. Court of International Trade and certain federal administrative agencies and departments.

Federal district courts, like county courts at the state level, are the trial courts of the federal judiciary. This level of courts tries civil and criminal cases. Federal district courts have original jurisdiction over all crimes against the United States, all civil actions arising under the Constitution, laws or treaties of the United States where the issue in controversy exceeds ten thousand dollars and cases involving citizens of different states or citizens and aliens where the value of the controversy exceeds ten thousand dollars. Other cases in which federal district courts have original jurisdiction include admiralty, maritime and prize cases, review and enforcement of orders and actions of certain federal administrative agencies and departments, and other cases prescribed by Congress by law. Trials can be held without juries if all parties agree. When a jury trial is demanded, twelve jurors must serve and the decision must be unanimous.

Congress may give concurrent or exclusive grants of jurisdiction to different federal courts. For example, Congress has the authority to give federal district courts concurrent original jurisdiction with the U.S. Supreme Court over cases involving foreign ambassadors and over some cases in which a state is a party to a suit. Although Congress may permit concurrent state and federal jurisdiction at the discretion of the litigants, this flexibility does not negate the superior claim to federal jurisdiction should the parties disagree.

Avenues to Supreme Court Review

The highest tribunal, the U.S. Supreme Court, has both appellate and original jurisdiction. It rarely exercises original jurisdiction, however, partly because of the desire to share its power with lower federal courts and partly due to the Eleventh Amendment. Most of the cases that appear before the Supreme Court involve appellate review from the federal circuit courts of appeals. There are three principal avenues for appellate jurisdiction at Supreme Court level: certification, writ of appeal and writ of certiorari. Certification is the least used method and occurs when a lower court requests that a higher court instruct it on any civil or criminal case (see table 4-2).

The second method of having a case reviewed by the Supreme Court, the writ of appeal, is theoretically a matter of a statutorily granted right. Presumably, the Supreme Court must review cases reaching it through this method. Since 1928, however, the Supreme Court has been given considerable discretion to evaluate the writ of appeal and decide whether the issue raised by the appellee is of a significant federal nature. If the issue lacks importance according to this standard, the Supreme Court may refuse the petition. As a result, fifty to sixty percent of all writs of appeal are rejected. One of the two most common types of cases reviewed by Supreme Court via this method are those wherein a state court of last resort rules in favor of a state law or a portion of a

Table 4-2
The Structure of Appeals to the U.S. Supreme Court

CERTIFICATION

Lower courts ask the Supreme Court for technical instructions

WRIT OF APPEAL

Two most commonly used methods:

When a state court of last appeal has ruled in favor of a state
law or provision against a challenge that it conflicts with
the federal Constitution, federal law or federal treaty

When a special three-judge court has granted or denied an in-
junction in a proceeding which normally would be heard by
the Supreme Court

WRIT OF CERTIORARI

Review depends on the discretion of the Supreme Court

Applies to all cases, except those where writ of appeal is the
remedy and which raise a substantial federal question

Where decisions of a lower court involve the application or
interpretation of the federal Constitution, a federal law
or a federal treaty

---

state constitution in the face of a substantial challenge that it is in conflict with the federal Constitution, a federal law or a federal treaty. A
second type of case which sometimes reaches the Supreme Court by
writ of appeal concerns the granting or denial of injunctions by U.S.
district courts or by one of the special three-judge district courts (Abraham 1983, 24–30).

Under the third method, the writ of certiorari, the Supreme Court
orders a lower court whose decision is being disputed to send them the
records of a case so that the Supreme Court can decide whether the
law has been correctly applied. This is the most frequently used method
of achieving appellate review by the U.S. Supreme Court. Four judges
must agree to grant a writ of certiorari. The reason for this "rule of
four" is so that a substantial number (although not necessarily a majority of justices) should consider the case important enough to review.
Each year the Court receives about four thousand petitions and chooses

to hear only about one-tenth. Even Supreme Court justices do not agree on the meaning of denial of a writ of certiorari. While the immediate impact is to let a lower court decision stand, some justices contend that denial signifies Supreme Court agreement with the lower court decision while other justices argue that denial does not imply higher court agreement.

JUDICIAL ACTIVISM VERSUS STRICT CONSTRUCTIONISM

The U.S. Constitution does not explicitly mention judicial review but some framers of the Constitution expected the courts to exercise it. For example, in Federalist Paper No. 78, Alexander Hamilton stated that the courts should void laws that contradicted the Constitution. During that time, some state courts had such authority. However, the Constitution does not explicitly grant courts the ability to declare laws or the actions of governmental officials unconstitutional. In the U.S. Supreme Court case of *Marbury v. Madison* (1803), the Court asserted its right to judicial review.

The Background of *Marbury v. Madison*

Judicial review was born out of an extremely partisan environment. The background of the case of *Marbury v. Madison* clearly explains how Chief Justice John Marshall justified the birth of judicial review. In 1800 President John Adams, a Federalist, was defeated by an arch political rival, Thomas Jefferson. Jeffersonians also won control over Congress. Adams and other Federalists, realizing that both Congress and the presidency were lost, tried to pack the judicial branch with "safe and loyal" Federalists (Hyneman 1963, 75).

Adams, with the assistance of the lame-duck Federalist Congress, enacted legislation that enabled him to appoint fifty-nine federal judges and have them confirmed in the Senate. As fate would have it, Adams appointed his own secretary of state, John Marshall, to the office of Chief Justice. Marshall, still secretary of state, was supposed to deliver the commissions to the new judicial appointees. Due to last minute pressures and preparations for the inauguration of Thomas Jefferson (at which Marshall had to swear in the incoming president), Marshall failed to deliver seventeen of the forty-two commissions for District of Columbia justices of the peace.

When Jefferson and the new secretary of state, James Madison, discovered the undelivered commissions, Jefferson was livid at the Federalists' attempts to pack the judiciary and ordered Madison not to deliver the commissions. Without the signed commissions, the new appointees were unable to prove they had ever been appointed. Among the disappointed appointees were William Marbury and three colleagues. They petitioned the Supreme Court for a writ of mandamus—a writ that orders government officials to carry out an assigned duty. In this instance, the writ was to order Secretary of State Madison to deliver the commissions.

Thus, Chief Justice Marshall had to rule on the case of *Marbury v. Madison*. Marshall was on the horns of a dilemma and it seemed that no matter how he ruled the authority of the Supreme Court or the position of Federalists in the judiciary would be undermined. If Marshall issued the writ, Jefferson would predictably tell Madison to ignore it and the Supreme Court would be unable to enforce it. If the Chief Justice did not issue the writ, it would appear that the Supreme Court was giving in to Jefferson. Caught between a rock and a hard place, Marshall devised an ingenious solution.

Marshall, with the Court's unanimous support, declared Section 13 of the Judiciary Act of 1789 unconstitutional because Congress in this act had given the Court illegal authority by permitting the Supreme Court to issue a writ of mandamus. This power represented a statutory addition to the Court's original jurisdiction, and original jurisdiction could only be changed by a constitutional amendment (as it had once been altered by the Eleventh Amendment). Although Marshall insisted that Marbury and his colleagues had a right to their commissions, he reasoned that the Court could not order the Jefferson administration to deliver the commissions because the provision of the Judiciary Act that granted the Court that authority was illegal. In this manner, the principle of judicial review was established, giving the Supreme Court broadened power to declare void those laws which contradicted the Constitution. Marshall sacrificed the commissions and established judicial review instead. The Jeffersonians got what they wanted but the Federalists got something greater.

Today the power of judicial review is awesome. It is a very effective tool in the hands of the judiciary of the United States and more particularly those of the Supreme Court. Although for many years the dominant belief about the Supreme Court was that it did not legislate but rather "found" the law, many scholars now acknowledge that the Supreme Court does indeed make policy. Neutral principles and precedent do not pose sufficient restraints on the Court when it chooses to legislate.

The Case for Judicial Restraint

All judges exercise some discretion, but not all judges legislate to the same extent. Some judges accept the doctrine of judicial restraint while others eschew it and become activists. Restrained judges contend that the judiciary branch is the least democratic since justices are appointed, not elected, and should avoid overturning or overruling decisions by the other two branches. Why trust judges whose futures are not linked to the ballot box more than legislators who are subject to election and reelection (Graglia 1982, 155)?

Proponents of judicial restraint also argue that since most justices are generalists and lack the expertise of bureaucrats or legislators in various substantive policy areas, judicial power should be curbed. If an error in judgment is made at the Supreme Court level, it is more difficult to correct than other forms of judicial action. Those adhering to the philosophy of judicial self-restraint go to great lengths to allow the legislative and executive branches to act or not act or to maintain the upper hand (Kurland 1971, 5).

The Case for Judicial Activism

Judicial activists, on the other hand, do not feel constrained by such arguments. More frequently activist judges are outraged at injustices and are quite willing to declare statutes or actions of government officials unconstitutional. Proponents of judicial review claim that labeling the Supreme Court undemocratic is unfair given the shortcomings of the other branches of government as well as state governments. Some branch of government has to police the unwise choices made by politicians and the electorate, so why not allow the Supreme Court to do so (Miller 1982, 172)? Any polity requires some degree of consensus on the values that have overall importance to the general population.

Judicial activism is justifiable because such a consensus cannot be reached without conscious and conscientious thought. The Court can articulate these tacit and commonly accepted values whereas some of the other branches may be tempted to do what is politically expedient instead. Typically, judicial activism has been aimed at protecting civil liberties and rights. Less concerned about adhering to technical procedure, activist judges generally want to obtain policy-specific results.

Eras of Judicial Restraint and Activism: The Implications

Several justices stand out as advocates of judicial restraint. These include Oliver Wendell Holmes, Louis Brandeis, Harlan F. Stone and Felix Frankfurter, who argued that the Supreme Court should use judicial review sparingly and that maximum respect should be given to legislative acts. These justices exercised a greater degree of restraint than the average members of their Court and were less likely to strike down congressional legislation than state and municipal legislation.

Holmes, Brandeis and Stone, however, exercised judicial restraint on behalf of liberal causes, whereas Frankfurter's dissents inclined in favor of conservative interests.

The implications of these trends suggest that although restraint is an effort to remain outside of "legislating" policy, the actual refusal to become involved in policymaking is in effect an agreement with policies made by other political bodies. The exercise of restraint may vary according to the ideological leanings of individual justices. In addition, justices may persuade other justices to adopt a position of judicial restraint. Changes in the composition of a Court may limit or increase the ability of a justice to support a restrained stance (Champagne and Nagel 1982, 303–318).

Even though the Courts of some eras are more activist than others, the Court has not overruled federal statutes regularly. Prior to 1860, only two statutes were invalidated. In the sixty years between 1860 and 1920, the Court struck down thirty-five statutes. The period of greatest activism occurred in the 1920s and 1930s, two decades during which the Court overturned fifteen and thirteen statutes respectively. Another activist period occurred during the 1950s and 1960s, a twenty-year period when the Court struck down twenty-two federal statutes (Baum 1981, 161).

Although there is a tendency to associate restrained judges with conservatism and activist judges with liberalism, this does not always apply. For example, in the 1950s and the 1960s, the Supreme Court was both liberal and activist, but in the early 1930s it was activist and conservative (Wasby 1978, 20–22). During the twenties, the Court was headed by William Howard Taft and many of its decisions were designed to protect private business from government regulations. Taft was followed by Charles Evans Hughes. Under his direction as Chief Justice the Court continued its conservative activism striking down much of the New Deal legislation until the Roosevelt court-packing plan of 1937 pressured the middle-of-the-road swing judges to change their views. By contrast, the activism of the Warren Court under the stewardship of Earl Warren between 1953 and 1969 was liberal in its extension of civil rights to minorities and defendants.

Thus the Supreme Court has been largely activist, whether liberal or conservative, during most of the twentieth century. As Richard Neustadt (1976) stated in his study of presidential power, "nowadays all Supreme Courts are activist." Particularly in the twentieth century, there has been a need of the Court to adapt to changing technology and modern life by adopting the mores of the modern day. Activism may be limited only by a plea for modesty from those who sponsor the philosophy of judicial restraint (Schick 1982, 37).

THE EXPANSION OF CIVIL RIGHTS

The policy area of civil rights is concerned with equality of rights for all people regardless of their sex, race or ethnic background. Contained in the Declaration of Independence is the notion that "all men are created equal." Although Thomas Jefferson knew that all men were not necessarily equal in talent, intellect or other abilities, he meant to emphasize that all men should be given equal rights and should be considered equal before the law.

From a modern perspective, civil rights would include the right to vote and participate in politics, the right to have access to the economic system, and equal access to social institutions such as schools and the military. Yet the Declaration's refined words did not extend to slaves or women. While the colonials possessed a spirit of egalitarianism, they advocated equality for white males only. Across time, however, there has been a gradual expansion of civil rights for minority groups that have suffered discrimination.

Civil Rights for Racial Minorities

The involvement of the U.S. Supreme Court in civil rights for blacks is long-standing, dating back to issues from the days of slavery. In the *Dred Scott* case (1857), Chief Justice Taney ruled that no blacks, slave or free, were citizens, and that blacks had no citizenship rights. Furthermore, Taney struck down the power of Congress to control slavery in U.S. territories thereby allowing slavery to expand into states that Congress had already declared to be free states where slavery would not be permitted.

In 1883, two decades after the Civil War and the official end of slavery, the Court ruled on five separate suits affecting the rights of blacks, and collectively called the *Civil Rights Cases* (1883). These cases arose in response to the Civil Rights Act of 1875 which prohibited racial discrimination in jury selection and public accommodations. In these cases, the public accommodations portions of the 1875 act were challenged. The Court recognized that the Fourteenth Amendment forbade discrimination by states but it made no mention of discriminatory acts committed by individuals. Since the Civil Rights Act prohibited discrimination by individuals and private businesses, the Court ruled that the act had overstepped congressional authority and was therefore unconstitutional.

Civil rights for blacks were set further back in the case of *Plessy v. Ferguson* (1896). This case arose as a challenge to an 1890 Louisiana state law requiring segregation of passengers on railroads. Plessy, an

American who was one-eighth black, was arrested for trying to sit in a white section of a railroad car. He claimed that the Louisiana statute was unconstitutional under the Fourteenth Amendment, but the Court disagreed and established the "separate but equal" doctrine which allowed separate public facilities for the races as long as they were equal.

The doctrine of racial segregation was further extended in *Cummings v. Richmond County Board of Education* (1899), a case which addressed the issue of whether blacks could attend white high schools if their school districts were too poor to maintain a separate high school for blacks. In this case only one white high school existed and a black, trying to gain admittance to it, was turned down by the Court, which extended the doctrine of "separate but equal" to "separate, even if nonexistent." Nine years later, in *Berea College v. Kentucky* (1907), the Court ruled in favor of a state law prohibiting private schools from educating blacks and white together (McDonald 1958, 154).

Starting in the era of the New Deal, the Court gradually began to shift away from the doctrine of "separate but equal." The state of Missouri separated the races through college, but rather than establish separate law and professional schools for blacks, it subsidized them to attend post-college training in other states. In *Missouri ex rel Gaines v. Canada* (1938), a black from Missouri sought to attend a white law school in the state. The Supreme Court declared that the Missouri law was unconstitutional under the equal protection clause and Missouri was forced to establish a separate law school for blacks.

One method employed in the past by the Democratic party in the South to deprive blacks of the right of suffrage was the all-white primary in which blacks were denied partisan membership. This prevented them from voting in the Democratic primary. Since in most of the South, one-party politics was the norm, denial of the right to vote in the primary prevented black participation in electoral outcomes. By the end of World War II, the Supreme Court had become more supportive of civil rights for blacks. It struck down the all-white primary in *Smith v. Allright* (1944), arguing that the Democratic party was in essence an agent of the state and was therefore subject to the Fifteenth Amendment.

During the late 1940s and the 1950s, the Court followed the trends begun in *Missouri ex. rel. Gaines v. Canada,* of moving away from the doctrine of "separate but equal." This may be seen in the cases of *Sipuel v. Oklahoma* (1948), *Sweatt v. Painter* (1950) and *McLaurin v. Oklahoma State Regents* (1950). In the *Sipuel* case, which was similar to the *Gaines* case, the Court ordered Oklahoma to provide a separate but equal law school for a black woman and stressed the need for equality in facilities. In *Sweatt v. Painter,* the state of Texas had established a separate black law school but it was inferior to the white law school at the University of Texas in the size of its faculty and the quality of its library and student body. The court ruled that the black law school had to be improved. The Court nearly overturned the "separate but equal" doctrine in the *McLaurin* case in which Oklahoma had allowed a black student to attend a white graduate school but had segregated him from the rest of the students by designating separate sections of the library, cafeteria and classrooms for him. The Court struck down these segregation provisions, claiming that they interfered with the ability of the black student to exchange ideas with other students, a requisite for a good education. Although these cases fell short of invalidating the "separate but equal" principle, they made segregation at the graduate school level more difficult to implement.

Perhaps the most significant civil rights cases to aid blacks in the fight for equality were the two *Brown* cases in the 1950s. *Brown v. Board of Education I* (1954) arose as the result of a suit against Topeka, Kansas where Linda Brown, a black child, was not permitted to attend a segregated white school four blocks from her home. In *Brown I*, under the leadership of Supreme Court Chief Justice Earl Warren, the Court overturned the *Plessy* decision of "separate but equal" in the public schools by declaring that the separate but equal doctrine made black children feel inferior. In *Brown v. Board of Education II* (1955), the Court ruled on how to accomplish desegregation, concluding that local school boards should establish plans for desegregation under the supervision of federal district judges and "with all deliberate speed." Despite these court rulings, southern school boards were slow to respond and avoided court orders by closing public schools and placing white children in private schools. Consequently, desegregation was only implemented very slowly.

Additional decisions attacked the issue of desegregation in locations besides the public schools, including *Shelley v. Kraemer* (1948), *Holmes v. Atlanta* (1955), *Baltimore v. Dawson* (1955) and *Schiro v. Bynum* (1964). As a result of this series of Court decisions, racial segregation was banned in municipal bathing beach facilities, in public parks, at public athletic events, in state and county court houses and on city bus lines. Restrictive covenants, where white homeowners agreed not to sell their homes to blacks, were also struck down.

Another case, *Loving v. Virginia* (1967), dealt with the issue of interracial marriage which was prohibited at that time in the state of Virginia. The defendants were a racially mixed couple who were married in the District of Columbia and returned to Virginia to live. There they were arrested, convicted and sentenced to leave the state for twenty-five years. On the basis of the equal protection clause of the Fourteenth Amendment, the Court ruled that the freedom to marry or not to marry a person of another race was an individual choice and could not be regulated by the state.

Since desegregation of the public schools was occurring only slowly if at all in some areas, the court took a radical departure from the *Brown* decision in *Green v. County School Board of New Kent County* (1968). Under Virginia law, the New Kent County School Board gave students the freedom to choose the school they wished to attend. Three years after the establishment of the freedom of choice plan, seven-eighths of the black children chose to remain in all-black schools, while all of the white children chose to stay in all-white schools. In response, the Supreme Court rejected freedom of choice systems by holding that whatever system was devised, the results must be integration of public education.

Court involvement in specific remedies for public school segregation characterized *Swann v. Charlotte-Mecklenburg Board of Education* (1971) and *Milliken v. Bradley* (1974). In the *Swann* case, the court ruled that busing for the purpose of racial integration was appropriate within school districts where *de jure* segregation had been practiced. The Court dismissed complaints that busing would be detrimental for students, noting that thirty-nine percent of public school students in the nation were bused for reasons other than desegregation. Yet the Court chose not to extend busing to *de facto* segregation by requiring cross-district busing between predominantly black center cities and predominantly white suburbs. In the *Milliken* case, the Court rejected such a cross-district busing integration plan for metropolitan Detroit.

Another controversial area of Court involvement in civil rights for blacks involves racial quotas and affirmative action. Affirmative action and compensatory treatment are aimed at remedying past discrimination against blacks by employing measures to help them catch up to the current competitive standards of American society. The Supreme Court has not ruled clearly on the use of quotas to overcome past discrimination.

In the 1978 case of *Regents of the University of California v. Bakke,* a special set of circumstances arose. The University of California at Davis had set aside sixteen places for minority students in an effort to provide minorities equal opportunity. Bakke, a white engineer, sued the University when he twice applied for admission and was rejected while minority students whose qualifications were less than his were accepted. In this case the Court ruled that it was appropriate for the University to consider race as a factor in admissions but at the same time held that the quota system as established in this instance was unconstitutional.

In *Kaiser Aluminum and United Steelworkers v. Weber* (1979), where a white worker named Weber was not allowed into a job-training program despite his seniority over blacks who were admitted, the Supreme Court upheld the quotas. The Kaiser Aluminum and Chemical Company and the Steelworkers union agreed to set aside half of the job-training openings in Kaiser's training program for blacks. The Court upheld this quota system, arguing that the private company had voluntarily adopted the plan and that this industry had a past record of discrimination for which it should compensate. Pertaining more directly to the issue of seniority is the case of *Memphis Firefighters v. Stotts* (1984). In *Stotts* the Court allowed employers to lay off workers with less seniority, which disproportionately affected blacks since they were usually the last hired (Fallon and Weiler 1984, 1–5).

The Court's Treatment of Other Ethnic Minorities

The 1980 census showed that fifteen million Hispanics resided in the United States at that time. Hispanics did not endure slavery, but due to their darker skin color they have been subject to various forms of discrimination. As have blacks, Hispanics have encountered discrimination in voting, education, jobs and housing.

Early in the twentieth century Hispanic children were excluded from some schools and were sometimes segregated into Mexican schools. By the 1940s, Mexican-Americans requested that they be regarded as "white," thereby avoiding segregation. Their wish was granted by the federal courts. This strategy proved useless, however, when the Supreme Court later declared segregation by race illegal, since many school districts claimed "integration" by moving Hispanics (now officially white) to black schools. In the 1970s many Hispanic public school children were placed in schools with over ninety percent minority student populations (San Miguel 1982, 710).

Because minorities such as blacks and Hispanics tended to live in poor areas and public schools are supported by local property taxes, minorities often had less funding for school facilities and teachers. In *San Antonio Independent School District v. Rodriguez* (1973), Hispanic parents recognized this problem and asked the Supreme Court for a remedy. The Court held that states did not have to equalize funding for schools from different districts, implying that Hispanics might receive a poorer quality education and thus at some point be denied equal opportunity in the "foot race" of life.

In 1980 approximately one and a half million native North Americans, most of whom were Indians, resided in the United States. Indians have endured discrimination of a different kind from blacks and Hispanics since they have in the past been viewed as belonging to a separate nation. The U.S. Constitution granted Congress the authority to regulate relations among the various Indian tribes. In the early 1830s as settlers moved west, the government promoted separation of Indians from whites by relocating the Indians on reservations. Under this policy, Indian tribes were to be governed by their own legal systems and tribal courts. In *Cherokee Nation v. Georgia* (1832) and *Worcester v. Georgia* (1832), Georgia was sued for applying state law to Indians. In these cases, the U.S. Supreme Court ruled that the federal government's jurisdiction over Indians was exclusive and states were precluded from controlling them. In the 1880s the official policy was changed to one of assimilation and attempts were made to abolish tribal governments and to force white life-styles. In the 1930s assimilation fell into disfavor and official policy shifted back toward tribal restoration. Indians still fall under the jurisdiction of tribal courts and tribal law. With the adoption of the 1968 Civil Rights Act, many citizen protections within the Bill of Rights were applied to tribal courts.

Civil Rights for Women

Women are not a minority but they have historically experienced legal discrimination based on their gender. The Supreme Court has played an important role in the expansion of rights for women. Overall the Court has been less important in the expansion of women's rights than it has been in the extension of rights to blacks and other racial minorities. A major reason for the less important role of the Court is that women's rights have mostly been broadened through legislation.

One area in which the Court was not very supportive was in the extension to women of the right to vote. In *Minor v. Happersett* (1875), the court ruled that the privileges and immunities clause of the Fourteenth Amendment was not sufficient justification for giving this franchise to women. Ultimately, women's attainment of the vote required the passage of the Nineteenth Amendment.

Many women's rights cases addressed by the Supreme Court have been concerned with employment. Early court decisions followed a trend of protectionism and upheld restrictions on the nature and conditions of employment for women. In *Bradwell v. Illinois* (1873), the Supreme Court upheld a state law preventing women from practicing law. The ruling in *Muller v. Oregon* (1908) upheld an Oregon law that prohibited laundries from making women work more than ten hours a day. *Goesaert v. Cleary* (1948) also upheld restrictions on female employment by ruling in support of a Michigan law prohibiting any woman except the wife or daughter of a bar owner from being a bartender. The Michigan law did not prohibit women from being waitresses. The restrictive attitude of the Court also spilled over into nonemployment areas. In *Hoyt v. Florida* (1961), a Florida law was upheld which gave women discretion in serving on juries but did not give men the equivalent choice.

Not until the 1970s did U.S. Supreme Court rulings begin to move away from the restrictive, protectionist trend of the past. *Reed v. Reed* (1971) was the first instance of the Court striking down a state law which discriminated against women. *Taylor v. Louisiana* (1975) overturned the precedent set in *Hoyt v. Florida. Phillips v. Martin-Marietta* (1971) ruled that employers could not discriminate against mothers of preschool children, despite fears that they might often miss work to care for their children. In *Stanton v. Stanton* (1975) the Court struck down a Utah law which required divorced fathers to support sons until they were twenty-one under the assumption that they would need support while being educated, while daughters had to be supported only until they were eighteen under the assumption that they would get married and be supported by their husbands. *Dothard v. Rawlinson* (1977) struck down arbitrary employer discrimination on the basis of height and weight, restrictions which handicapped women as they are typically shorter and lighter than men. By 1984 the Court had decided in *Hishon v. King and Spalding* (1984) that law firms could not refuse to hire or promote women. Not all recent decisions have been uniformly supportive of expanded women's rights, however. In *Grove City v. Bell* (1984), the Court distinguished between institutional federal support and individual support when they failed to apply Title IX prohibitions against discrimination in education programs to a private college.

Although many women have supported and fought unsuccessfully for an Equal Rights Amendment to the Constitution (ERA), women have achieved many aspects of legal equality through the Court. The Court, however, may not be a complete substitute for an Equal Rights Amendment since its rulings are made slowly and ponderously on a case-by-case basis. The ERA would require quick and thorough changes in the law whereas the Court might later be made up of justices less sympathetic to women's and minority rights. Attempts could be made to overturn prior favorable rulings, while a constitutional amendment cannot be repealed without widespread public approval.

THE EXPANSION OF CIVIL LIBERTIES

Beginning in the 1920s, the U.S. Supreme Court began to apply the Bill of Rights to states through a process now called the incorporation of the Bill of Rights into the Fourteenth Amendment. As originally passed, the Bill of Rights applied only to the federal government and not to state governments. The Fourteenth Amendment's equal protection and due process clauses clearly applied to the states. Through a series of lengthy cases, the Court engaged in a piecemeal process of interpreting the Fourteenth Amendment clauses to include the various freedoms protected in the Bill of Rights.

Most but not all of the Bill of Rights has been interpreted by the Court to apply to the states as well as to the federal government. Among those provisions not yet applied to the states through Court interpretation are the guarantee of a grand jury in criminal cases, the guarantee of a jury trial in civil cases and the prohibition of excessive bails and fines. In the process of incorporating the Bill of Rights into the Fourteenth Amendment, the Court has examined some freedoms (such as First Amendment liberties) more closely than others. A second factor in this process has been their multifaceted interpretations of what the various freedoms mean. For example, the Court has defined different standards for freedom of the written press compared to freedom of motion pictures and broadcasting. There are also gradations of free speech for individuals.

Almost a century earlier, the Court showed little inclination to expand the Bill of Rights to state governments. In *Barron v. Baltimore* (1833), the Court ruled that the Bill of Rights only applied to the federal government. The first major case in the incorporation trend was *Gitlow v. New York* (1925), in which the Court began to apply the Bill of Rights to the states by ruling that freedom of speech was part of the Fourteenth Amendment. In this case, the Court upheld a New York state law punishing criminal anarchy—the doctrine that government should be overthrown by force or violence—as constitutional and not a violation of freedom of speech. It established the "bad tendency" doctrine for assessing future violations. According to the "bad tendency" doctrine, legislatures, not courts, are most responsible for determining which speech should be outlawed.

In *Near v. Minnesota* (1931) the Supreme Court applied freedom of the press to the states. In this case, the city of Minneapolis tried to suppress the publication of scandalous, malicious and defamatory material in newspapers. A newspaper publishers association, fearing censorship, challenged the Minnesota law on the grounds of violation of freedom of press. The Supreme Court struck down the law by contending that it represented prior restraint of future issues. The most important freedom given to the press is freedom from prior restraint, the freedom not to be censored.

Powell v. Alabama (1932) addressed the issue of fair trials by states. In this case, some young black men convicted of raping two white girls were not allowed to see lawyers before and during their trial. The Court ruled that the Sixth Amendment guaranteed defendants the right to counsel, and that the failure of the Alabama trial court to permit defendants to procure an attorney before and during the trial in capital cases constituted a clear denial of due process and a fair trial (Pritchett 1984, 207–209).

The process of nationalizing the Bill of Rights through the Fourteenth Amendment continued in the area of free exercise of religion. In *Hamilton v. Board of Regents* (1934), the Court held that freedom of religion was protected by the First Amendment against invasion by the national government and by the states. This decision was confirmed in *Cantwell v. Connecticut* (1940). This case questioned the constitutionality of a Connecticut law which banned solicitation of money for religious or charitable reasons unless approved by the secretary of the public welfare council. This particular official had the authority to decide whether a fund-raising cause was truly a religious one. In a unanimous decision, the Supreme Court ruled that the statute violated religious freedom and the due process clause of the Fourteenth Amendment.

Not until 1947 in *Everson v. Board of Education* did the Supreme Court apply the establishment clause of the First Amendment to the states. The *Everson* case involved provisions by a New Jersey state law that authorized payments in the form of reimbursement to parents who paid school bus expenses to either public or private schools. The Court held that this statute did not breach the wall of separation of church and state and did not violate the establishment clause (Friendly and Elliott 1984; 116–117).

In the mid-to-late 1930s, there was a wave of anti-communism and fear of "un-American" ideas. As a result, many states enacted statutes to punish so-called seditious activities and to limit the rights of dissident political minorities. Despite intense public pressure, the Roosevelt Court sought to protect these minorities. *Dejonge v. Oregon* (1937) involved the constitutionality of an Oregon criminal syndicalist law. The defendant, Dejonge, was arrested and convicted of participation in a Communist political gathering. Chief Justice Hughes, holding for a unanimous court, maintained that the defendant had no record of advocating violence or forceful overthrow of the government and had not been charged with that kind of offense. Consequently, the Court reversed the conviction, claiming that "peaceful assembly for lawful discussion cannot be made a crime." The conviction under the Oregon statute violated the right to free speech and assembly (Kelly and Harbison 1976, 765–766).

Sixth Amendment trial rights were considered again in 1948 in the case of *In re Oliver*. The case came up in response to a Michigan judge's mishandling of a witness who testified before him in a closed and secret session. The judge assumed that the witness was lying, charged him with contempt, convicted him and sentenced him to jail for sixty days. The only people to witness this strange procedure were two other judges and the court staff. This trial had proceeded without counsel and the defendant was not informed about the nature or cause of the accusation against him. The Supreme Court struck down these proceedings as unconstitutional and in violation of the defendant's right to a public trial.

Ruling on the right to freedom of association in *NAACP v. Button* (1963) and *NAACP v. Alabama* (1964), the Court dealt with the issue of whether litigation was a form of political expression and whether states could ban the stirring up of litigation on the grounds of improper business solicitation. Typically the National Association for the Advancement of Colored People (NAACP) sought test cases and used them to improve the treatment of blacks in America. The Court held that such litigation was a form of political expression and that the effective advocacy of public and private views was enhanced by group association. Thus, freedom of association was applied to the states.

Early in American history, the English conception that a family's home was its castle flourished. Colonial resentment toward English writs of assistance led to the adoption of the Fourth Amendment. In 1961, the Court turned its attention to the issue of unreasonable searches and seizures of evidence. The exclusionary rule, first enunciated in *Weeks v. United States* (1912), bars the court from considering evidence obtained in violation of the Fourth Amendment.

The issues addressed in *Mapp v. Ohio* (1961) revolved around the evidence obtained by Cleveland police from Dolree Mapp. Mapp refused to allow the police, who were in search of a fugitive reportedly hiding in her house, to enter without a search warrant. The police reacted by forcing their way into her home without a warrant and arresting Mapp for being "belligerent." In the course of their search, the police found only a sack of pornographic materials. Mapp denied that the materials were hers and claimed that they had belonged to a former renter. Nonetheless she was tried and convicted for possession of obscenity. The Supreme Court, upon considering this case, applied the *Weeks* exclusionary rule to state courts as well as federal courts (Bartholowmew 1978, 269). In *U.S. v. Leon* (1984), the Court narrowed the meaning of *Mapp* by holding that illegally obtained evidence may be submitted to the Court if the police acted in "good faith" when acquiring a warrant.

The Court next considered the issue of cruel and unusual punishment. Cruel and unusual punishment was defined as torture or punishment grossly disproportionate to the crime committed. The Eighth Amendment, which forbids cruel and unusual punishment, was first applied to the states in 1962. The case of *Robinson v. California* (1962) involved a California statute that made drug addiction a crime. The statute only required that needle marks be present on the arm for a person to be labeled a drug addict: no proof of drug purchase or possession was necessary. The Court declared the statute unconstitutional under the Eighth Amendment, thus applying the "cruel and unusual" provision to the states.

Although trial rights were considered in *Powell v. Alabama* (1932) and *In re Oliver* (1948), where the Court examined the issues of fair and public trials, the Court had still not established the right to counsel of indigents in felony cases. In *Gideon v. Wainwright* (1963) Gideon was charged with illegal breaking and entering and requested a state-appointed lawyer since he could not afford one. The judge refused his request and he was tried and convicted even though the prosecutor presented a weak case against him. On appeal to the Supreme Court, the Court declared that Gideon was entitled to counsel and that lawyers were not a luxury but rather a necessity in criminal courts. The Court applied another Sixth Amendment provision to the states by holding that state courts must provide a lawyer to indigent defendants in felony cases.

Another criminal defendant right, the freedom from self-incrimination, was applied to the states in 1964. In its earlier consideration of this Fifth Amendment freedom in the cases of *Twining v. New Jersey* (1908) and *Adamson v. California* (1947), the Supreme Court had ruled in favor of state statutes that allowed unfavorable conclusions to be drawn from a defendant's refusal to take the witness stand. In *Mallory v. Hogan* (1964), the Court overturned the *Twining* and *Adamson* decisions by asserting that it was unjust to have different standards of self-incrimination at the federal and state levels. Due process demanded that states not imprison individuals solely on the basis that their refusal to testify might incriminate them.

Criminal defendant protections were further extended and applied to the states in *Pointer v. Texas* (1965). This case was concerned with the issue of the right of defendants to confront the witnesses testifying against them. In this particular case, a transcript of witness testimony from a preliminary hearing was introduced as evidence in a trial because the witness had left the state and was not able to testify in person. The Supreme Court declared that this procedure denied the defendant's right to confront the witness and was a violation of due process.

Besides criminal defendant rights, another area of major concern to the Supreme Court in the 1960s was the issue of privacy. The right to privacy is not mentioned in either the Constitution or the Bill of Rights. Although not overtly stated in the Constitution, rights to privacy are implied in various amendments. For example, the Third Amendment protects the privacy of the home from forced quartering of soldiers and the Fourth Amendment protects the privacy of individuals from illegal searches and seizures. The right to privacy was firmly established by the Warren Court in the case of *Griswold v. Connecticut* (1965) when the Court struck down a Connecticut statute that prohibited the distribution, use, or dispensing of information on contraceptives. The Court further extended the right to privacy to include abortion in the case of *Roe v. Wade* (1973).

The remaining cases in which the Bill of Rights was applied to the states during the 1960s and 1970s were concerned with the rights of criminal defendants. In *Parker v. Gladden* (1966), the Court used the

Fourteenth Amendment to apply to the states the Sixth Amendment provision which guarantees that the accused has a right to trial by an impartial jury. In *Klopfer v. North Carolina* (1967), it was held that the speedy trial provision of the Sixth Amendment applied to the states. Also in 1967 in the case of *Washington v. Texas*, the Sixth Amendment right to have a compulsory process for obtaining witnesses was incorporated through the due process clause and made binding for the states.

Not until 1968 did the Court rule that the states must have jury trials for all serious crimes. In *Palko v. Connecticut* (1937) the Court claimed that a jury trial was not a necessary requirement of due process. However, in *Duncan v. Louisiana* (1968), the Supreme Court overruled the *Palko* case by asserting that a trial by jury in criminal cases is fundamental to the U.S. scheme of justice.

In *Benton v. Maryland* (1969) the Court considered the Fifth Amendment protection against double jeopardy wherein a person may not be tried twice for the same crime. The Supreme Court ruling in the *Benton* case upheld a ban on double jeopardy and applied this principle to the states. A final protection of criminal defendants was applied to the states by the Burger Court in *Argersinger v. Hamlin* (1972). Here the Court unanimously held that when misdemeanors and petty crimes lead to imprisonment for any length of time, there exists the right to counsel. This extended the right to counsel for felony prosecutions which had been established in the *Gideon v. Wainwright* case.

In this manner, the Supreme Court has used the Fourteenth Amendment to nationalize the Bill of Rights. Through the application of the Bill of Rights to the states the Court has interpreted the Constitution to provide many important civil liberties and protections. In theory, the list of rights for criminal defendants is available to all defendants. In practice, however, trial court judges, police and prosecutors do not always abide by or support Supreme Court rulings. The impact of the extension and application of many Bill of Rights protections to the states may vary according to the state's compliance and interpretation of rulings (Johnson and Canon 1984).

SUGGESTED COURT REFORMS

The reform of the federal judiciary system has been a concern of judges and lawyers for many years. In the twentieth century, Chief Justice William Howard Taft and Chief Justice Warren Burger have been notable for their efforts to improve the efficiency and effectiveness of the system.

Taft, a former president who found his proper niche as Chief Justice, made determined efforts to modernize the administration of the federal courts. In 1922 he lobbied Congress and obtained their approval to create a Conference of Senior Circuit Justices which would meet annually to oversee the operation of the federal courts. The Chief Justice of the Supreme Court was to preside as chairman. Taft was also successful in getting support for a bill which gave the Supreme Court certiorari jurisdiction.

In 1939 Congress gave its blessing to a new Administrative Office of the United States Courts. According to Murphy and Pritchett (1986; 90) the same statute set up a judicial council in each circuit. The council was responsible for general supervision of all the district courts within that circuit and also provided for an annual conference in each circuit to be attended by all circuit and district judges as well as representatives of the bar.

In later years the Conference of Senior Circuit Judges was changed into the Judicial Conference of the United States, and its membership was enlarged by the addition of an elected district judge from each circuit. The conference now convenes twice a year and continues to exercise oversight and undertake planning for the court system. The Chief Justice still presides over the conference.

In 1967 the Federal Judicial Center was established. Among its activities is the conduct of seminars for newly appointed federal district judges. Congress has also provided for a court executive in each circuit and for state-federal judicial councils which provide a liaison in practically all the states between federal and state judges.

When Warren Burger was appointed Chief Justice in 1969, "the time was ripe for vigorous leadership," according to Tamm and Reardon (1985, 101). Although Burger, who retired as Chief Justice in 1986, was not a strong intellectual leader of the Court, he was an outstanding advocate of administrative reform in the court system. He led campaigns to change and strengthen the state courts and legal systems and raise standards for ethics and training in both law schools and the bar.

In his first meeting with the American Bar Association in August of 1969, Burger came in like a lion. He called for more modern court management methods, an Institute for Court Management (ICM) to train Court Administrators and a re-examination of the American penal system. He also criticized law schools for failing to prepare their students for the realities of the legal profession. Burger built a fire under the American Bar Association (ABA) and reforms began to occur. An ABA task force was set up to address the problem of training court executives. Within four months of Burger's speech an Institute of Court Management was set up. Two months later it was in operation. In December of 1970, thirty-one people received the first certificates from the Chief Justice himself. By 1980, 350 people had completed both phases of the program and seven of ten circuit executives in the federal courts of appeal were graduates of the ICM. At the state level there now were fourteen court administrators.

In 1971, at Burger's suggestion, a National Center for State Courts was established by state judges and judicial administrators to provide training and research services for state courts much the same way as the Federal Judicial Center does for the federal system.

By 1972 both the Congress and the President agreed that the Chief Justice needed administrative help. A law was passed which authorized the appointment of an administrative assistant to the Chief Justice at the same salary as a district judge. Mark Cannon, a Ph.D. in political science with extensive governmental experience, was chosen to be the first incumbent.

Also in 1972, a blue-ribbon committee headed by Paul Freund of the Harvard Law School addressed the issue of the Supreme Court's heavy work load. The Committee concluded that the Court was badly over-burdened and proposed that a new National Court of Appeals be established immediately below the Supreme Court to resolve conflicting rulings among the circuit courts. The new court would also screen appeals and pass on some 400 of the most important cases to the Supreme Court. The plan drew considerable criticism, including that of former Chief Justice Earl Warren who argued that it was important for the Court to be able to decide what cases to hear and that to deny justices control of their own dockets would severely damage the power and prestige of the highest court.

An alternative plan was proposed in 1975 by a federal commission chaired by Senator Roman Hruska. A new court, subordinate to the Supreme Court and composed of seven judges, would decide cases assigned by the high court and various courts of appeal. Burger approved the plan but it received little support otherwise. A revised and updated plan was offered by Burger in 1983. This was an "inter-circuit tribunal" which was slated to settle differences between federal courts of appeal and would be staffed by a rotating core of sitting judges. A somewhat similar suggestion was forwarded by Justice John Paul Stevens. He envisaged a new court whose sole task would be to screen certiorari petitions and select those that ought to be decided by the Supreme Court. His colleague, William J. Brennan, Jr., disagreed strongly and said that it would destroy the role of the Court as the Founding Fathers had envisioned it.

In spite of widespread agreement that the Supreme Court was overloaded, none of these proposals gained much support. Murphy and Pritchett (1986) observe that "a recent decline in the number of cases filed with the Court and in its backlog makes reorganization even less likely."

In 1973, Burger's administrative assistant Mark Cannon proposed a Judicial Fellows Program to parallel those in the legislative and executive branches. It was subsequently established for the purpose of adding new and creative staff assistance to Cannon's office, the Federal Judicial Center and the Administrative Office of the United States Courts. It also assists scholars by exposing them to experience in working for and studying judicial administrators.

Among other innovations which received strong backing from Chief Justice Burger was the Conference of Metropolitan Chief Justices, the use of videotaped dispositions and court reporter management at the district level, and the so-called "individual calendar" which provided that all aspects of a case be assigned to one judge immediately after the case is filed. The "individual calendar" reduces judge-shopping, focuses responsibility on one judge and enables that judge to familiarize himself with the background of the case prior to trial. Burger generally pushed for more emphasis on modern management principles, new techniques and technological devices, and for receptivity to innovation. The result has been a marked increase in the rate of case disposition per judge.

The Federal Magistrates Act of 1968 set in place a new system of magistrates with broader jurisdiction than those who served under the old system of United States Commissioners. As a result, over half of the federal district courts now delegate a major portion of their pre-trial duties to the new federal magistrates, and another quarter of the district courts do so on occasion. Burger applauded the act and encouraged the further broadening of the magistrates' jurisdiction. The magistrates are appointed by district court judges for four and eight year terms and are required to have a law degree.

A major overhaul of the federal judiciary system occurred in 1978 under President Jimmy Carter. The Omnibus Judgeship Act of that year created 117 new district judgeships and thirty-five new positions on the Courts of Appeal. Carter filled those positions through the wide use of state selection commissions which recommended qualified candidates. A number of well-qualified woman and minority judges were appointed.

Another major reform has been the effort to reduce the use of the three-judge District Courts which are required for suits which seek injunctions on grounds of unconstitutionality, or which call for the enforcement, operation or execution of both federal and state statutes which deal with the apportionment or reapportionment of legislative districts. They are also required in cases involving courts impaneled by a specific act of Congress, such as the Civil Rights Act of 1964, the Voting Rights Act of 1965 as amended, or the Campaign Fund Act of 1974. These three-judge courts require two district judges plus an appeals court judge. Any appeals go straight to the Supreme Court. Their work load has tripled in the past decade and according to Henry J. Abraham (1980, 170–171), "they have unquestionably added to the judicial work load, in general, and to the Supreme Court, in particular." Justice Burger was a leading spokesman for their abolition and in 1976 the Congress restricted the type of case in which they may be impaneled. This resulted in a decrease of almost fifty per cent in their case load during a two-year period.

Burger was also instrumental in founding the National Center for State Courts which seeks to reduce friction between state and federal courts, and the National Institute of Justice which provides general assistance to state courts. He consistently opposed the expansion of federal jurisdiction and upheld the principles of federalism as a way to protect federal courts from further overloading.

In his last appearance before the American Bar Association in August of 1986, Burger chastised the profession for not policing itself better and told the group that if they didn't do so, the government would do it for them. He also praised the ABA for revising its code of Judicial Ethics and its Model Rules of Professional Conduct.

All in all, Burger was a leading advocate of judicial reform in the great tradition of Justices Taft, Vanderbilt and Hughes. Whether his successor Chief Justice William Rehnquist will carry on this tradition throughout the bicentennial years of the Constitution remains to be seen. That the need for judicial reform is real and the task great is beyond dispute. If justice delayed is justice denied, then clearly a judiciary system which is overloaded, outmoded and maladministered is a system which is unjust, unstable and potentially dangerous to the nation.

REFERENCES

Abraham, Henry J. 1983. *The Judiciary: The Supreme Court and the Governmental Process.* 6th ed. Boston: Allyn and Bacon, Inc.

——. 1980. *The Judicial Process.* 4th ed. New York: Oxford University Press.

Bartholowmew, Paul C. 1978. *American Constitutional Law (Volume II): Limitations on Government.* 2nd ed. Totowa, N.J.: Littlefield, Adams and Co.

Baum, Lawrence. 1981. *The Supreme Court.* Washington, D.C.: Congressional Quarterly Press.

Champagne, Antony, and Stuart S. Nagel. 1982. "The Advocates of Restraint: Holmes, Brandeis, Stone, and Frankfurter." In *Supreme Court Activism and Restraint.* Stephen C. Halpern and Charles M. Lamb, eds. Lexington, Mass.: D.C. Heath and Co.

Fallon, Richard H., Jr., and Paul C. Weiler. 1984. *"Firefighters v. Stotts:* Conflicting Models of Racial Justice." In *1984: The Supreme Court Review.* Philip B. Kurland, Gerhard Casper, and Dennis J. Hutchinson, eds. Chicago: University of Chicago Press.

Friendly, Fred W., and Martha J. H. Elliott. 1984. *The Constitution: That Delicate Balance.* New York: Random House.

Graglia, Lina A. 1982. "In Defense of Judicial Restraint." In *Supreme Court Activism and Restraint.* Stephen C. Halpern and Charles M. Lamb, eds. Lexington, Mass.: D.C. Heath and Co.

Hyneman, Charles S. 1963. *The Supreme Court on Trial.* New York: Atherton Press.

Johnson, Charles A., and Bradley C. Canon. 1984. *Judicial Policies: Implementation and Impact.* Washington, D.C.: Congressional Quarterly Press.

Kelly, Alfred H., and Winfred A. Harbison. 1976. *The American Constitution: Its Origin and Development.* 5th ed. New York: W. W. Norton and Co.

Kurland, Philip B. 1971. *Mr. Justice Frankfurter and the Supreme Court.* Chicago: University of Chicago Press.

McDonald, Forrest. 1958. *We the People: The Economic Origins of the Constitution.* Chicago: University of Chicago Press.

Miller, Arthur S. 1982. "In Defense of Judicial Activism." In *Supreme Court Activism and Restraint.* Stephen C. Halpern and Charles M. Lamb, eds. Lexington, Mass.: D.C. Heath and Co.

Murphy, Walter F., and C. Herman Pritchett. 1986. *Courts, Judges and Politics.* 4th ed. New York: Random House.

Neustadt, Richard E. 1976. *Presidential Power: The Politics of Leadership With Reflections on Johnson and Nixon.* 2nd ed. New York: Wiley.

Pritchett, C. Herman. 1984. *Constitutional Civil Liberties.* Englewood Cliffs, N.J.: Prentice-Hall, Inc.

San Miguel, Guadaloupe. 1982. "Mexican American Organizations and the Changing Politics of School Desegregation in Texas." *Social Science Quarterly* 63:701–715.

Schick, Marvin. 1982. "Judicial Activism on the Supreme Court." In *Supreme Court Activism and Restraint.* Stephen C. Halpern and Charles M. Lamb, eds. Lexington, Mass.: D.C. Heath and Co.

Tamm, Edward A., and Paul C. Reardon. 1985. "The Office of the Chief Justice." In *Views From the Bench.* Mark A. Cannon and David M. O'Brien, eds. Chatham, N.J.: Chatham House Publishers Inc.

Wasby, Stephen L. 1978. *The Supreme Court in the Federal Judicial System.* New York: Holt, Rinehart, and Winston.

Chapter Five

The Constitution Under Pressure: The Amendment Process

THE SIGNIFICANCE OF CONSTITUTIONS

Modern constitutions have arisen from a desire by new governments to start anew. For example, newly created countries in Eastern Europe after World War I, such as Czechoslovakia and Hungary, had just been released from an empire and were free to create constitutions and set up a means of governance. In France (1789) and the Soviet Union (1917), revolutions represented a break with the past and new principles of government gave expression to change. The circumstance of great war losses in Germany after 1918 caused discontinuity with the past and necessitated a fresh start. The circumstances behind the creation of new constitutions vary, but overall the countries desire to start again and to outline the governing principles of their proposed new systems (Wheare 1966).

Constitutions fulfill several functions in addition to establishing a framework for governance. They typically identify who will govern and the process by which those leaders will be selected. They may specify the scope of powers for the government, for parts of the government and for specific officials within it. Some constitutions attempt to create procedures for emergencies and crises as well as for routine operations of government. The relationships between levels and branches of government may be delineated in varying degrees. Liberal constitutions identify and protect the rights and liberties of individual citizens (Wheare 1966; Strong 1963).

Constitutions differ from laws in several ways. First, constitutions are typically the supreme authority, establishing boundaries and parameters within which the laws must fall. While constitutions deal with the principles of governance, laws deal with the details. Constitutions focus on governmental processes, defining basic powers; laws may attempt to regulate the daily behavior of citizens and government officials. Laws are easier to pass, revoke or modify than are constitutions. Constitutions, in intent if not in practice, are more permanent than laws, often requiring extraordinary majorities and multiple levels of approval to be amended. If a legislative act or any other rule-making authority conflicts with the terms of constitutions, in most instances such acts or rules will be void (Barber 1984; Miller 1981).

THE SIGNIFICANCE OF CONSTITUTIONAL AMENDMENTS

Since the U.S. Constitution was ratified, many changes have occurred in the United States. Such changes as technological advances, the growing population of the country, the diverse standards of public morality and the transformation of the party system from a source of factions to an informal instrument of governance have placed pressure on the Constitution. How is a government, which has undergone such dramatic changes, accommodated by a document that was drafted two hundred years ago? The Founding Fathers, deliberately vague when they drafted the Constitution, also recognized that no amount of drafting skill could dispense with the need for revision. In order for the Constitution to adapt to unforseen circumstances, the amending clause was included in the Constitution (Prichett 1971).

Two methods have been used to change the U.S. Constitution during the 200 years it has served as the framework for government. The first is the formal amendment process which changes the actual language of the Constitution, and the second is the process of judicial review in which the courts reinterpret or expand the meaning of existing Constitutional language through opinions and rulings (Ely 1980; Hirschfield 1962).

The two methods of constitutional change are interrelated. The small number of formal amendments to the U.S. Constitution was linked to the development of judicial review in 1803. Judicial review has been used more frequently as a method of constitutional change, despite the fact that the amendment process was expressly delineated in the Constitution while judicial review was not. Judicial review has eventually been accepted as a better method for change than amending the Constitution (Schmidhauser 1963; Mendelson 1966; Carr 1970).

The rarity of amendments in the twentieth century may support the supposition that U.S. citizens are satisfied with governance by legislation, administration and judicial review. In comparison to these routine processes, the infrequently used amendment process often appears hazardous. Because amendments become necessary when other modes of change fail, they tend to address extreme circumstances. In such instances, amendments can account for significant changes in methods of governance or in individual rights and freedoms (Vose 1972).

The study of Constitutional amendments is important for a variety of reasons. First, Constitutional amendments may constitute permanent changes in the basic framework of government. Also, they may constrict or expand individual liberties. Frustrated and dissatisfied with routine methods of change, advocates of Constitutional amendments may seek a permanent change as a strategy of last resort.

THE AMENDMENT PROCESS

Some legal scholars argue that the Founding Fathers included an amendment process in the U.S. Constitution to reduce the need for revolution and to establish a routine method for reforming the government when change was needed. Article V of the U.S. Constitution delineated the ways in which the Constitution could be amended and how proposed constitutional amendments could be ratified, granting the amendment authority both to Congress and the states. There are two methods for proposing constitutional amendments. The first, the only method used to date, calls for a two-thirds vote in both Houses of Congress. The other method requires Congress to call a constitutional convention when requested by two-thirds of the state legislatures. Controversy surrounds the second method: how would such a constitutional convention be run? Might delegates to such a convention try to establish a new form of government (Tugwell, n.d.; Edel 1981)?

Once an amendment has been initiated, it must be ratified by the states. There are two methods for ratifying amendments: by the approval of legislatures in three-fourths of the states or by ratifying conventions in three-fourths of the states. The method of ratification by conventions in three-fourths of the states has been used only once. Thirty-six state conventions approved the Twenty-first Amendment which repealed prohibition in 1933 (Livingston 1956, Brown 1935). Many recent amendments include congressionally imposed time limits upon state ratification, typically seven years.

The issue of popular sovereignty is also relevant to the amendment process. Legal scholar Walter Dellinger (1986; 16) argues that since states are treated equally in the amendment process and are not weighted by population, state approval of a proposed amendment does not require a majority of the population. The amount of popular support that an amendment requires for ratification depends principally on whether it is opposed by small or large states or some combination of the two. Even if an amendment has the support of thirty-seven states comprising ninety-six percent of the population, it can be defeated by thirteen of the smallest states containing less than four percent of the total population. If the thirty-eight smallest states constituting only forty percent of the population support an amendment opposed by the twelve largest states (who hold sixty percent of the population) the amendment will pass without majority support.

During the decade of the 1980s, the percentage of the population required for ratification varied from forty to ninety-six percent, depending upon whether support came from the smaller or the larger states. While the exact percentage varies across time with relative population shifts between the states, the underlying principle remains: constitutional amendments favored by smaller states may be approved with less than a majority of popular approval, while constitutional amendments favored by larger states may require extraordinary popular margins to be passed.

STRUCTURE OF GOVERNMENT CONSTITUTIONAL AMENDMENTS

There are two types of constitutional amendments: those which institute structural changes in the government and those which effect individual liberties. The structural amendments are concerned primarily with the principles of limited government such as the separation of powers doctrine, checks and balances and the principle of federalism. There are seven "structure of government" constitutional amendments, far fewer than the civil liberties amendments which are nineteen in number. The structural amendments are the Tenth, Eleventh, Twelfth, Sixteenth, Twentieth, Twenty-second, and Twenty-fifth Amendments (see table 5-1).

The Tenth Amendment, ratified in 1789, was part of the Bill of Rights but, unlike the other nine, it dealt with the structure of government rather than civil liberties. The Tenth Amendment reserved powers not specifically delegated to the national government to the states. Its inclusion was important in ratification politics following the 1787 Convention. It was included to assuage states' righters.

The Eleventh Amendment, an example of an amendment dealing with the principle of federalism, was proposed as the result of a Supreme Court decision in 1792 which extended the Court's jurisdiction over suits initiated by a citizen of one state against another state. Adherents to state sovereignty requested an amendment prohibiting such suits. (Livingston 1956; Edel 1981).

Of the other structure of government amendments, the Twelfth Amendment, ratified in 1804, modified the electoral college by placing

Table 5-1
Constitutional Amendments Affecting the Structure of Government

AMENDMENT		PURPOSE
1791	Tenth	Gives reserve powers to the states not specifically delegated to the national government.
1795	Eleventh	Prohibits equity suits initiated by citizens of one state against another state.
1804	Twelfth	Requires electors in the electoral college to cast separate sets of ballots for president and vice president.
1913	Sixteenth	Allows for a progressive federal income tax.
1933	Twentieth	Moves presidential inaugural from March 4 to January 20, and beginning of new Congress to January 3.
1951	Twenty-Second	Establishes a two term limit on presidents.
1967	Twenty-Fifth	Establishes a procedure for filling a vice presidential vacancy between presidential elections by allowing the president to nominate a candidate who must be confirmed by both houses of Congress; creates a procedure for temporary transfer of presidential authority when the incumbent president is disabled.

the election of the president and the vice-president on separate ballots, requiring electors to cast one set of ballots for the president and a second set for the vice-president.

In 1913, the Sixteenth Amendment, another structure of government amendment, modified Congressional taxing power to allow for a progressive income tax where tax revenues collected within a state were not proportionate to population as stipulated earlier. In the long run, this amendment greatly enhanced national power over the states by providing the federal government with an elastic tax whereby revenues grew at a more rapid rate than the revenues from the more regressive taxes employed by the states.

Also in 1933, the states ratified the Twentieth or "Lame Duck" Amendment. To reduce the amount of time an incumbent president not reelected for an additional term would be a lame duck, this amendment modified the Twelfth Amendment by moving assumption of the presidential office after the November election from March 4 to January 20. The period between the election and the assumption of power by the newly elected Congress was also shortened by moving the start of the new Congress to January 3. Another structural amendment, the Twenty-second, establishes a two-term limit on presidents.

The last structure of government amendment, the Twenty-fifth Amendment ratified in 1967, established a procedure for selecting a vice-president should the office become vacant between presidential elections. In this event, the president nominates a vice-president who takes office upon confirmation by a majority vote in both houses. The Twenty-fifth Amendment also creates a procedure to transfer presidential power temporarily upon mental or other disability. Should the president inform the president pro tempore of the Senate and the speaker of the House of Representatives in writing of an inability to discharge presidential duties, or should the vice-president and a majority of the cabinet or some other body legally designated by Congress declare in writing that the president is incapacitated, presidential power will be temporarily transferred to the vice-president.

CIVIL LIBERTIES CONSTITUTIONAL AMENDMENTS

The remaining nineteen amendments generally expand individual liberties and protect the individual from excessive use of power by state and federal governments. Five of the eleven constitutional amendments passed since 1900 expanded individual freedoms by allowing increasing numbers of the population to have voting privileges (Edel 1981). Amendments expanding individual liberties include the first nine amendments in the Bill of Rights and the Thirteenth, Fourteenth, Fifteenth, Seventeenth, Eighteenth, Nineteenth, Twenty-first, Twenty-third, Twenty-fourth, and the Twenty-sixth Amendments (see table 5-2).

The first nine amendments in the Bill of Rights, ratified in 1789, primarily restricted the powers of the national government to intrude on or restrict individual liberties (see chapter one). Major protection. in the Bill of Rights include freedoms of religion, speech, the press, peaceful assembly, petitioning government officials, and prohibitions against state establishment of a religion (First); the right to bear arms (Second); freedom from unreasonable searches and seizures (Fourth); and the right to a grand jury and due process in criminal proceedings, protection against self-incrimination and double jeopardy, and compensation for property seizure (Fifth).

Other protections of individual liberties in the Bill of Rights include the right to a speedy trial, an impartial jury, the right to be informed of the nature of charges, to confront witnesses, subpoena power for defendants, and the right to counsel (Sixth); the right to trial by jury in common law cases (Seventh); freedom from excessive bail and fines and from cruel and unusual punishment (Eighth); and a protection of

Table 5-2
Constitutional Amendments Affecting Civil Liberties

	AMENDMENT	PURPOSE
1791	First	Freedom of religion, speech, press, assembly, and to petition the government for grievances.
1791	Second	The right to bear arms.
1791	Third	Prohibits peacetime quartering of soldiers.
1791	Fourth	Prohibits unreasonable searches and seizures.
1791	Fifth	The right to a grand jury, due process, protection against self incrimination and double jeopardy, and just compensation for property seizures for public use.
1791	Sixth	The right to a speedy trial and an impartial jury, to be informed of charges and to confront witnesses, and to counsel.
1791	Seventh	The right to trial by jury in common law cases.
1791	Eighth	Prohibits excessive bail and fines, and cruel and unusual punishments.
1791	Ninth	Provides protection of individual rights not specifically enumerated in the Constitution.
1865	Thirteenth	Abolishes slavery and involuntary servitude.
1868	Fourteenth	Provides due process and equal protection under the laws, and prohibits the abridgment of privileges and immunities of citizens.
1870	Fifteenth	Gives blacks the right to vote.
1913	Seventeenth	Provides for direct election of U.S. Senators
1919	Eighteenth	Prohibits the sale, manufacture, transportation, importation of, or exportation of alcoholic beverages
1920	Nineteenth	Gives women the right to vote.
1933	Twenty-First	Repeals prohibition.
1961	Twenty-Third	Provides presidential electors for the District of Columbia.
1964	Twenty-Fourth	Abolishes poll taxes.
1971	Twenty-Sixth	Gives eighteen year-olds the right to vote.

individual rights not explicitly enumerated in the Constitution (Ninth).

The Thirteenth Amendment (ratified in 1865), the Fourteenth (adopted in 1868), and the Fifteenth (approved finally in 1870), are often called the Civil War Amendments; together they expanded the rights of blacks and naturalized citizens significantly. The Thirteenth Amendment abolished slavery. Through equal protection, due process, and privileges and immunities clauses, the Fourteenth Amendment restricted the power of the states to infringe upon individual liberties, including those of blacks. The Fifteenth Amendment gave black males the right to vote.

In 1913, ratification of the Seventeenth Amendment provided for the direct election of U.S. Senators. Previously the election of U.S. Senators by their respective state legislatures allowed citizens only indirect input into this important choice. Direct election expanded citizen power at the national level.

The Eighteenth Amendment, ratified in 1919, is an anomaly, and not easily labeled either as a structure of government or a civil liberties amendment. Since this amendment prohibited the sale, manufacture, transportation, importation, or exportation of alcoholic beverages, it probably affected civil liberties most. Unlike other civil liberties amendments, the Eighteenth restricted rather than expanded individual freedoms. The Eighteenth Amendment was repealed in 1933 with the ratification of the Twenty-first Amendment.

Not until 1920, with the ratification of the Nineteenth Amendment, did women in the United States secure the right to vote. This amendment expanded the electorate by approximately fifty percent and consequently popularized the election process greatly. Further expansion of the electorate by constitutional amendment did not occur until 1961 when the passage of the Twenty-third Amendment authorized presidential electors from the District of Columbia. Until that time, residents of the nation's capital could not vote in presidential elections.

In 1964 the Twenty-fourth Amendment was ratified. Its impact was to further expand the freedom of individuals to participate in governance by prohibiting use of poll taxes for federal elections. Poll taxes were frequently used in the South to prevent blacks and poor people from voting. The last expansion of the electorate occurred in 1971, when the Twenty-sixth Amendment gave the right to vote to eighteen-year-olds. The previous age limit on voting was twenty-one.

Conservatives might argue that not all civil liberties amendments have expanded individual freedom. For example, the Thirteenth Amendment, which abolished slavery, could be viewed in two ways depending on whether or not one was a slaveholder. Also, the First Amendment is often interpreted ambiguously vis-à-vis the expansion of individual liberty. Those who desire prayer in public schools claim the establish-

ment clause, as interpreted by the Supreme Court, violates their freedom to pray. Yet those who oppose prayer in public schools assert that
the Supreme Court properly interpreted the establishment of religion
clause in order to protect personal liberty.

There is further controversy over whether the Fourteenth Amendment was used to expand or contract individual liberties in the *Roe v.*
Wade abortion case of 1973. Pro-choice advocates applauded the decision, stating that it expanded liberty by giving women the freedom to
choose what they wanted to do with their own bodies. On the other
hand, pro-life advocates, concerned with the rights of the unborn, protested that the Supreme Court decision infringed on those rights. Clearly
cogent arguments exist, however, that the net effect of civil liberties
amendments, including the First, Thirteenth and Fourteenth, was to
expand individual freedom.

TRADITIONAL EXPLANATIONS
OF POLITICAL CHANGE

Why have these constitutional changes come about? Political science
literature has suggested two categories of variables as potential predictors of political system outputs: socioeconomic factors and political factors. Most of the literature exploring the relative importance of political and economic factors focuses on state-level public policy, and many
analyses have examined V. O. Key's hypothesis that welfare spending
would be higher in states with two-party competition than in states with
one-party dominance (Key 1949).

Using a limited set of variables, early findings by Dawson and Robinson (1963) indicated that public welfare programs appeared to be related more to social and economic factors than to political factors. Other
scholars found interparty competition to have little independent impact
on policy outcomes, and concluded that a state's socioeconomic environment has a great deal of influence over its policies (Dye 1966; Fry
and Winters 1970; Winters 1976; Hofferbert 1968). The socioeconomic
perspective was challenged by Jennings (1979) who found party competition to have an impact on welfare spending. In deriving conclusions
about the superior explanatory power of economics, most studies have
used financial output variables.

Some evidence, however, suggests that political factors as well as economic factors are important for explaining constitutional change. There
are several reasons why political factors might have as important an
impact on constitutional change as economic factors.

Constitutional change, especially in the initiation stage, transpires at
the federal level. Groups which have been too small or impotent to
effectively mobilize at lower levels of government are sometimes able

to reach the critical mass for an impact at the federal level by pooling resources. Welfare groups and other groups which speak for the poor, for example, have historically been more effective in the halls of Congress than in the halls of many state legislatures.

At the federal level, the stakes involved in political outcomes are increased, providing further incentives for groups to become involved in political conflicts. The greater ability of various groups to mobilize at the federal level heightens the importance of politics at that level. Previous studies which found economic factors to be most important have focused on the state legislation. Constitutional change, however, may be sensitive to both economic and political factors. Changing a constitution is an action which sometimes raises basic questions and assumptions about the role of government and of the individual in society. Political conflict may be inevitable.

MODELS OF CONSTITUTIONAL CHANGE

Two different models of constitutional change have been developed to explain structure of government amendments and civil liberties amendments. Each has four stages, resulting in a constitutional amendment in stage four. The two models differ, however, in stages one, two and three. In stage one, the precipitating factor for structure of government amendments is a political triggering event, while the precipitating factor for civil liberties amendments is technological innovation. Since technological innovations are a major contributor to economic growth and are instrumental in significant long-run improvements in productivity, economics is a major causal factor in the initiation and ratification of civil liberties amendments, while politics is a major causal factor in the initiation and ratification of structure of government amendments.

The process model for structure of government amendments is more elite-based, while the model for civil liberties amendments is more popularly based. In stage two, for structure of government amendments, the political triggering event and recognition of a structural problem has an impact primarily on politicians and other prominent elites, while for civil liberties amendments, the precipitating technological innovation has a profound impact on the behavior and attitudes of average citizens.

In stage three, for structure of government amendments, political coalitions begin to form among salient elites, both in Congress at the national level and in the states, especially in the state legislatures. By contrast, for civil liberties amendments, grass roots political movements are formed or, if they already exist, are given new life by the attitudinal and behavioral changes caused by the precipitating technological innovation. Stage four for both models results in constitutional change (see table 5-3).

The stage one political triggering event for structure of government amendments focuses attention upon the structural weakness in the government process. Spreading awareness of the problem and building motivation to change the weakness among relevant politicians and political elites is characteristic of stage two. As awareness and motivation spread, political coalitions build up in stage three to demand a formal system response to the problem, highlighted by the political triggering event. Lobbying and concern for good government culminate in the initiation and ratification of a constitutional amendment in stage four. Clearly the process is a long one, not only due to the number of stages, but also because of the amount of time each stage can take. The time required may range from a few years to many years or even decades.

Table 5-3
Models of Constitutional Change

STAGES OF CHANGE FOR STRUCTURE OF GOVERNMENT AMENDMENTS

(Elite-Based Constitutional Change)

Political triggering event	Widespread awareness of structural problem	Formation of political coalition	Constitutional change
Stage I	Stage II	Stage III	Stage IV

STAGES OF CHANGE FOR CIVIL LIBERTIES AMENDMENTS

(Popular-Based Constitutional Change)

Techno-logical Innovation	Behavioral & attitudinal change	Political movements demands	Constitutional change
Stage I	Stage II	Stage III	Stage IV

For civil liberties amendments, the precipitating event in stage one is technology because technology provides a basis for social organization which, in turn, affects behavior and attitudes. New technologies have an impact on the way individuals relate to each other as well as on production. Technological advances also affect opportunity structures and the degree to which weaker segments are excluded from decision making. After technological innovation in stage one has induced behavioral and attitudinal changes in stage two, political movements arise in stage three to push for formal recognition of expanded opportunities. When successful, these movements result in legal and constitutional change in stage four.

Why are the first stages of the constitutional amendment process different for structure of government amendments than for civil liberties amendments? Structure of government amendments are usually technical in nature, refining and improving the process of government. These amendments have little immediate impact on the daily lives of citizens but rather are designed to improve the efficiency and effectiveness of government. The precipitating event for these amendments is typically a political event or series of events highlighting an inadequacy in the current method of selecting public officials or administering governmental affairs. The weakness or problem in the governmental process may have been readily apparent before the occurrence of the political triggering event, but the motivation to overcome inertia and push through a constitutional reform would have previously been lacking. The precipitating political event highlights the importance of the problem, makes cognizance of the problem widespread and provides the motivation to correct the structural deficiency.

Civil liberties amendments deal with the basic and daily relationships between major groups in society. The general thrust of civil liberties amendments is to prevent the group or groups in power from exploiting or continuing to exploit less powerful groups. Why would a powerful group suddenly alter a pattern of dominance and interaction toward a powerless group, relinquishing the control it once enjoyed? Such a shift in power is so major and substantial that only fundamental changes in the economic, technological and cultural bases of society make it possible.

As one of the most important factors in economic growth and as the major contributor to significant improvements in productivity, technological innovation typically precedes and precipitates such a fundamental shift in power. The time lag between the development and dissemination of the technology and the resulting constitutional change may be lengthy. The formation of political coalitions in stage three, as well as behavioral and attitudinal changes in stage two, are a necessary part of the process, but the precipitating event is a technological change which does one of two things: either the new technology makes the previous exploitation of the powerless group by the powerful group no longer profitable and therefore no longer desirable; or else the new technology provides the disadvantaged group with a new power base from which it can impel greater equality and recognition from the legal and governmental systems.

POLITICAL TRIGGERING EVENTS FOR STRUCTURAL CHANGE AMENDMENTS

Ratification Politics and the Tenth Amendment

The political triggering event for the Tenth Amendment was the ratification politics surrounding the adoption of the 1787 Constitution (see table 5-4). The content of the Tenth Amendment was debated in the First Congress which set about the task of enacting a Bill of Rights which had been promised during the ratification battle to assure adequate support for the new Constitution. States' righters and Anti-Federalists proposed limiting the federal government to those powers expressly delegated by the Constitution. However, James Madison, other moderates and some Federalists who desired effective government, be-

Table 5-4
Political Triggering Events for Structure of Government Amendments

AMENDMENT	POLITICAL TRIGGERING EVENT
Tenth	Politics of ratification of the Constitution.
Eleventh	U.S. Supreme Court case of Chisholm v. Georgia.
Twelfth	Rising strength of political parties, president and vice president of opposite political parties in 1796, and the election tie of 1800.
Sixteenth	Increasing inadequacies of excise taxes and customs duties as methods of financing governemnt, and Supreme Court blockage of federal income tax legislation.
Twentieth	Unresponsiveness of Republican controlled Congress to the Great Depression.
Twenty-Second	Republican reaction to four terms for Roosevelt.
Twenty-Fifth	Eisenhower's illnesses and Kennedy's assassination.

lieved that some federal powers must be implicitly admitted. They preferred a version of the amendment which reserved for the states powers not explicitly delegated to the national government (Burns 1982, 46). Eventually the attitudes of the Anti-Federalists changed sufficiently to accept the proposed compromise between doing nothing, leaving fewer overt limits on national power, and the original amendment (which they preferred) giving states greater power. The Federalists prevailed in the political movement to get both the Constitution and the Bill of Rights adopted.

Chisholm v. Georgia and the Eleventh Amendment

The adoption of the Eleventh Amendment represented the only time in U.S. history that the federal judiciary had its power directly curtailed by constitutional amendment (Kelly and Harbison 1976, 181). The 1793 U.S. Supreme Court case of *Chisholm v. Georgia* is the political triggering event that prompted the Eleventh Amendment. This case concerned the right of the federal judiciary to call a state as defendant and to make judgements about its rights and liabilities. In Article III, the Constitution gives federal courts direct jurisdiction over "controversies between a state and citizens of another state." During the ratification debates of the Constitution in several states, prominent Federalists promised Anti-Federalists that this portion of Article III would be applied only to cases in which the state consented to be sued. However, federal suits were instituted against states by citizens of other states.

In *Chisholm v. Georgia,* citizens of South Carolina successfully sued the state of Georgia in federal court against its will for the recovery of property. Angry sentiments of Anti-Federalists increased, especially in states where similar suits were pending. Georgia refused to implement the U.S. Supreme Court decision. The day after the decision, the Eleventh Amendment was introduced in Congress. Four years lapsed before the Anti-Federalists succeeded in ratifying the Eleventh Amendment among the states, but their political coalition eventually prevailed.

The Election of 1800 and the Twelfth Amendment

The rising strength of political parties and the political maneuvering surrounding the election of 1800 triggered the process of constitutional change which resulted in the Twelfth Amendment. The framers of the Constitution had not anticipated the development of political parties and had assumed that control of the federal government would be entrusted to nonpartisan elites. No mention of political parties was made in the Constitution itself and no recognition of political parties was given in voting procedures for president and vice-president.

Under the original balloting method specified in the Constitution for those two offices, each elector simply casts two votes for two men without distinguishing between the vote for president and the vote for vice-president. This left open the possibility that a president of one political party and a vice-president of the opposing party might be elected simultaneously, a possibility which became reality in 1796 when John Adams, a Federalist, was elected president and Thomas Jefferson, a Republican, was elected vice president. The original balloting method also allowed for ties for the presidency between men of the same party. This occurred in 1800. The lengthy political battle which ensued in the House of Representatives spread awareness of the problems in the existing balloting method and prompted the initiation and ratification of the Twelfth Amendment.

Inadequate Federal Revenues and the Sixteenth Amendment

Over a century passed before another structure of government amendment was passed. At the beginning of the twentieth century, revenues from tariffs and excise taxes had not kept pace with the economic growth of the country, causing presidents to propose new revenue sources to Congress. Theodore Roosevelt recommended a federal income tax in 1907, and a proposal for a federal income tax was introduced in every session of Congress after 1905. Liberal nationalists and progressives favored a graduated tax for redistributive as well as revenue purposes. The U.S. Supreme Court, however, constantly blocked income tax legislation, declaring such provisions unconstitutional. The growing confrontation in Europe and realization that the United States might be drawn into it began to affect domestic tax politics. As concern over these problems heightened, the Sixteenth Amendment was initiated by Congress in 1909 and was ratified by the states in 1913.

**Congressional Unresponsiveness and
the Twentieth Amendment**

The Lame Duck Amendment, the Twentieth Amendment, altered the structure of government by moving forward the formal assumption of office and power of both the president and the Congress to January dates, bringing it closer to the November election. This amendment reduced the lame duck period between the election and the exit from office for retiring incumbents of both branches of government (Morris et al. 1971, 562). The triggering political event was the unresponsiveness of the Republican-controlled Congress between 1929 and the Great Depression. The failure of President Hoover's policies to bring about relief from the Depression caused a crisis of confidence in Congress and the presidency. Anxious to implement a rapid change in leadership when the public mandated it, a coalition of Democrats and agrarian Republicans in Congress initiated the Twentieth Amendment, which was ratified in 1933.

Roosevelt's Four Terms and the Twenty-Second Amendment

Franklin Roosevelt's extraordinary four-term election to the office of president triggered the adoption of the Twenty-second Amendment in 1951. Sometimes called "the Republicans' revenge on Roosevelt," the Twenty-second Amendment states that "no person shall be elected president more than twice." Republicans resented being precluded from the White House and its prerequisites of office, including the power to appoint federal judges and political appointees in the federal bureaucracy. Republican partisans were joined by Democrats who feared that the presidency could come to resemble a dictatorship if no formal constitutional limits were imposed on the length of service. Awareness of these problems spread through the political elites and resulted in the Twenty-second Amendment.

Eisenhower, Kennedy, and the Twenty-fifth Amendment

Presidents had been disabled before the 1950s. When Woodrow Wilson suffered a stroke in his second term in office, his wife virtually became acting president. However, the immediate political triggering events for the Twenty-fifth Amendment, which deals with presidential disability and succession, were Eisenhower's illnesses while in the White House, and Kennedy's assassination which left open the vice presidency once Johnson assumed the presidency. Eisenhower suffered a mild heart attack on September 24, 1955, causing him to be hospitalized for three weeks. Less than a year later, on June 9, 1956, he was hospitalized again after an attack of ileitis and underwent surgery. On November 25, 1957, he suffered a minimal stroke (Schlesinger 1983). These illnesses created concern among the political elites, especially in Congress under Senator Birch Bayh's leadership, over the need to develop appropriate and official procedures for dealing with presidential disabilities. Similarly, the vacancy in the vice-presidency when Kennedy was killed drew attention to that problem. The Twenty-fifth Amendment was designed to address both presidential disability and succession.

TECHNOLOGICAL INNOVATIONS TRIGGERING CIVIL LIBERTIES AMENDMENTS

What is technology? In a general sense, technology consists of a society's knowledge of how to make or do things. More narrowly, technology involves the application of research for practical concerns, either industrial or commercial (Smithsonian 1978, 86). Ogburn (1950) has argued that technological innovation explains social change. Distinguishing between material culture (technology) and adaptive culture, Ogburn contends that changes in material culture force change in social organization and customs. Since social organization and customs do not change as quickly as material culture, there is a cultural lag between the introduction of a new technology and the response of social institutions to it. Material inventions may be of three types: tools, weapons, or technical processes. Invention, in turn, is influenced by the culture. It may be mechanical or social and it results from three factors—mental activity, demand and the presence of other cultural elements. This model of technology driven by social change and eventually culminating in legal change, is particularly appropriate to civil liberties amendments (See table 5-5).

The Beginning of the Industrial Revolution and the Bill of Rights

According to Thomas Jefferson, "Science is more important in a republican than in any other kind of government" (Meier 1981, 20). Jefferson believed that technology was compatible with and conducive to a democratic republican government and also served to build up a sense of U.S. nationalism. Technology achieved a new level of importance in

Table 5-5
Technological Innovation Triggering Civil Liberties Amendments

AMENDMENT	TECHNOLOGICAL INNOVATION
First Nine Amendments	Beginning of the industrial revolution.
Civil War Amendments (13th, 14th, 15th)	Expansion of the industrial revolution.
Seventeenth	Enhanced communication and electricity.
Prohibition (18th & 21st)	Automobile
Nineteenth	Barrier methods of birth control.
Expansion of the electorate (23rd, 24th, 26th)	Television

the United States as well as throughout the rest of the world during the Industrial Revolution.

The precise dates of the Industrial Revolution are subject to debate, but some consider the beginning period to have lasted over a century between 1660 and 1815. During this period, the factory system began, experimentation with steam power to pump water was commenced, coal mines reached new depths as pumping systems improved, and the first practical steam engines were invented. In the 1760s, a spinning jenny was perfected which greatly improved the speed with which raw cotton was transformed into thread, as well as the quality of the output. The mercantile system of commerce began to decline and the free enterprise system began to emerge.

With the decline of mercantilism and feudalism, attitudes and behavior evolved toward new liberal values emphasizing individual rights in the political sphere and private property in the economic sphere. Although many liberal philosophers such as Locke and Adam Smith were English, liberal values were particularly strong in the United States. By the time of the Philadelphia Convention, these values were so strongly held that many states refused to ratify the new U.S. Constitution without a promise of the inclusion of the protections of civil liberties in the Bill of Rights.

In the case of the Bill of Rights, the technological changes brought about by the beginning of the Industrial Revolution in stage one of its development contributed to the growth of a liberal political philosophy emphasizing individualism in stage two. In stage three, the ideals of the revolution supporting freedom from government oppression were supported by Anti-Federalists, who desired a Bill of Rights, and Federalists, who feared the 1787 Constitution would be overturned without it. In this instance, the new technologies represented by the beginning of the Industrial Revolution held forth the promise, if not yet the actualization, of a more economically independent United States. As technology spread, the colonies would no longer be dependent on Britain for finished goods and finer manufactured products because they could produce those products domestically. Technological innovations in this instance gave greater economic and ultimately greater political power to the formerly disadvantaged group, the colonists. This fueled the Revolution, the resulting liberal 1787 Constitution and the individual protections in the Bill of Rights.

The Expansion of the Industrial Revolution and the Civil War Amendments

The Industrial Revolution entered a more mature phase between 1815 and 1918. The technological inventions in the early to mid-1800s contributed to cultural and economic changes underlying the American Civil War and to the resulting Civil War Amendments to the U.S. Constitution. Technology dissemination in the first half of the nineteenth century was not uniform throughout the country. For example, the total output of pig iron in 1860 was approximately 859,000 tons, of which only 26,000 tons were produced in the South (Oliver 1956, 278). Similarly, of over 11,000 tons of steel produced nationwide, 9,000 were produced in Pennsylvania. Because of the dissemination of the sewing machine in the North, that area dominated in clothing production. Northern production of armaments also far outstripped production in the South.

These and other less dramatic technologies transformed the North from an agricultural to an industrial society, while the South remained primarily agricultural. Never dependent upon slave labor because they used cheap immigrant labor instead, the North needed slavery even less with industrialization. The expansion of the Industrial Revolution in the North in stage one of the constitutional change process contributed to the growth of the urbanization and its accompanying attitudes and behaviors. Urban lifestyles in stage two provided fertile ground for the growth of the abolitionist movement in stage three. After the bloody, prolonged and extraordinarily costly Civil War, in which the industrial power of the North finally prevailed over the manpower of the South, the Thirteenth, Fourteenth and Fifteenth Amendments were passed. Many southern states actually ratified these Civil War Amendments in an attempt to shorten Reconstruction.

In the case of the Civil War Amendments, the new technologies accompanying the expansion of the Industrial Revolution in the North made the continued exploitation of blacks through the institution of slavery uneconomical in industrialized regions. Historians now disagree about how economical slavery was in the South, and how long its practice would have continued had the war not occurred. However the industrialization of the North, which clearly made slavery uneconomical in that region, also gave it the supplies and economic base to win the war and enforce its views through the Civil War Amendments.

Enhanced Communication, Electricity and the Seventeenth Amendment

Enhanced communication in the form of the telegraph and telephone, as well as the spread of electric power to households, contributed to rapid dissemination of information about politics and to greater citizen interest in national political affairs. By 1844, Samuel F. B. Morse was able to construct a working telegraph line between Washington, D.C. and Baltimore, an event which symbolized the beginning of a revolution in communications in the United States. By the 1860s lines crossed the country and were spreading to other countries. Building on the technology employed in the telegraph, Alexander Graham Bell set out to design a device that would transmit the human voice, a feat first achieved in 1875. The telephone spread rapidly and 54,000 were in service by 1880 in the U.S. By 1890, the number of phones had increased to 234,000, and other rapid dissemination continued, with 1.3 million phones in 1900 and 7.6 million in 1910.

Accompanying the growth of improved communications technologies was the simultaneous electrification of America. Thomas Edison patented the electric light bulb in 1880. By 1881 he had invented a method to generate electricity and to distribute it within an extended area. By 1882, Edison had opened the Pearl Street Central Station in New York City, the world's first system of extensive distribution of electric energy. This event marked the beginning of the electric age. By 1900, electric lights were found in many homes and electricity began to be used to improve communications.

These inventions contributed to a more informed citizenry, both directly and through improvements in the information contained in the newspapers, as well as through the increase in the speed with which they were produced. Citizens began to form impressions of a government controlled by powerful, monied and corrupt corporations and interests. They joined political movements such as the Progressives and the Populists who pushed for reforms. First Populists, then the Bryan Democrats and eventually liberal Republicans and Progressives advocated direct election of senators to make the Senate more responsive to average citizens and less responsive to powerful corporations and interests. The Seventeenth Amendment was introduced into Congress and successfully passed the House in 1893, 1894, 1898, 1900, and 1902, but was ignored or voted down in the Senate in each of those years. After the Lorimer incident, first revealed in the *Chicago Tribune* in 1911, Senate resistance to direct election was minimized after the *Tribune* revealed that corporations had bribed state legislators to select Lorimer to be a U.S. Senator. Initiated by Congress in June 1911, the Seventeenth Amendment was ratified in May of 1913 (Sundquist 1986, 55).

Improved communications technologies, facilitated by the development of electricity, enhanced the power of the average citizen by providing speedier and more complete access to political information. This created a climate, in stage two of the change process, where derogatory attitudes toward the corrupting influence of large corporations and special interests developed. This robber baron era represented the raw exercise of corporate and monied power. Although the Sherman Antitrust Act was passed in 1890, its impact was minimal and its effectiveness was not bolstered until after the ratification of the Seventeenth

Amendment and the passage of the Clayton Antitrust Act in 1914. This anti-corporate climate activated reform movements in stage three which succeeded only after numerous attempts to dilute the strength of corporate power by direct election of U.S. Senators.

The Automobile and Prohibition

The prohibition movement had been sporadically active in American politics since the Civil War, but did not gain great support until just before World War I. Only five states passed statewide prohibition acts prior to 1900. After 1900, prohibition spread quickly as part of the progressive era, its progress partially attributable to the political acumen of the Anti-Saloon League. By 1916 nineteen states were dry and many of the remaining states had local option laws. Congress first adopted prohibition legislation in 1917 as part of wartime food control measures. In December of that same year, the Eighteenth Amendment was initiated by Congress and submitted to the states for ratification. By January of 1919, this constitutional amendment was ratified.

Given that prohibition was a long standing movement, sometimes overlapping with the women's movement for suffrage, why was it successful in the period immediately following World War I and not before? The climate of the time was one of moral and social reform. Cultural changes preceding this period facilitated the reform climate which gave final victory to the prohibition movement in the form of a constitutional amendment. Urbanization and technological developments undermined traditional values and the sense of community, creating flux in everyday life and social patterns.

More than any other technology, the automobile altered the traditional family structure and contributed to the demise of the extended family by enabling young adults to move to better jobs in distant communities without completely severing contact with their relatives at their home. By 1900, the United States had developed a technological base upon which the automobile industry could be built. Petroleum technology facilitated an abundant supply of kerosene and gasoline. In 1900 Henry Ford began efforts to design a low-cost, useful car. By 1903 he had organized the Ford Motor Company. He had designed a practical car, the Model T, by 1908. Several engineering improvements soon followed, including the first self-starter in 1911. The standardization system and adoption of the assembly line method of production reduced costs so that tens of thousands of wage earners were able to purchase Model Ts.

The first stage, therefore, of the constitutional change process resulting in the Eighteenth Amendment was a rapid growth in American technology around 1900 and the introduction of the automobile shortly thereafter. The automobile contributed to an already existing trend toward urbanization and the erosion of traditional family values. These changes alarmed prohibitionists who saw alcohol as a major evil contributing to these social changes. Particularly active were religiously affiliated prohibition groups such as the Women's Christian Temperance Union and the Temperance Society of the Methodist Episcopal Church. The prohibitionist movement was able to capitalize on other reform movements occurring in the same period, such as the women's suffrage movement and the reform wave against machine politics, to achieve passage of the Eighteenth Amendment.

More than any other amendment, the Eighteenth Amendment invaded privacy and attempted to regulate living patterns and daily behavior. Americans in droves, including President Harding, reacted adversely and seemed to take perverse delight in violating the amendment. Saloons were replaced by speakeasies—private clubs that served liquor illegally. Bootleggers flourished and made black-market fortunes. The annual bootlegging intake of Al Capone, a well known Chicago gangster, was estimated at sixty million dollars. After fourteen years of widespread lawbreaking by average citizens as well as gangsters, the difficulty of enforcing moral absolutes in an increasingly urban, technological, and secular society became apparent. Prohibition was repealed with the adoption of the Twenty-first Amendment in 1933.

Birth Control and the Nineteenth Amendment

Barrier methods of birth control were the technological innovation which precipitated the Nineteenth Amendment, which gave women the right to vote. With the vulcanization of rubber in the mid-nineteenth century, mass production of cheap and effective condoms became feasible. Female barrier methods included the diaphragm and the cervical cap, both developed in the late 1800s. By 1900 spermicides were also widely available in many countries. Although the Comstock laws prohibited the dissemination of contraceptives and contraceptive information, many upper-class women who were active in the women's movement at the turn of the century travelled abroad and thus secured access to birth control information and devices.

As birth control technologies become more reliable, women gained greater control over their own bodies, allowing them to separate sex from procreation for the first time in history. Controlling the number and timing of the children they bore allowed women to express demands for political rights and greater equality in the work place. Birth control technology gave the disadvantaged group—women—greater power for making demands upon the existing establishment. Changing attitudes of women caused many to join the women's suffrage movement as the push for political rights became increasingly focused on the right to vote.

By 1914, nine states plus the territory of Alaska had enfranchised women through state law. President Wilson asked Congress for a suffrage amendment in September of 1918. Congress was reluctant, causing the suffragettes to stage rallies, engage in hunger strikes and picket the White House. In June of 1919, Congress proposed the amendment. Ratification by the states occurred in August of 1920.

Television and the Expansion of the Electorate

During the 1960s and early 1970s, three constitutional amendments were passed which expanded the electorate. The Twenty-third Amendment gave presidential electors to the District of Columbia; the Twenty-fourth removed the poll tax as a barrier to voting; and the Twenty-sixth lowered the age for voting from twenty-one in most states to eighteen. The technology which propelled this electorate expansion was television. Although television had been invented before World War II, it was too expensive for most families at that time.

Beginning in the early 1950s, however, television spread rapidly and experienced phenomenal growth. As of January 1946, there were ten thousand television sets in the U.S. By April 1951, five years later, twelve million sets were in operation throughout the country (Settel and Laas 1969, 69). By the early 1960s, 2.7 million color televisions had been sold. Throughout the 1960s, the amount of daily household viewing time increased steadily from five hours and three minutes in 1960 to five hours and fifty-six minutes by 1970 (Bowers 1973, 29).

Television has had a significant impact on attitudes and values. Comstock (1980, 57) argues that television increased the participation of the general public. Television has helped to reinforce and crystallize opinion as well as to change opinion. For example, public opinion polls have shown that voter interest in politics increased from 45 percent to 57 percent after 115 million people witnessed the 1960 presidential debates. The percentage of the electorate that voted increased from 60.4 percent in 1956 to 64.5 percent in 1960.

Not only did television increase general voter interest in politics, but it affected comparatively disadvantaged groups such as blacks and the young as well. Through television, blacks were able to get a close view of middle-class white society. Every day blacks were struck by comparisons between the economically better-situated middle-class white family and their own more constricted and impoverished circumstances. Greater awareness of this relative gap contributed to the discontent which fueled the civil rights movement in the early 1960s.

The movement was protracted and its activities, including planned marches and rallies as well as unplanned violence, were covered in painstaking detail through the eye of the television camera. Television coverage of the activities of the civil rights demonstrators fortified blacks and repulsed many whites, contributing to attitude changes in both groups and helping to produce two civil rights related constitutional amendments as well as major legislation. In 1961, the Twenty-third Amendment granted presidential electors to the increasingly black city of Washington, D.C. In 1964, with the ratification of the Twenty-fourth Amendment, the poll tax, a major impediment to voting for blacks and poor whites, was struck down.

Television also had a galvanizing impact on the protest of American youth against the Vietnam War during the latter part of the 1960s. This impact was twofold. Television covered in graphic detail the missions and battles in the Vietnam military arena, projecting images of violence and death half-way around the world into U.S. living rooms every night. Vietnam was the first true television war. Television also covered the growing protest movement at home, and, by its coverage, affected the attitudes of the young in particular and the general public toward the war. The attitude change produced the protest movement which eventually succeeded in securing U.S. troop withdrawal.

Impressed by the violent images projected by television, youth and their supporters began to ask this question: if they were old enough to die why were they not old enough to vote? U.S. youth had also fought and died in previous wars but the question of giving greater political power to young adults had not arisen, since television was not present to project the costs that the young were paying on the battlefield. The Twenty-sixth Amendment was ratified in 1971 as an outgrowth of the Vietnam War and its portrayal on television. In all three cases of the expansion of the electorate through the Twenty-third, Twenty-fourth and Twenty-sixth Amendments, television aided the comparatively disadvantaged groups of blacks and youth by providing them with new information and awareness. On occasion it also gave them an effective and powerful medium for expressing their own views.

CONCLUSIONS

Constitutional amendments may be one of two types: changes in the structure of government or expansions of civil liberties. In two hundred years of American history the latter have outnumbered the former. Civil liberties amendments are driven by technological innovation while structure of government amendments are triggered by political crises. Since technology is constantly changing, demands for expansions in civil liberties have been more numerous than the demands for alterations in the structure of government. Not only have amendments altering the structure of government been less numerous, but they have refined rather than radically restructured the basic governmental institutions and processes. Americans continue to revere the governmental framework set forth by the founders and the concepts of separation of powers and checks and balances that it embodied.

REFERENCES

Barber, Sotirios A. 1984. *On What the Constitution Means.* Baltimore: Johns Hopkins University Press.
Bowers, Robert T. 1973. *Television and the Public.* New York: Holt, Rinehart and Winston, Inc.
Brown, Everett S. 1935. "The Ratification of the Twenty-First Amendment." *American Political Science Review* 29:1008–1009.
Burns, James MacGregor. 1982. *The Vineyard of Liberty: The American Experiment.* New York: Alfred A. Knopf.
Carr, Robert K. 1970. *The Supreme Court and Judicial Review.* Westport, Conn.: Greenwood Press.
Comstock, George. 1980. *Television in America.* Beverly Hills, Calif.: Sage Publications.
Dawson, Richard E., and James A. Robinson. 1963. "Inter-Party Competition, Economic Variables, and Welfare Policies in the American States." *Journal of Politics* 25:265–289.
Dellinger, Walter. 1986. "The Process of Constitutional Amendment: Law, History, and Politics." *News for Teachers of Political Science* 49:16–19.
Dye, Thomas. 1966. *Politics, Economics, and the Public: Policy Outcomes in the American States.* Chicago: Rand McNally.
Earle, Valerie A. 1984. "The Federal Structure." In *Founding Principles of American Government: Two Hundred Years of Democracy on Trial.* George J. Graham, Jr. and Scarlett G. Graham, eds. Chatham, N.J.: Chatham House Publishers.
Edel, Wilbur. 1981. *A Constitutional Convention: Threat or Challenge?* New York: Praeger Publishers.
Ely, John Hart. 1980. *Democracy and Distrust: A Theory of Judicial Review.* Cambridge, Mass.: Harvard University Press.
Fry, Brian R., and Richard F. Winters. 1970. "The Politics of Redistribution." *American Political Science Review* 64:508–522.
Hirschfield, Robert S. 1962. *The Constitution and the Court: The Development of the Basic Law Through Judicial Interpretation.* New York: Random House.
Hofferbert, Richard. 1968. "Socio-economic Dimensions of the American States: 1890–1980." *Midwest Journal of Political Science* 12:401–418.
Jennings, Edward T. 1979. "Competition, Constituencies, and Welfare Policies." *American Political Science Review* 73:414–429.
Kelly, Alfred H., and Winfred A. Harbison. 1976. *The American Constitution: Its Origin and Development.* 5th ed. New York: W. W. Norton and Co.

Key, V. O., Jr. 1949. *Southern Politics in State and Nation.* New York: Random House.

Livingston, William S. 1956. *Federalism and Constitutional Change.* Oxford: Clarendon Press.

Meier, Hugo A. 1981. "Thomas Jefferson and a Democratic Technology." *Technology in America: A History of Individuals and Ideas.* Carroll W. Pursell, Jr., ed. Cambridge, Mass.: MIT Press.

Mendelson, Wallace. 1966. *The Constitution and the Supreme Court.* 2nd ed. New York: Dodd, Mead, and Co.

Miller, Arthur Selwyn. 1981. *Democratic Dictatorship: The Emergent Constitution of Control.* Westport, Conn.: Greenwood Press.

Morris, Richard B., William Greenleaf, and Robert H. Ferrell. 1971. *America: A History of the People.* Chicago: Rand McNally & Co.

Murphy, Paul L. 1972. *The Constitution in Crisis Times 1918–1969.* New York: Harper & Row, Publishers.

Ogburn, William F. 1950. *Social Change with Respect to Culture and Original Nature.* Rev. ed. New York: Viking Press.

Oliver, John W. 1956. *History of American Technology.* New York: The Ronald Press Co.

Pritchett, C. Herman. 1971. *The American Constitutional System.* 3rd ed. New York: McGraw-Hill.

Rottschaeffer, Henry. 1948. *The Constitution and Socio-Economic Change.* Ann Arbor, Mich.: University of Michigan Law School.

Schlesinger, Arthur M., Jr., ed. 1983. *The Almanac of American History.* New York: G. P. Putnam's Sons.

Schmidhauser, John R., ed. 1963. *Constitutional Law in the Political Process.* Chicago: Rand McNally & Company.

Settel, Irving, and William Laas. 1969. *A Pictorial History of Television.* New York: Grosset and Dunlap, Inc.

Smithsonian Institution. 1978. *The Smithsonian Book of Invention.* New York: W. W. Norton and Co.

Strong, C. F. 1963. *A History of Modern Political Constitutions.* New York: Capricorn Books.

Sundquist, James L. 1986. *Constitutional Reform and Effective Government.* Washington, D.C.: The Brookings Institution.

Tugwell, Rexford G. 1976. *The Compromising of the Constitution (Early Departures).* Notre Dame, Ind.: University of Notre Dame Press.

Vose, Clement E. 1972. *Constitutional Change: Amendment Politics and Supreme Court Litigation Since 1900.* Lexington, Mass. D.C. Heath and Company.

Wheare, K. C. 1966. *Modern Constitutions.* London: Oxford University Press.

Winters, Richard. 1976. "Party Control and Policy Change." *American Journal of Political Science* 20:597–636.

Chapter Six

The Constitution and Representation: Malapportionment and Dissatisfaction

PHILOSOPHICAL VIEWS OF REPRESENTATION

Even great minds disagree about the nature and meaning of representation. One of the framers of the Constitution, James Wilson, claimed that representation involved constant communication between the people and those charged with administering public affairs (Chelf 1977, 3). James Madison, another framer, believed that diversity in human talents and capabilities would lead to a variety of interests in society, and that these multiple and shifting interests, which were often based on economic concerns, might conflict. An early pluralist, Madison contended that these shifting factions played an important role in representation.

One old and formalistic view derived from the philosophy of British political theorist Thomas Hobbes, is that a representative is someone who has been authorized to act, and the represented are responsible for the consequences of the action. Under this view, the rights of the representative are expanded, while the rights of the represented are shrunk. After the authorization, any action of the representative is perceived as "representing" the constituency (Pitkin 1967, 39).

According to philosophers who believe in the concept of ascriptive representation, true representation only occurs when the composition of the legislature corresponds to that of the whole nation. John Adams, an adherent to this concept during the American Revolution, contended that the legislature should be an exact portrait of the people at large, with the same thoughts, feelings, and reasoning. This approach differs greatly from the formalistic approach because it depends upon the representative's characteristics and upon the representative being rather than doing something.

Another perspective on representation is the accountability viewpoint. This school of thought argues the representative must be responsible to the electorate. Carl Friedrich, a supporter of this school, has reasoned that if A represents B, then A is answerable to B in both word and action. Accountability theorists tend to equate representative government with popular sovereignty (1950, 263–264). Symbolization theorists, on the other hand, view the representative as a symbol for the nation and the unity of the state.

Edmund Burke, a conservative theorist, has argued that political representation manifests particular interests. The legislature should perform as a natural aristocracy governing the masses, according to Burke, who viewed the masses as incapable of governing themselves. Representatives were to be men of superior abilities and were not compelled to consult the wishes of their constituents. The legislature should pursue and act in the national interest (Burke 1949, 301).

Burke distinguished between actual and virtual representation. Actual representation consisted of representation of the whole nation by parliament. Virtual representation existed when a town or region did not have an individual representative of their views, but rather had their interests articulated in parliament by some other member from some other constituency. In essence, virtual representation was collective in nature and did not require a specific one-on-one correspondence between representative and constituency. Burke's views of representation coincided with the broader interpretation of the conservatives, who regarded society as an organic whole. Each class performed a specialized and particular function, just as differentiation of parts of the body is necessary to a live organism. The continuation of this functional specialization was crucial for the maintenance of stability and order, both strongly valued by conservative political philosophers.

In contrast to Burke, the liberal definition of representation contended that constituents were individuals, not interests or classes. Representation therefore was based on rational, economically independent persons. Representation on the basis of population, such as that in the U.S. House of Representatives, reflects this liberal view.

The *Federalist Papers*, authored by Alexander Hamilton, John Jay and James Madison, expressed a modified liberal view of representation in the United States. Representative government was seen as a replacement for direct democracy due to the difficulties of assembling great numbers of people in a single place. Under this modification, interests still played a role in representational politics. In contrast to Burke, who perceived interests in broad benevolent terms wherein the welfare of the nation was promoted, Madison viewed factions as narrow and potentially disruptive. Separation of powers helped to check the disruption of factions.

EMPIRICAL VIEWS OF REPRESENTATION

In modern times, political scientists have paid particular attention to policy congruence between members of Congress and their constituencies. Measuring the degree of congruence has proved difficult for several reasons: constituency opinion may not be stable on any given issue and random samples are costly and often difficult to obtain. Several indicators have been used as surrogates of constituency opinion, including simulations, referenda voting and aggregate national survey data. Each indicator has drawbacks. Simulation outcomes may be difficult to verify, referenda may occur intermittently and only on selected issues, and aggregate national survey data may not reflect state- or district-level opinion.

Several studies have attempted to examine the strength between roll call voting by members of Congress and estimates of constituent opinion. The relationship between the two is the strongest when Congressional roll call votes are collapsed into broad policy dimensions, such as welfare policy or civil rights. If a constituency is considered to be supportive of their member of Congress, the relationship between representative and represented is also stronger. The relationship is weaker when specific votes on single bills are scrutinized (Jacobson 1983, 184–185).

Fenno (1978, 232–247) has examined the various constituencies of members of Congress, arguing that there is more to representation than policy congruence. Fenno and others claim that members represent their constituents in other ways besides policy agreement, such as helping them cope with the federal bureaucracy, producing pork barrel benefits for the district, and enabling local governments and other groups to gain access to federal programs. Fenno contends that the home styles of members of Congress are more important than their Washington styles in representation. Two-way communication is essential to Fenno's view of representation, and includes the relative importance members place upon constituent access to them.

Fenno differentiated between multiple constituencies. The largest, most diverse and least cohesive is the geographic constituency which comprises the entire district. The reelection constituency is composed of those voters the representative believes will support him while the primary constituency is composed of his strongest supporters. The people who interact with the representative intimately and often daily and whose activities may be directed toward helping him get reelected are his personal constituency.

Fenno argues that members of Congress also differentiate between these various constituencies and place greater importance upon those which are crucial to their election and reelection. To Fenno, the act of getting elected cannot be separated from the act of representing. "If the congressman cannot win and hold the votes of some people, he cannot represent any people. Further, he cannot represent any people unless he makes an effort to know who they are, what they think, and what they want." Candidates learn this crucial information by campaigning (Fenno 1978, 233).

CRITICISMS OF REPRESENTATION

American electoral politics has been criticized for producing flawed representation. Great representative responsiveness to individuals and their problems coexists with great collective irresponsibility in policy information. According to Jacobson (1983, 190), members of Congress place greater emphasis on constituent service as policy issues confronting them become more divisive. The collective irresponsibility is most evident when members express concern over mounting deficits and growth of government but insist on funding programs that benefit their individual constituencies (Fiorina 1977, 39–44).

Perversely, representatives spend more time assuming and publicizing symbolic positions than finding and testing real solutions to national problems due to their fear of angering any important political group. If individual members cannot be held responsible for the institutional decisions of Congress, then a critical part of representation is missing. Responsiveness without responsibility results in inadequate representation (Mayhew 1974, 174–177).

CONSTITUTIONAL IMPEDIMENTS TO PARTICIPATION

Fearful of widespread popular participation in the fledgling American nation, the framers of the Constitution rejected direct democracy and imposed several impediments to popular control in the republican form of government which they created. Among impediments to participation at the federal and state levels were a right to vote limited to white male property owners, election of U.S. Senators by state legislatures and the selection of the president by the electoral college. Over the years, some of these restrictions have crumbled.

Property Requirements and the Franchise

When classical liberals favored property qualifications for the franchise of the vote, the qualifications were justified on the assumption that property was the best indicator of capacity, stability and good will in the individual. Poor individuals were assumed to have no will of their own. However, the idea of greater popular control began to gain momentum. The Vermont Constitution of 1777 was one of the first state constitutions to permit suffrage to all men without a property-holding requirement. This practice continued when Vermont was admitted to the Union in 1791. Other states successively liberalized their voting requirements, including Kentucky in 1799, New Jersey in 1807, Maryland in 1810 and Connecticut in 1818 (Hofstadter et al. 1967, 263).

By the 1820s and 1830s, with the rise of Jacksonian Democracy, the concept of property requirements was becoming obsolete. Frontier states, notably in the West, gave suffrage to all adult males. In the West land was plentiful and its easy attainability made the old property requirements meaningless. Government by the common man, instead of government by the aristocracy, was more firmly introduced at the national level by Andrew Jackson (Bailey and Kennedy 1983, 222).

Direct Election of U.S. Senators

Another method of limiting popular control which the framers employed was the election of U.S. Senators by the state legislatures. By 1828, a constitutional amendment had been introduced into the U.S. House of Representatives to provide for direct election of Senators. Forty years later, President Andrew Jackson, in a message to Congress, supported this reform. A belief that the role of the U.S. Senate was to represent the states, not the people, prevented change for many years. The Senate's nonlegislative functions, including the ratification of treaties and the confirmation of presidential appointments, further contributed to the belief that the Senate should not be popularly elected.

The Civil War eliminated the idea of the states as sovereign political entities and eroded the idea that the Senate represented the states as sovereign governments. Economic unrest spread in the late nineteenth century and resulted in a critical examination of the method of electing Senators. The reformers of that time viewed the Senate as composed of corporate lawyers, corrupt state bosses and millionaires. By 1912 twenty-nine states had conducted senatorial primaries. Since senators who were chosen by this method generally became supportive of a constitutional amendment for direct election, the Senate's institutional resistance to reform weakened and reformers succeeded in ratifying the Seventeenth Amendment in 1913.

The Electoral College and Presidential Elections

A third impediment to popular control—the use of the electoral college in electing the U.S. president—still exists. The delegates to the

1787 Convention allowed each state to select a number of electors equal to its total number of members in the U.S. House and Senate. Initially most electors, like U.S. senators, were selected by state legislatures, but states were granted an option of selecting electors by popular vote. Difficulties with the electoral college system in the elections of 1796 and 1800 gave impetus to the passage of the Twelfth Amendment which provided separate ballots for electors for president and for vice-president.

After the ratification of the Twelfth Amendment in 1804 many states began to change their methods of choosing electors. Initially a mixture of systems was used. One method continued to be appointment by the state legislature. Another method was election from local districts. Some states used a third method of a winner-take-all general-ticket system. Various constitutional amendments were introduced into Congress to standardize the method of selecting electors but none were adopted. Across time, however, most states moved to popular election of electors. By 1836, South Carolina was the only state which did not employ a general-ticket method for popular selection of electors (Sayre and Parris 1970, 28).

The electoral college makes possible the selection of a president who did not receive a majority of the popular vote—an event which has happened in two elections. In the presidential election of 1824, during a period of factionalism, none of the four presidential candidates obtained a majority of votes in the electoral college. At the time, six states did not even record the popular vote for president. Although Andrew Jackson had the largest plurality of the recorded popular vote (forty-two percent) he won the electoral vote in only seven states. One of his opponents, John Quincy Adams, won the electoral vote in thirteen states, but received only thirty-two percent of the recorded popular vote. Jackson received a total of ninety-nine electoral votes compared to Adams's eighty-four electoral votes. The election was thrown into the House of Representatives which chose Adams as president after Henry Clay, one of the candidates, gave his support to Adams in return for being named secretary of state. This election, however, raised questions about the possibility of electing a president who received less than a majority of the popular vote and of the electoral college vote.

Between 1789 and 1984, fifteen elections resulted in the selection of a president who did not win a majority of the popular vote. Other electoral college victors with less than a majority popular vote included James K. Polk who gained 49.6 percent of the popular vote in 1844, Zachary Taylor with 47.3 percent in 1848, James Buchanan with 45.6 percent in 1856, and Abraham Lincoln who received only 39.8 percent of the popular vote in a four-man race in 1860. After the Civil War, presidents without a majority of the popular vote were elected in 1876,

1880, 1884, 1888, 1892, 1912, 1948, 1960, and 1968. In all, a total of fifteen elections resulted in the election of a nonpopularly-elected president. In all but four of these, more than two presidential candidates were on the ballot (see table 6-1).

Two elections in the post-Civil War period were particularly troublesome: those of 1876 and 1888. In 1876 Democrat Samuel J. Tilden officially received 50.9 percent of the popular vote and Rutherford B. Hayes, the Republican, received only 47.9 percent, yet Hayes was elected president. Political bargaining contributed to Hayes's victory. This occurred toward the end of Reconstruction, while federal troops were still occupying three southern states: Louisiana, South Carolina and Florida. Controversy over the vote count in these three states and in Oregon made the winner uncertain.

Subsequent information has caused historians to believe that Tilden had won the popular vote in Florida and should have received that state's four electoral votes, which would have made Tilden the winner of the electoral college. However, given two sets of popular vote returns from the contested states—one set from the Democrats showing Tilden the winner and a second set presented by the Republicans showing Hayes the victor—Congress established a commission consisting of five representatives, five senators and five Supreme Court Justices, which was to decide the final outcome. In the political negotiations that followed, the commission determined that Hayes was the winner, and placated the southern states by pledging to provide subsidies to southern railroads and to reduce the federal military presence in those states. Tilden, the loser, charged that the commission was illegal and violated the constitutional power of the House of Representatives to select the president in the case of disputed returns (Hofstadter et al. 1967, 479; Sayre and Parris, 1970, 31).

Another hotly contested election occurred in 1888. In this election, Benjamin Harrison received the majority of electoral votes but did not win the majority of the popular vote, receiving 47.8 percent in comparison to Grover Cleveland's 48.6 percent. He carried many of the large competitive states where there was a concentration of electoral votes. As in 1876, charges of voting irregularities were levied, but Cleveland, an incumbent president, decided not to contest the electoral college outcome.

In addition to the criticism that the electoral college permits the election of a president without a majority of the popular vote, the unit rule in the electoral college gives the most populous states an advantage during a presidential campaign. To secure a majority of electoral college votes, candidates must focus campaign time, activities and perhaps promises of future help upon the more heavily populated states with their larger blocks of electoral votes.

Table 6-1
Presidential Elections in Which the Winner of the Electoral College Did Not Receive a Majority of the Popular Vote

YEAR	ELECTORAL COLLEGE WINNER	PERCENTAGE OF THE POPULAR VOTE	
1824	Andrew Jackson	42.2	*
1844	James K. Polk	49.6	*
1848	Zachary Taylor	47.3	*
1856	James Buchanan	45.6	*
1860	Abraham Lincoln	39.8	*
1876	Rutherford B. Hayes	47.9	
1880	James A. Garfield	48.3	*
1884	Grover Cleveland	48.5	*
1888	Benjamin Harrison	47.8	
1892	Grover Cleveland	48.6	*
1912	Woodrow Wilson	41.8	*
1916	Woodrow Wilson	49.3	
1948	Harry Truman	49.5	*
1960	John F. Kennedy	49.9	
1968	Richard Nixon	43.4	*

* Indicates elections with three or more presidential candidates

Proponents of a multi-party system contend that the electoral college, along with the single-member district method of electing members of Congress, promotes a two-party system to the detriment of smaller third parties. Under the unit rule winner-take-all system, third parties have virtually no chance of securing an electoral college victory.

Another criticism of the electoral college is that electors are not legally bound to cast their electoral votes in accordance with the popular vote. One state, Alabama, passes a law requiring electors to cast their votes for the nominee of their party's national convention. The Alabama Supreme Court struck down this provision, ruling that electors should be able to exercise their discretion in voting for president. Typically electors do vote in accordance with the popular vote but they do so out of custom rather than legal or constitutional obligation. In 1976 a Ford elector voted for Reagan, and in 1968 an Alabama elector voted for "Bear" Bryant, a University of Alabama football coach. Although no faithless elector has ever made a difference in the outcome of an election, the possibility of this occurrence, especially in a close election, remains.

Some critics of the electoral college contend that it affects the nomination process. Candidates from large states are more likely to be selected than those from small states, and the size of the home states of possible vice-presidential nominees becomes a factor in the ticket balancing that occurs in vice-president selection. Because of these and other criticisms, opponents of the electoral college argue that it is outdated and should be abolished. So far, their views have not prevailed. Since U.S. citizens rarely think about their method of selecting presidents in the interstices between presidential elections, only a political crisis or a triggering event would be likely to precipitate constitutional reform.

Proposed Reforms in the Electoral College

Several reforms have been suggested to correct the problems created by the electoral college. One reform would be the total abolition of the college and substitution of a direct popular vote. Popular vote totals would simply be aggregated to determine the winner. The direct vote plan usually provides that if no candidate received at least forty percent of the popular vote, a runoff election would be held.

A second plan, the National Bonus Plan, retains the electoral college structure, but weights it heavily toward the winner of the popular vote. The candidate with the most popular support nationwide would automatically receive a pool of 102 electoral votes—two additional electoral votes for each state and the District of Columbia. This expands the total number of electoral votes from 537 to 639. The candidate receiving the majority of the expanded number of total votes would win the electoral college and become president. If no one received a majority of the electoral votes a runoff would be held between the two candidates receiving the largest blocs of popular votes.

Arguing that the general-ticket method of allocating votes within the electoral college favors liberals, many conservatives support a reform called the district plan. Introduced in Congress in 1969, the plan calls for the same number of total electoral votes and the same allocation of votes as currently exists among the states under the present system.

Within each state, however, all but two electors would represent single-member geographic districts smaller than the state at large. State legislatures would draw the electoral districts using a one-person one-vote criterion. Two electors would represent the state at large. Authors of the original plan anticipated that electoral districts would coincide with U.S. House districts and that the voting arrangements would closely parallel voting for the U.S. House and Senate. This plan would greatly localize presidential election politics by reducing the geographic area from which electors would be selected (Sayre and Parris 1970, 144).

Under the proportional plan the electoral college would be abolished, but state electoral votes would be retained and allocated according to the proportion of the popular vote candidates receive in each state. This plan closely approximates a direct popular vote, but aggregates votes by party by state. A joint session of Congress would select the president if no candidate received at least forty percent of the electoral votes.

One of the least radical plans, the automatic plan, retains the current method of aggregating votes, state by state, with the winner of the popular vote in each state receiving all the electoral votes from that state. The automatic plan, however, removes the possibility of faithless electors and elector discretion by abolishing the office of elector. Electoral votes would be automatically allocated to the winner of each state's popular vote.

REPRESENTATION VERSUS DIRECT DEMOCRACY

Some scholars argue that as technology advances, the need for representative democracy will diminish and will be superseded in many instances by direct democracy devices. Others contend that representation and a republican form of government should not and will not be replaced and present several arguments in favor of republican representation. Proponents of limited participation believe that apathy, more likely to be present in a republican government, is good for political stability and makes disagreement easier to accept (Berelson et al. 1956; Dahl 1956).

A second argument in favor of representation is that representatives have greater expertise and by virtue of their superior knowledge and greater amount of time devoted to public affairs are better qualified than the average citizen to make decisions about public policy and political outcomes. Yet a third argument focuses on the tension between majority rule and minority rights. A representative democracy permits minorities to mobilize more easily and thwart majority preferences more readily. This allows minorities to protect themselves from being stripped of civil liberties and other basic rights.

On the other hand, proponents of direct democracy cite several advantages for the greater popular control that direct democracy devices provide. In a cross-national study including the United States, Almond and Verba (1963) discovered a positive correlation between a sense of political efficacy and political participation. By providing greater opportunity for participation, direct democracy devices might be a means for increasing political effectiveness. Those who argue for participatory democracy usually believe that people are inherently good and should have the opportunity to protect themselves and make decisions.

Rousseau (1984) viewed participation as a method of educating citizens and providing them with an opportunity to learn political skills such as compromise, cooperation and deliberation. Rousseau argued that lack of participation produced apathy, rather than the reverse, and argued that the only reason that citizens are apathetic and ignorant about politics is because they have been denied opportunities to participate directly. Direct democracy also enhances freedom by increasing the control citizens have over their lives and environment. Participatory democracy also promotes a sense of community.

Direct democracy, especially direct legislation, provides a safety value by allowing voters a chance to address issues that might otherwise stagnate and cause a stalemate in legislative politics (Magleby 1984, 28). Another argument supportive of direct democracy is that citizens know their own preferences better than do representatives, and therefore should have the power to make decisions to implement those preferences.

Several types of direct democracy devices have been used in the United States, including initiatives and referenda. The state constitutional amendment initiative is proposed by popular petition and then submitted to the voters for approval. The direct statutory initiative allows statutes to be proposed directly by voters through petition and then submitted to voters. The indirect statutory initiative involves the legislature as well as the citizens. First citizens propose a statute to the legislature through petition. The proposal may become law in one of two ways: either by securing majority approval in the legislature, or failing that, by resubmission to the voters for majority popular approval. Originally employed in California, this method was repealed in that state in 1966. Referenda are a fourth form of direct democracy. Under this form, statutes are originally passed by the legislature and then submitted to the voters for final majority approval before enforcement occurs (Lee 1978, 89).

In the United States, the referendum has never been used at the national level, yet the states adopted the device early as a method for approving constitutions. Since the progressive era, the states have served as experimental laboratories for direct democracy. Except for constitutional referenda, which have been used by each state since its admittance into the union, other direct democracy devices are most common among the western states (see table 6-2). The other forms spread more slowly. South Dakota in 1898, Utah in 1900 and Oregon in 1902 all pioneered the initiative for constitutional amendments and ordinary

Table 6-2
Direct Democracy Devices in the States

NEITHER REFERENDA OR INITIATIVE	REFERENDA ONLY	INITIATIVE ONLY	BOTH REFERENDA AND INITIATIVE
Northeast:	Southeast:	Southeast:	Northeast:
Connecticut	Kentucky	Florida *	Maine
Delaware	Maryland		Massachusetts
New Hampshire		Midwest:	
New Jersey	Southwest:		Southeast:
New York		Illinois *	
Pennsylvania	New Mexico		Arkansas
Southeast:			Midwest:
Alabama			Michigan
Georgia			Missouri
Louisiana			Nebraska
Mississippi			North Dakota
North Carolina			Ohio
South Carolina			South Dakota
Tennessee			
Virginia			Southwest:
West Virginia			
			Oklahoma
Midwest:			
			West:
Indiana			
Iowa			Alaska
Kansas			Arizona
Minnesota			California
Wisconsin			Colorado
			Idaho
Southwest:			Montana
			Nevada
Texas			Oregon
			Utah
West:			Washington
			Wyoming
Hawaii			

* Indicates initiative used only for constitutional amendments statutes. Nineteen additional states followed their lead between 1906 and 1918. From 1918 to 1959, the states were quiescent in expanding the use of direct democracy devices. Since 1959, four more states have added the use of initiative (Ranney 1978, 69).

THE ROLE OF POLITICAL PARTIES IN REPRESENTATION

Functions of Political Parties

Political parties, though not mentioned in the U.S. Constitution, have nevertheless emerged as a unifying force in U.S. politics. Traditionally, political parties have performed several functions which expedite the representative process. Among these is the aggregation of diverse and heterogeneous interests. Parties act as vehicles for assembling voters of different interests under a large and unifying umbrella. This function is more important in a two-party system such as that in the United States, than in a multi-party system where the greater number of parties diminishes the impetus toward intra-party aggregation. Thus, parties provide symbols of identification, and promote unification and loyalty.

A second major function of political parties is to socialize voters into the democratic participatory process. Through political parties, citizens are offered opportunities to learn political skills by offering arguments, voting at precinct meetings, and participating in campaigns. Parties also transmit knowledge and shape the values of their members by controlling political debate.

Leadership recruitment is perhaps one of the most important functions of political parties. The primary goal of political parties is to win elections, a goal facilitated by the recruitment of attractive and articulate candidates. Several factors, in turn, affect which party will be joined by ambitious youth intent on a political career: their parents' political party, their current economic status, their philosophical outlook, the opportunity for advancement within the party in the region or state and the likelihood of exercising meaningful power if elected to office.

Political parties help to finance campaigns. U.S. parties are heavily dependent upon contributions from wealthy members, a feature which has helped Republicans more than Democrats. However, other methods include direct mail campaigns, telephone solicitations, telethons and other media events, and fund-raising events. In the 1980 presidential campaign, the Democratic national and state committees contributed to Democratic candidates (or spent on their behalf) $6.7 million. Republican national and state committees spent or contributed over $10.0

million more than the Democrats, for a total of $16.9 million (Sorauf 1984, 325).

In that same election, the Democratic National Committee (DNC) spent a total of $14.9 million on all elections while the Republican National Committee (RNC) spent a total of $71.0 million, 4.8 times more than the DNC. Democratic congressional committees spent $2.0 million while Republican congressional committees spent $25.6 million, 12.8 times more than their Democratic counterparts. Republican senatorial committees also outspent Democratic senatorial committees: $21.9 million by the Republicans, which was 13.7 times more than the $1.6 million spent by the Democrats. Overall, with a total of $118.6 million, Republican party organizations at all levels outspent the Democratic organizations (with $18.6 million) 6.4 times (Crotty 1985, 91).

Political parties formulate and publicize policy options by offering platforms which take stands or push solutions for controversial issues on the national agenda. These platforms summarize for voters the nature of the party coalition. The development of party platforms coincides with presidential elections, although party leaders may individually articulate stands on issues during nonpresidential years.

In the past, political parties performed social services for members, a function which has diminished and been largely replaced by government programs. Especially for newly arrived immigrant groups living in large urban areas, parties were an important organization for smoothing the transition from the country of emigration into life in the United States. Party bosses controlled jobs through patronage and dispersed other social benefits to needy members in return for electoral loyalty. Eventually, the spread of civil service systems, the growth of welfare, unemployment, compensation, social security, other social programs and the demise of the old style party bosses undercut this function. However, in comparison to parliamentary democracies, the U.S. political system retains a large number of government jobs filled by political appointment, especially at the national level. Political parties continue to play some role in filling these jobs.

Characteristics of the U.S. Party System

The foremost characteristic of the U.S. party system is the fact that there are only two major political parties. Both the current major parties on the political scene today are quite old. The Democratic party dates back directly to the Democratic Republican party of Thomas Jefferson, which shortened its name to Democrats in the 1830s under Andrew Jackson. The current Republican party began in the 1850s shortly before the Civil War. It gained national stature under Abraham Lincoln. Its ideological, if not organizational roots are grounded in the Federalist party which became the National Republicans briefly in the 1820s and the Whig party in the 1830s.

Throughout U.S. history, third parties have appeared on the national and regional political scene but have had minor roles, typically exhibiting a longevity of no more than two or three elections. Third parties have been short-lived, despite their ability to capture five percent of the popular vote in one-third of the presidential elections and ten percent of the vote in one out of five presidential contests (Rosenstone et al. 1984).

Third parties often spring up when the major parties fail to address issues of great salience for the voter, and third-party voting often reflects the reactions of citizens to their social and economic environment. Third parties typically derive their power by affecting the national agenda. The rise of third parties sometimes forces the major parties to deal with issues which they had previously ignored.

Electoral structure and the number of political parties are closely correlated. The single-member district system coupled with either a majority or plurality criterion for obtaining office is typically correlated with a two-party system. Under the single-member district system, geography is the primary basis for differentiating voters and constructing electoral districts. Furthermore, only one member in the legislature can be selected from each geographic unit. Single-member district systems, by definition, are winner-take-all rather than proportional representation systems.

In a winner-take-all system, the candidate who receives a majority or plurality (depending upon the criterion employed) becomes the officeholder. All other candidates lose. Under a proportional representation system, broader geographic units are typically the basis for electoral contests. Parties gain a number of seats in proportion to their vote total in the election. Third parties have little or no chance of securing seats under a winner-take-all system, whereas they may gain and hold seats in a proportional representation system. Under a parliamentary system, where proportional representation systems are typically found, even a small block of seats may provide great power if the small party becomes a linchpin in forming a coalition minority government.

Subsidiary reasons why third parties have experienced a short life span on U.S. political soil include socialization and voter access to information. The portrayal of elections by the media, education systems and by parents as contests between Democrats and Republicans reinforces the voter's perception of the two-party norm. Voter access to information about third parties may be limited and voters may find the process of acquiring information costly, falling back on traditional knowledge bases and voting patterns. Since third parties rarely get more than five percent of the total vote in presidential elections, they usually do not qualify for public financing in the next presidential race.

A second major characteristic of U.S. political parties is their non-ideological, centralist orientation. Downs (1957) and Page (1978) argue that the distribution of public opinion interacts with the electoral system to influence the ideological orientation of political parties. Unimodal opinion distributions (where the majority of voters hold moderate or middle-of-the-road opinions on issues, with only a few voters on the extreme right or extreme left) coupled with a winner-take-all single member district system, often produce non-ideological centralist parties where the distinctions between the parties are muddy and there is much ideological overlap. Since candidates must usually capture a majority of the opinion and since unimodal opinion distributions characterize many issues in U.S. politics, most voters are clustered in the middle of an ideological continuum. Both major parties also strive to stay close to the ideological center, as to stray too far to the left or right would be to invite defeat.

The two-party system also contributes to the nonideological and centralist nature of U.S. political parties. In multi-party systems, parties sometimes have sharp ideological distinctions, and the negotiations involved in interest aggregation may occur across parties, thus forming coalition governments. In two-party systems, each party has to appeal to the widest number of voters and often covers a broader ideological spectrum. The negotiations involved in interest aggregation occur within, rather than across parties. In a two-party system, the parties tend to resemble each other and may offer less distinctive choices to the voters.

Parties in the United States are highly decentralized, resembling a truncated pyramid with no definitive governing body at the apex. Pomper and Lederman (1980, 43) argue that if there is a concentration of power in U.S. parties, it is most likely to be at the subnational level, and that concentrations there may be suspect: "Even the truncated pyramid is not a solid piece of granite. There are faults in the stone, and there are many protected enclaves of power in which individual politicans and local groups reside." The decentralized nature of U.S. political parties reflects the decentralization of its federalistic governmental structure. Rewards are not concentrated at the national level, so consequently the political battle between parties over the distribution of rewards is not concentrated either (see table 6-3).

Both major parties have national committees where representation approximates a confederate system with each state receiving about equal power, regardless of its size. Reforms in the Democratic National Committee (DNC) in 1972 not only doubled its size, making it almost twice as large as the Republican National Committee (RNC) but also brought about the abandonment of the confederate system of allocating seats.

Table 6-3
Organizational Structure of U.S. Political Parties

NATIONAL INSTITUTIONS:

(1) National Convention

(2a) National   (2b) National
     Chairperson   Committee

STATE INSTITUTIONS:

(1) State Conventions

(2) State Committees

(3) Congressional District Committees

LOCAL INSTITUTIONS:

(1) County Committees

(2) Intermediate Committees
    (City, Legislative, Judicial)

(3) Ward and Precinct Committees

(4) Party Members

The replacement selection method adopted by the DNC gave weight to both population and party support within each state.

Formally, the national conventions choose the members of the national committees, but the selection usually represents a ratification of decisions already made by the states. Chairs and other officers of the national committees do not have to be selected as state members to the committee, but rather are elected by and may be removed by the committee. Shortly after the national convention presidential candidates are generally given the prerogative of selecting the person to head the national committee, a choice which the committees will ratify without question. National committees usually have greater discretion in selecting other officers.

National committees usually meet only two or three times a year, and do more than just selecting executive committees. Often the executive committees have parochial interests which divert attention from building a strong national party. The functions of national committees and chairpersons vary, depending on the hold of their party on the White House. National chairs may be managers of the president's campaign and mobilizers of support if their party is in power. If their party is out of power, the national chair may heal old wounds, mediate intra-party fights, assist in payment of old campaign debts, raise campaign monies, and receive party organizations around the country.

State parties differ in their decision making and often vary in their method of selecting members for the national committees. Several factors have contributed to a decline in state party power, decentralizing power even below the state party level to candidates' personal campaign organizations and to individual voters. Presidential nominees are increasingly selected by direct primaries rather than party caucuses, and the rising importance of the media in campaigns has enabled candidates to win with little or no party support. Other centrifugal forces within states that diminish cohesion within state parties include regional differences, rural-urban splits, ethnic and racial groupings, religious differences, loyalty to local leaders, liberal-conservative preferences, and political factions.

Criticisms of Political Parties

Several criticisms have been levied at U.S. political parties. Critics have often described the two major parties as "Tweedledee" and "Tweedledum" to emphasize the centralist, middle-of-the-road positions they take on most issues. The voter is provided with limited choices when the two viable candidates take similar and sometimes almost identical positions. Even when the candidates in a political race do take different positions, those positions are often very close together ideologically.

A second criticism of U.S. parties focuses on their lack of cohesion. Given their nonideological and decentralized nature, there is little to bind elected officials of the same party into a cohesive political organization. Burns (1967) and Broder (1971) have both observed that the lack of cohesion within U.S. political parties contributes to an absence of party discipline and to failure to deliver the promised platforms. Party platforms are often ten to fifteen times the length of the Declaration of Independence. Frequently they are not read, and they are often ignored by the congressional party. Even presidential candidates reserve the right to disagree with specific planks. Still, approximately three-fourths of campaign pledges are redeemed by presidents during their administrations.

An absence of party discipline diminishes accountability to the voter, since any individual politician may not be able to deliver on campaign promises to approve, modify, or cut programs. Even if elected officials attempt to implement their campaign promises, they may be blocked by other politicians in their own party, as well as by members of the opposing party.

Not only are U.S. political parties criticized for their inability to deliver on their platforms, the platforms themselves are often critiqued for being uninnovative centralist compromises developed to satisfy competing interests. The members of platform committees are often selected to be geographically representative of the voters, and often embody many of the conflicts that exist in the general population. Platforms sometimes appear to be exercises in semantics rather than clear statements of commitment. In fact, they are primarily campaign documents designed to manipulate symbols that energize and mobilize winning coalitions.

The decline of political parties parallels the rise of political action committees (PACs) as a method of funding increasingly personalized electoral campaigns. As political parties have diminished in importance, a power vacuum has been created which the PACs have partially filled. Critics of political parties argue that this has enhanced the role of special interests in determining legislative outcomes. Sabato (1985) concludes that political parties and PACs have developed a symbiotic relationship of peaceful coexistence and even mutual benefit. PACs need information about potential candidates and congressional contests which only political parties can provide, while parties need PAC money for their candidates.

Political Party Reforms

Critics of U.S. political parties have suggested several reforms to correct their inadequacies. Burns (1967) presented a six-point program to revitalize, reform, and reenergize political parties in the United States. Burns contends that the national government, rather than the state governments, should control national elections. (Currently, states write and enforce election laws for national and state elections.) Second, the national parties must build grass-roots memberships by placing more emphasis on party clubs and less emphasis on party committees. A third suggested reform is the organizational merger of presidential and congressional parties at the national level, possibly by structuring ballots to facilitate straight party-ticket voting at the national level. The development of new party leadership in Congress should be facilitated by removing the seniority rule as the basis for leadership selection. Financing parties and their candidates on a mass, popular, systematic basis might be achieved by an extensive dues-paying membership. Finally, better organization of the opposition party would provide voters with a clearer, more distinct choice.

Since political parties are not discussed in the U.S. Constitution, most of Burns's suggestions for reforming parties could be achieved without amending the constitution. Massive changes in electoral laws and a shift of power over elections might require a formal amendment, but even that would depend on Supreme Court interpretation. In recent times, legislation has been used to achieve more modest electoral reform, requiring states to allow citizens who have recently immigrated from other states to vote in national elections after a state residence of one month. Legislation was also the vehicle used to diminish racial discrimination through the 1965 Voting Rights Act. Some of Burns's reforms deal with the internal organization of Congress, another area where reform is not likely to occur by constitutional amendment since Congress has the constitutional authority to legislate its own organization and operating rules.

INCREASE IN VOTER APATHY

Several indicators point to an increase in voter apathy and alienation from U.S. political institutions in the modern era. One indicator is a declining turnout in recent elections. In the mid-nineteenth century voter turnout as a percentage of those eligible to vote was approximately eighty percent in presidential elections. Voter turnout declined to fifty-three percent in the 1984 presidential race. In the twentieth century, participation rose slightly after women were enfranchised in 1920, peaking in 1960 when sixty-three percent of those eligible to vote did so. Since that election, voter turnout has dropped ten percentage points.

Turnout in presidential years has typically been higher than turnout in nonpresidential years, but total turnout has paralleled a decline in presidential elections. In the period between 1960 and 1978, voter turnout in the United States was lower than in Italy, Austria, Denmark, Australia, West Germany, Norway, Britain, Japan, Canada, or France.

A second indicator of the growth in disillusionment with traditional political institutions has been the increase in the number of citizens who are independents and identify with no political party. Since 1966 the percentage of independents rose from twenty-eight percent to a high of thirty-eight percent in 1978. Throughout this period, the number of voters who were self-identified independents actually exceeded the number of voters who were self-identified Republicans.

A long-term fifteen-year decrease in levels of trust in government and public institutions is a third indicator of increasing alienation and apathy. Watergate and Vietnam contributed to this long-term decline in confidence in the government. Data from the National Election Studies show that levels of trust for all races were approximately fifty percent in 1958. By 1980, forty percent expressed distrust in government. The increase in distrust and dissatisfaction closely parallels a decline in the confidence of average voters in their ability to participate effectively in the political process (Flanigan and Zingale 1983, 172-173).

Some scholars argue that levels of interest in national and local elections may vary according to differences in media coverage. However, media coverage does not explain the long-term decline in turnout, since media coverage of all races, particularly presidential races, has been increased at the same time turnout has been declining. A more probable explanation of the long-term decline in turnout and the increase in apathy and alienation is a decline in the effectiveness of a single vote for a geographically based candidate as a means of expressing voter preferences on issues.

When the government is only involved in a few policy areas, there is a higher probability that one of two candidates will reflect a voter's composition of policy preferences. As the number of policy areas increases, the probability of either of two candidates reflecting any single voter's preferences on all of the issues drops exponentially. The number of possible sets of combinations of issue outcomes across the policy areas in which government is involved is a function of both the number of issues and the number of positions which can be taken on each issue. If there are two issues, each of which has two outcomes (a pro and a con position) the total number of sets of outcomes is 2^2 or 4. For example, in the early years of the country, two controversial issues were free trade and the gold standard. The four possible combinations of policy preferences on these two issues are: support free trade and stick to the gold standard, support free trade and abandon the gold standard, abolish free trade and stick to the gold standard, and abolish free trade and abandon the gold standard.

This logic may be extended to a larger number of issues and to a larger number of outcomes for each issue. If there are three issues, each with a pro and a con outcome, then the total number of combinations of policy preferences is 2^3 or 8. If the number of issues increases to four, the number of total combinations of policy preferences increases to 2^4, or 16. The rate of increase is exponential as the number of issues increases.

In general, the formula for the number of combinations of policy preferences, C, is O^I where O equals the number of outcomes or stands likely to arise in political debate for each issue, and I equals the number of issues addressed in the political and governmental arena. If the number of outcomes for each issue increases to 3, then the total combination of policy outcomes for two issues is 3^2, or 9. For three issues, with three outcomes each, the number of combinations is 3^3 or 27.

The probability, P, that a single candidate would reflect any particular combination of preferences (even if his or her own positions on these issues were known) is the reciprocal of the number of total combinations of policy preferences, such that P equals 1/C. If there are eight possible combinations, the probability of a single candidate reflecting any one of these combinations is 1/8 or .12. If there are 27 combinations, the probability of a single candidate reflecting any one of these special preference distributions is 1/27 or .03. Clearly, as the number of combinations increases, the probability that a single candidate will reflect any one of these combinations decreases (see table 6-4).

Which has the greater impact on growth in C (the total number of combinations of policy preferences)—an increase in the number of issues, I, or an increase in the number of options for each issue, O? The rate of increase in C is the first derivative of the function for C, C', such that $C = O^I$ IMPLIES $C' = I \times O^{I-1}$. Table 6.5 examines the behavior of the first derivative for C first as O increases while I is held constant, and then as I is increased while O is held constant. Clearly, increasing I, the number of issues, has a far greater impact on the rate of increase in C than does increasing O, the number of options for each issue (see table 6-5).

Geographic winner-take-all representation systems force voters to collapse all their preferences on issues into a single vote for a single candidate who, in turn, is to represent the voter on all policy dimensions. As the number of issues increases, the number of possible combinations of policy preferences increases, and the reciprocal, the probability that any candidate will reflect any particular combination or preferences, decreases. Similarly, as the number of outcomes for each issue increases, the number of preference combinations also increases and the probability of congruence between any voter and any candidate decreases.

The expansion of the role of government has especially increased the number of policy issues addressed by government and, in many instances, the number of outcomes each issue may have. The result has been a decline in voter ability to express preferences by voting. This has produced a decline in voter turnout, increased voter apathy and alienation and, in some instances, a rise in the power of single-issue interest groups as a method of expressing at least the most salient of a voter's preference.

Table 6-4
Decrease in Probability of a Candidate Reflecting a Voter's Preferences with Increases in the Number of Issues and the Number of Positions for Each Issue

O	I	C	P
2	2	4	.2500
2	3	8	.1250
2	4	16	.0625
2	5	32	.0312
2	10	1,024	.0010
2	15	32,768	.00003
3	2	9	.1111
3	3	27	.0370
3	4	81	.0123
3	5	243	.0041
3	10	59,049	.00002
3	15	14,348,907	.00000007
4	2	16	.0625
4	3	64	.0156
4	4	256	.0039
4	5	1,024	.0009
4	10	1,048,576	.00001
4	15	1,073,700,000	.0000000009

Total number of combinations of policy preferences equals C

such that $C = O^I$ and $P = 1/C$

where C = total number of combinations of policy preferences

O = number of outcomes for each issue

I = number of issues

P = probability of a single candidate reflecting any one of the possible combinations of voter preferences

LINKING PUBLIC OPINION, LEGISLATIVE ISSUES, AND REPRESENTATION

Representation is a process rather than a specific single action. The process typically begins with the formulation of public opinion among citizens. Public opinion, in turn, helps shape the legislative agenda and

Table 6-5
The Impacts of Increasing the Number of Issues and Issue Options on the
Rate of Increase in the Total Number of Combinations of Policy
Preferences

I	O	$C' = I \times O^{I-1}$
INCREASING O, I CONSTANT		
2	2	$2 \times 2^1 = 4$
2	3	$2 \times 3^1 = 6$
2	4	$2 \times 4^1 = 8$
2	5	$2 \times 5^1 = 10$
2	6	$2 \times 6^1 = 12$
2	7	$2 \times 7^1 = 14$
2	8	$2 \times 8^1 = 16$
2	9	$2 \times 9^1 = 18$
2	10	$2 \times 10^1 = 20$
INCREASING I, O CONSTANT		
2	2	$2 \times 2^1 = 4$
3	2	$3 \times 2^2 = 12$
4	2	$4 \times 2^3 = 32$
5	2	$5 \times 2^4 = 80$
6	2	$6 \times 2^5 = 192$
7	2	$7 \times 2^6 = 448$
8	2	$8 \times 2^7 = 1,024$
9	2	$9 \times 2^8 = 2,304$
10	2	$10 \times 2^9 = 5,120$

Note: $C = O^I$ IMPLIES $C' = I \times O^{I-1}$

where C' is the first derivative or rate of

change in C

the structure of issues in legislative negotiations. The structure of legislative issues, in turn, affects the type of representation which occurs.

Types of Public Opinion Issues

In the early stages of policy formulation and agenda setting, public policy issues may be characterized as one of three types: divisive, negotiable, or unifying. These categories represent an underlying continuum of political behavior of affected groups and elites along which most public policy issues fall.

Unifying issues often reflect unimodal public opinion distributions

where constituent opinion converges in agreement. Most unifying issues tend to be consensus-maintaining issues which reinforce the status
quo. Unifying issues typically evoke positive emotions, and may be coupled with the use of positive emotion-laden symbols. Despite this use
of emotion-laden symbols, unifying issues are often of low salience to
constituents. The intensity of public opinion is often modest as well.
Little interest group activity surrounds this type of issue, since political
change is rarely a concern. Little or no effort is made to pass significant
legislation. Unifying issues often include themes of national unification
and patriotism. Examples include campaigns to spur national growth
and to make or keep the country strong, and displays of national power
(see table 6-6).

Public opinion on negotiable issues is often multimodal. Negotiable
issues are characterized by continuous issue positions and a range of
policy options which typically represent incremental changes from the
status quo. Consensus, if not initially present, is negotiable, and compromise is likely. Negotiable issues are of moderate salience to constituents. The intensity of public opinion is also moderate. Unlike both
unifying and divisive issues, which are characterized by the use of emotion-laden symbols, negotiable issues are more likely to be characterized
by the use of impact analyses and evaluation studies. Interest groups
typically employ traditional political tactics such as lobbying and financing campaigns to influence the outcome of negotiable issues. The political battles surrounding negotiable issues are most likely to occur over
methods to achieve change. Proponents usually seek to pass statutory
legislation. Negotiable issues often include economic and financial proposals. Examples include budgetary bills, appropriations, tax changes
and regulations.

Divisive issues are often characterized by intensely held bimodal
opinion, where the issue is of high salience to constituents. If opinion
is not evenly bimodal, the opinions held by the smaller group are
particularly intense and members of this less dominant group may be
particularly vocal. With divisive issues, options are often dichotomous,
mutually exclusive, and extreme. Controversy and conflict surround
divisive issues. Unlike unifying issues which are characterized by the
use of positive emotion-laden symbols, or negotiable issues, where symbol manipulation is secondary to some semblance of objectivity, divisive
issues are characterized by the use of negative emotion-laden symbols
(Edelman 1964). Interest groups often resort to grass-roots mobiliza-
tion to achieve their policy goals. With divisive issues, political battles
emerge over whether to achieve change, rather than over how to achieve
change (as with negotiable issues). With divisive issues, intense preferences often lead antagonists to seek constitutional changes which, once
in place, would require extraordinary majorities to modify. Divisive is-

Table 6-6
Characteristics of Public Opinion

UNIFYING ISSUES

    Public opinion tends to be unimodal
    Congruence of issue positions
    Agreement on policy options
    Options tend to maintain the status quo
    Consensus maintaining
    Low salience to constituents
    Low intensity of public opinion
    Use of positive emotion-laden symbols
    Low interest group activity
    Political change not a concern
    Little effort directed toward passing legislation
    Include themes of national unification and patriotism

NEGOTIABLE ISSUES

    Public opinion tends to be multimodal
    Continuous issue positions
    Range of policy options
    Options represent incremental change
    Consensus negotiable
    Moderate salience to constituents
    Moderate intensity of public opinion
    Use of impact analyses and evaluation studies
    Interest groups use traditional political tactics
    Political battles over how to achieve change
    Proponents usually seek to pass statutes
    Include economic and financial proposals

DIVISIVE ISSUES

    Public opinion tends to be bimodal
    Dichotomous issue positions
    Extreme mutually exclusive policy options
    Options represent extreme change
    Conflict typical
    High salience to constituents
    High intensity of public opinion
    Use of negative emotion-laden symbols
    Interest groups use grassroots mobilization
    Political battles over whether to achieve change
    Proponents usually seek constitutional change
    Include civil liberties, moral, and social issues

sues typically include civil liberties and moral and social concerns (Tatalovich and Daynes 1981; Monroe 1975). Examples include school prayer, abortion, gun control, capital punishment, civil rights for blacks and women, affirmative action and euthanasia.

Financial Impacts and Models of Representation

Public opinion on proposed policies affects the development of those issues in legislative settings. Pennock (1979) has developed a legislative typology for analyzing issues with financial and redistributive impacts. His typology has four issue categories: proposals with (1) generalized benefits and generalized costs, (2) generalized benefits and particularized costs, (3) particularized benefits and generalized costs, and (4) particularized benefits and particularized costs.

Proposals with generalized benefits and generalized costs are usually consensual. Almost everyone believes in such programs as national security or protection of private property. The second category includes regulatory policy which provides examples of issues with generalized benefits and particularized costs. In this category, pressure group activity by affected groups may be intense, but is typically over the degree rather than over the principle since there is broad consensus on the benefits.

Conflict over proposals with particularized benefits and generalized costs is usually minimal, since benefits are typically directed toward groups assumed to be deserving, such as veterans or college students, while costs are dispersed. Issues are rare where both benefits and costs are particularized and the beneficiaries differ from those bearing the costs. One example is legal requirements for racial quotas. Since participants perceive the issue as a zero sum game, conflict is intense.

Implicit in Pennock's categories are linkages between different models of representation and different types of financial impacts (see table 6-7). If benefits are generalized, politics will play a role in determining the level and distribution of those benefits. Conflict in the case of generalized benefits is not over the question of whether benefits will occur, but rather over how to shape the benefit structure to the mutual satisfaction of all participants in the legislative process. The appropriate model of this political process is a bargaining model where logrolling and compromise are evident. This type of benefit structure closely parallels Lowi's distributional policy (Lowi 1979). With this type of benefit structure, the possibility of negotiation and compromise heightens the importance of political factors of representatives and constituents relative to social characteristics. Political factors include party identification patterns of representatives and constituents, presidential vote in the constituency, liberalism and conservatism of representatives and constituents and number of terms served by the representatives. Social characteristics include ethnic and racial composition, region, education and religion.

If benefits are particularized, conflict is more apparent. Some gain and others do not. Who gains depends upon the mesh of the social

Table 6-7
Financial Impact and Models of Representation

TYPE OF FINANCIAL IMPACT	MODELS OF POLITICS AND OF REPRESENTATION
Generalized benefits	Political characteristics Bargaining model
Particularized benefits	Social characteristics Environmental model
Generalized costs	Representatives characteristics Trustee model
Particularized costs	Constituency characteristics Delegate model

characteristics of various constituencies with the criteria espoused in the political rhetoric of the day. An environmental model of politics is appropriate where social factors of constituents and representatives supersede political characteristics in determining policy outcomes.

Costs may also be generalized and particularized. Generalized costs are compatible with a trustee model of representation where representatives follow their consciences. With a generalized cost structure, everyone experiences some pain. The consciences, value systems and expert judgements of legislators must establish the level of pain to be borne, based on previous experiences of the legislators. With generalized costs, representative characteristics are more important than constituency characteristics in determining legislative outcomes.

Particularized costs, on the other hand, imply a delegate model of representation, where representatives try to reflect constituency opinion. With particularized costs, some constituencies gain in a relative way while others lose absolutely. The zero-sum politics involved with the focused pain of particularized costs make constituency characteristics important in determining policy outcomes.

The models of politics and representation attached to various ideal benefits and costs may be applied to Pennock's categories (see table 6-8). Where both benefits and costs are generalized, the bargaining model of politics and the trustee model of representation are applicable. Political factors outweigh social factors; representative characteristics outweigh constituency characteristics. When benefits are particularized and costs are generalized, an environmental model of politics and a trustee model of representation apply. The environmental model implies that

Table 6-8
Types and Characteristics of Legislative Issues

		COSTS	
		Generalized	Particularized
BENEFITS	Generalized	Political and Representative Factors	Political and Constituency Factors
		(Bargaining and Trustee Models)	(Bargaining and Delegate Models)
		Generated from unifying public opinion issues	Generated from negotiable public opinion issues
	Particularized	Social and Representative Factors	Social and Constituency Factors
		(Environmental and Trustee Models)	(Environmental and Delegate Models)
		Generated from negotiable public opinion issues	Generated from divisive public opinion issues

social factors outweigh political factors in determining policy outcomes, while the trustee model implies that representative characteristics supersede constituency characteristics.

Policies where benefits are generalized and costs are particularized may be characterized by the bargaining model of politics, where political factors dominate social factors. This type of benefit and cost structure may also be correlated with the delegate model of representation, where constituency characteristics supersede representative characteristics. Environmental protection, where industries are regulated and pay a cost for the general benefit of all, may be a policy area where the bargaining model and the delegate model are likely to prevail. Although the regulated industry may eventually pass the costs on to the consumer, the costs are initially particularized and the benefits that accrue are initially generalized.

The environmental model of politics and the delegate model of representation apply to particularized costs and benefits. With both particularized costs and benefits, social and constituency characteristics are more important in determining policy outcomes. The requirement of racial or minority quotas is a policy issue where there are particularized costs and benefits. Where quota systems are applied, the advantaged group, usually white males, are denied the right to compete for all available job slots in the public and private sector and must allow disadvantaged groups access to a percentage of the open positions. In this instance, the white males would bear the costs while the disadvantaged persons would enjoy generalized benefits.

The benefit and cost structure of legislative issues may also be linked to models of public opinion. Legislative issues with both generalized costs and benefits are typically generated from unifying public opinion issues. This type of legislative issue is noncontroversial and not divisive, due to perceptions that everyone benefits and everyone pays.

Negotiable public opinion issues may result in legislative issues where either costs are generalized and benefits are particularized, or when benefits are generalized and costs are particularized. For each of these benefit cost structures some groups gain relative to others, but some benefits or costs are widely dispersed. This wide dispersion prevents the alienation of specific groups and makes bargaining possible.

By contrast, when costs and benefits are both particularized, no common benefit or pain is widely dispersed. Groups are fragmented and less willing to bargain. Divisive issues in public opinion tend to result in legislative issues with particularized benefits and particularized costs. Such issues are also highly correlated with attempts not only to force change by statute but also to seek constitutional change.

THE CONSTITUTION AND MALAPPORTIONMENT

History of Malapportionment

One criticism of the current geographic basis for constitutional representation is that sometimes in history, malapportionment has occurred so that the one-person one-vote criterion has been violated. After the 1787 Convention, state legislatures used widely different apportionment practices. Most of the states admitted to the union at that time employed population as the basis for apportionment. However, several states followed the "federal plan" where one house of the state legislature was based on population and the other was based on land units. The remaining states, while using population as the foundation for apportionment, modified population-based representation by requiring that every county have at least one representative, and that no county have more than a maximum set number of representatives.

With the rise of the progressive movement in the twentieth century, land-based plans for representation were increasingly criticized as mass shifts in population to urban areas and growth in industrial centers produced great disparities in the power of individual votes in different areas of the states. Rather than try to address these disparities, in several states with rurally dominated legislatures, the rural elite tried to maintain their power by strengthening land-based apportionment. The 1920 census showed that for the first time in U.S. history, a majority of U.S. citizens lived in urban areas. This precipitated a crisis over malapportionment. For the first and only time, Congress refused to reallocate representatives among the states after the immediately preceding census (Hardy 1981, 18; Jewell 1962, 3).

As long as major apportionment decisions remained in the hands of malapportioned legislatures, the system proved resistant to change. At first federal courts were removed from and uninvolved in the reapportionment controversy. Even in 1946, in *Colegrove v. Green,* the U.S. Supreme Court refused to strike down a congressional districting plan in Illinois that gave one district nine times the population of another district. Felix Frankfurter, in his presentation of the *Colegrove* majority opinion said "the courts ought not to enter into this political thicket," and the issue was ruled nonjusticiable.

The Interventionist Role of the U.S. Supreme Court

Sixteen years after the *Colegrove* case, in the 1962 decision of *Baker v. Carr,* the U.S. Supreme Court reversed its position and decided that malapportionment was a justiciable issue. By remanding the case to a lower court, however, the Supreme Court refused to specify what levels of population disparity would be tolerable. Two years later, in 1964, two more landmark malapportionment cases were handed down. In *Wesberry v. Sanders,* Georgia's congressional district plan was struck down for violating the one-person one-vote doctrine. In *Reynolds v. Sims,* the court ruled that in bicameral state legislatures, both houses must be districted substantially on the basis of population (McKay 1965, 98).

These three major cases produced many citizen suits charging malapportionment in state legislatures. As a result, many states tried to address the long-neglected redistricting issue. By March 1964, twenty-six states had passed new apportionment plans. Three states, Alabama, Oklahoma, and Tennessee, were reapportioned under court-drafted plans. Several states redistricted after they received court threats to postpone elections or to require all legislators to run for reelection at large. Most states witnessing these examples of judicial scrutiny and intervention began to undertake redistricting voluntarily.

By 1973, the U.S. Supreme Court began to re-examine the application of the one-person one-vote criterion, particularly at the congressional vote level. In *White v. Weiser,* the court ruled that equality in congressional districting was an absolute requirement by favoring a plan so closely based on population that the largest district in the state exceeded the smallest by only four hundred voters. However, Connecticut's redistricting plan for its state legislature was upheld in *Gaffney v. Cummings* despite a 7.8 percent variance in population between the largest and the smallest districts. In *Mahan v. Howell,* the court upheld an even larger discrepancy of 16.4 percent for the Virginia state legislature.

This new approach of relaxing the standards of precise mathematical equality gave states increased discretion in selecting which factors beyond population should govern redistricting. The new approach was also open to criticism in the 1980s, since it made possible increased chances for state legislatures to gerrymander with impunity.

Politicans realize district lines affect their future careers as incumbents and their ability to thwart possible challengers. Thus, gerrymandering for a partisan advantage occurs often. State legislators may seek to maintain their incumbencies by drawing "safe" districts. Powerful legislative leaders may try to bolster their power by rewarding supporters with more favorable districts and by punishing opponents with more "competitive" districts (Hardy et al. 1981, 22).

In *Kirkpatrick v. Preisler* (1969), the Supreme Court ruled that a district plan which, in an earlier period, would have been acceptable and considered "equal," was unfit if political or personal advantage could be gained. This approach, rather than diminishing the competition for partisan advantage, has actually heightened it. Legislative majorities in state legislatures use the judicial emphasis on precise equality to justify drawing oddly shaped districts that range across county and other subdivision lines.

In recent times, the Court has become even more involved in the areas of political gerrymandering and minority dilution. In June 1986, the Supreme Court ruled in *Davis v. Bandemer* that a partisan gerrymander violates the equal protection clause only when intentional discrimination against an identifiable political group and an actual discriminatory effect on that group can be proven. For the first time, political gerrymandering became justiciable (Kilpatrick 1986, 2b). Another case decided in June 1986, *Thornburg v. Gingles,* dealt with the issue of minority dilution. The Court held that in order for minority group voters to establish that multimember districts impair their ability to elect representatives of their choice, they must show that the group is large enough to make up a majority in a single-member district, that the group is politically cohesive, and that it has sufficient majority votes to be strong enough to usually defeat a minority's preferred candidate.

Malapportionment and Dissatisfaction

Of course, the issue of malapportionment in the U.S. Senate has not been placed on the political agenda, since to do so would question the very constitutional bases of states themselves. Yet relative disparities in the power of different citizens in voting for U.S. senators have worsened across time. In 1790 the largest state, Virginia, with a population of 747,000 was 12.7 times larger than the smallest state, Delaware, with a population of 59,000. The power of a voter in Delaware was thus approximately 12.7 times greater than the power of a voter in Virginia. By contrast, in 1980 the largest state was California with a population of 24 million, while the smallest state, Alaska, had a population of .4 million. The disparity of voting power in 1980 had increased to 60 times.

Even beyond the problems of malapportionment and redistricting, geographic representation may be criticized for forcing voters to collapse policy preferences into a single vote. The U.S. Supreme Court has not dealt with this issue, nor has it been framed as a constitutional issue. Geographic representation and redistricting in most legislative issues except the U.S. Senate remain constitutionally supported and intact.

REFERENCES

Almond, Gabriel A., and Sidney Verba. 1963. *The Civic Culture*. Princeton, N.J.: Princeton University Press.

Bailey, Thomas A., and David M. Kennedy. 1983. *The American Pageant*. 7th ed. Lexington, Mass.: D.C. Heath and Co.

Baker, Gordon E. 1955. *Rural Versus Urban Political Power: The Nature and Consequences of Unbalanced Representation*. Garden City, N.Y.: Doubleday and Co., Inc.

Berelson, B. R., P. F. Lazarsfeld, and W. N. McPhee. 1956. *Voting*. Chicago: University of Chicago Press.

Broder, David. 1971. *The Party's Over*. New York: Harper and Row.

Burke, Edmund. 1949. *Burke's Politics*. Ross J. S. Hoffman and Paul Levack, eds. New York: Alfred A. Knopf, Inc.

Burns, James MacGregor. 1963. *The Deadlock of Democracy: Four-Party Politics in America*. Englewood Cliffs, N.J.: Prentice-Hall, Inc.

Chelf, Carl P. 1977. *Congress in the American System*. Chicago: Nelson-Hall, Inc.

Crotty, William. 1985. *The Party Game*. New York: W. H. Freeman and Co.

Dahl, Robert. 1956. *A Preface to Democratic Theory*. Chicago: University of Chicago Press.

Downs, Anthony. 1957. *An Economic Theory of Democracy.* New York: Harper and Row.

Edelman, Murray. 1964. *The Symbolic Uses of Politics.* Urbana, Ill.: University of Illinois Press.

Fenno, Richard F., Jr. 1978. *Home Style: House Members and Their Districts.* Boston: Little, Brown and Co.

Fiorina, Morris P. 1977. *Congress: Keystone of the Washington Establishment.* New Haven: Yale University Press.

Flanigan, William H., and Nancy H. Zingale. 1983. *Political Behavior of the American Electorate.* 5th ed. Boston: Allyn and Bacon, Inc.

Friedrich, Carl J. 1950. *Constitutional Government and Democracy.* Boston: Ginn and Co.

Hardy, Leroy, Alan Heslop, and Stuart Anderson. 1981. *Reapportionment Politics: The History of Redistricting in the 50 States.* Beverly Hills, Calif.: Sage Publications.

Hofstadter, Richard, William Miller, and Daniel Aaron. 1967. *The United States: The History of A Republic.* Englewood Cliffs, N.J.: Prentice-Hall, Inc.

Jacobson, Gary C. 1983. *The Politics of Congressional Elections.* Boston: Little, Brown and Co.

Jewell, Malcolm E., ed. 1962. *The Politics of Reapportionment.* New York: Atherton Press.

Kilpatrick, James J. 1986. "One More Political Thicket." *The State.* Columbia, S.C.: July 6.

Lee, Eugene C. 1978. "California." *Referendums: A Comparative Study of Practice and Theory.* David Butler and Austin Ranney, eds. Washington, D.C.: American Enterprise Institute for Public Policy Research.

Lowi, Theodore J. 1979. *The End of Liberalism: The Second Republic of the United States.* 2nd ed. New York: W. W. Norton and Co.

McKay, Robert B. 1965. *Reapportionment: The Law and Politics of Equal Representation.* New York: The Twentieth Century Fund.

Magleby, David B. 1984. *Direct Legislation: Voting on Ballot Propositions in the United States.* Baltimore: Johns Hopkins University Press.

Mayhew, David R. 1974. *Congress: The Electoral Connection.* New Haven: Yale University Press.

Monroe, Alan D. 1975. *Public Opinion in America.* New York: Dodd, Mead and Co.

Olson, David M. 1980. *The Legislative Process: A Comparative Approach.* New York: Harper and Row, Publishers.

Page, Benjamin I. 1978. *Choices and Echoes in Presidential Elections: Rational Man and Electoral Democracy.* Chicago: University of Chicago.

Pennock, J. Rolland. 1979. "Another Legislative Typology." *Journal of Politics.* 41:1206-1213.

Pitkin, Hanna Fenichel. 1967. *The Concept of Representation.* Berkeley: University of California Press.

Pomper, Gerald M., with Susan S. Lederman. 1980. *Elections in America: Control and Influence in Democratic Politics.* 2nd ed. New York: Longman.

Ranney, Austin. 1978. "The United States of America." *Referendums: A Comparative Study of Practice and Theory.* David Butler and Austin Ranney, eds.

Washington, D.C.: American Enterprise Institute for Public Policy Research.

Rosenstone, Steven J., Roy L. Behr, and Edward H. Lazarus. 1984. *Third Parties in America: Citizen Response to Major Party Failure.* Princeton: Princeton University Press.

Rousseau, J. J. 1948. *The Social Contract.* London, England: Oxford University Press.

Sabato, Larry J. 1985. *PAC Power: Inside the World of Political Action Committees.* New York: W. W. Norton & Co.

Sayre, Wallace S., and Judith H. Parris. 1970. *Voting for President: The Electoral College and the American Political System.* Washington, D.C.: The Brookings Institution.

Sorauf, Frank J. 1984. *Party Politics in America.* 5th ed. Boston: Little, Brown and Co.

Tatalovich, Raymond, and Bryon W. Daynes. 1981. "From Abortion Reformed to Abortion Repealed: The Trauma of Abortion Politics." *Commonweal* 108:644-649.

Vogler, David J., and Sidney R. Waldman. 1985. *Congress and Democracy.* Washington, D.C.: Congressional Quarterly Press.

Chapter Seven

Too Much Separation of Powers? Presidential Versus Parliamentary Government

When the United States declared its independence from Britain, the English monarch was still a potent force in British politics although the power of Parliament was growing. The authors of the U.S. Constitution copied many features of the British system with some modifications and limitations. One major aspect replicated in the United States Constitution was separation of powers, especially between the executive and legislative branches. Yet the British parliamentary system continued to evolve. The monarch became merely a ceremonial head of state while the decision-making power was diverted to the position of Prime Minister, a member of Parliament and leader of the majority party. This evolution was not inhibited by a written Constitution with a formal and stringent amendment process such as that specified in the U.S. Constitution.

Critics of separation of powers argue that a parliamentary system which combines executive and legislative functions is more modern and efficient than a system which constitutionally separates executive and legislative branches. This chapter will examine the merit of those claims. Yet separation of executive and legislative powers is only one of several structural differences between Congress and parliamentary governments. Most parliamentary systems are effectively unicameral, with a defunct or merely advisory upper house. Political parties play a heightened role in policymaking in parliamentary systems and committee status is less important than in Congress. The implications of each of these structural differences will be examined. Criticisms of parliamentary government will also be explored, including the continued dependence of parliamentary systems, especially those modeled on the British system with single member districts, on geography as a basis of representation.

THEORIES OF GOVERNMENT STRUCTURE

Political scientists have long been fascinated with and debated the utility of various governmental structures. Concern with the differential impacts of varying governmental forms was at the heart of the structural functionalism school of inquiry. When the sometimes obfuscating verbiage of structural functionalism was stripped away, the central issue remained concern with the mapping of social structures, including governmental structures, onto the functions performed.

Eastonian systems theory (named after political scientist David Easton) extended the concern with governmental structures and placed its focus upon form into a broader systems framework. Governmental forms were part of the black box in systems diagrams labeled "conversion processes and institutions." These "conversion processes and institutions," including governmental structures, were influenced by demands and supports fed into the system and, in turn, had an impact on policy outputs (Easton 1966).

Unfortunately, systems theory in its earlier state never proceeded beyond typologizing system components. This early systems theory created a framework for comparative measurements of political systems. Nonetheless, it fell far short of a rigorous theory. In contrast to the typologies of Eastonian systems analysis, a rigorous theory consists of a set of coherent, consistent and empirically testable propositions where each proposition is a hypothesized relationship between two or more theoretical concepts.

Several data limitations have handicapped scholars attempting more rigorous examinations of the relative merits of different government structures (Blondel 1973, 23-28). Documentation of important legislative proceedings is often difficult to obtain. Proceedings of subcommittees, committees and full debates may be only partly published or not published at all. In studying the U.S. system and, to an even greater extent, the legislatures of other western nations, scholars may experience difficulty obtaining access to member voting records and vote totals.

Another data-gathering limitation is the lack of information about informal activities of national legislators. This kind of information often has to be collected through participant observation, in-depth interviews and surveys—often slow and costly methods. Since legislators may manipulate their colleagues in ways that they might not wish to mention, legislator inhibitions on revealing information contribute to this problem. Researchers, consequently, must often face the fact that many informal activities cannot be recorded.

In comparing systems, other methodological problems also arise. For example, similar procedures may perform different functions in various systems. The question hour in many parliamentary systems may be a way for legislators to introduce a bill while in other systems its primary function may be to provide a forum for the opposition party to question the party in power. To cope with this problem of the same activity fulfilling different functions in cross-national comparison, scholars often devise functional equivalents for each of the legislatures under investigation.

Perhaps the biggest methodological difficulty in the comparative study of national legislatures is to establish the degree of influence each wields upon its environment. There are two ways in which the study of influence can take place: using cross-sectional data to tap the number of people involved in legislative activity, the degree to which sections of the national population are involved in a problem, the money spent and other resources employed; and using times series data to examine change across time. Difficult as it sometimes is to collect adequate cross-sectional data, collecting time series data is often even more arduous.

Lack of hard data on legislative performance in many countries, even including the United States, forces scholars to resort to more subjective judgments about the relative merits of different kinds of systems. These subjective observations and conclusions are necessarily colored by the different economic, social and cultural contexts of the scholars and the legislatures they are observing. While both congressional and parliamentary studies are often subjective, they have substantially increased the knowledge of students of legislatures. Often unable to predict future legislative behavior, and sometimes unable to explain past behaviors, scholars have begun the long, labor-intensive and difficult task of laying the foundation for better theory through describing the variants of national legislatures around the world. In scholarly descriptions of modern democracies, presidential and parliamentary democracies appear to be on two distinct and separate branches of the evolutionary tree.

THE STRUCTURE AND OPERATIONS OF CONGRESS IN A PRESIDENTIAL SYSTEM

Decentralization and Multiple Decision Points

The most outstanding operational and structural characteristics of the U.S. Congress are its decentralization and its multiple decision points. In order for the average bill to become a law it must be: (1) introduced in both the House of Representatives and the Senate; (2) referred by both houses to separate committees where hearings are held and recommendations are made; (3) debated and passed in both chambers; (4)

sent to a conference committee if the two versions passed in separate houses are different; (5) approved by each house; and (6) signed into law by the president. Some bills, which overlap into more than one committee jurisdiction in each house or must be sent to subcommittees, have even more obstacles to final passage.

The passage of legislation is extremely difficult under such a decentralized system. The multiple decision points through which a bill must pass require majority coalitions at each gate to push the measure along (Oleszek 1984, 12). There is a complex division of labor in Congress. Responsibilities for specific policy areas are delegated among numerous committees and subcommittees. There are 269 committees and subcommittees in both houses of Congress. Broader issues, like the national defense, education and health care are divided into smaller sub-issue categories for committee consideration.

Congressional Committees and the Norm of Seniority

Not only are committees divided according to issues, but there are structurally differentiated types of committees that are used for a variety of purposes. There are four major types of congressional committees: standing, select, conference and joint. Standing committees are permanent, whereas select committees are special committees created to study and investigate a specific problem and usually dismantled soon thereafter.

Since most bills must be sent to a standing committee for consideration, this committee usually plays the most important role in determining the fate of a bill. In the legislative process, conference committees are used to reconcile differences in bills that have passed through both chambers. Conference committees consist of an assortment of members from the standing committees that had original jurisdiction over the bill in both houses. The least-convened committee is the joint committee. Joint committees facilitate joint action and the coordination of standing committees from two different chambers. Most joint committees do not report legislation but rather conduct studies.

Congressional committees are strong and independent since some of them have existed since the early days of the Republic. The jurisdictions of the committees in the two chambers are clearly delineated in the standing rules of the 1946 and 1970 reorganization acts. The committees decide which bills will be reported to the floor for debate and which will be placed on the back burner of the congressional agenda. Favorable committee reports do not necessarily ensure the passage of the bill on the floor but the more favorable the report from committee, the greater the probability for passage (Jewell and Patterson 1986, 142; Dyson and Soule 1970, 626-647).

In the Eighty-ninth Congress (1965–1967), 26,566 measures were introduced, 4,200 were reported from committee and 810 became public law. A similar trend continued in the Ninety-seventh Congress: although fewer measures were introduced (only 13,240), 1,877 were reported from committee and 473 became public law. Thus, the committee system as a gatekeeper of what is debated and what is not debated remains extremely important (Oleszek 1984, 74).

On most congressional committees, the chairperson is the most influential leader. Committee chairs have the ability to set timetables for hearings and specify the time and place of work sessions. Chairs also preside over committee hearings, control committee staff resources and set the agenda. The success of the chairperson may depend on a variety of factors. For instance the formal powers of chairs are generally enhanced by the formation of political support bases (Fenno 1973, 114-137). The environment of the committee may or may not be hospitable to the committee chair. In part, a chairperson's influence depends on the ideological make up of committee members.

Seniority is a basic norm of Congress. Congressional use of seniority is widespread and does not apply only to the assignment of committee chairpersons. In fact, seniority is a norm that seeps into every aspect of congressional operations. As members are ranked according to length of uninterrupted service, prerequisites are distributed among the most experienced. For example, office space, as well as seating at official dinners, is assigned on the basis of seniority.

In more recent years two major developments have affected the operation of Congress. Subcommittees in the House have been given more autonomy and authority. As a result of these two developments, committee chairs have been weakened and party leaders have been somewhat strengthened. Greater subcommittee independence increases overall decentralization in decision making in Congress. The greater independence and authority given to subcommittees in the 1970s was designed to give more members an opportunity to contribute to the decision-making process. Designed to check the power of committee chairs, the subcommittee system has resulted in an even greater diffusion of power (Davidson 1981, 109).

Another development concerns the seniority system. Seniority in earlier periods of congressional history meant the automatic selecting of committee chairs who were members of the majority party and who had the longest continuous years of service. Since the 1970s new rules established by the party caucuses require the review of committee chair performance at the beginning of each Congress. Appointment to committees solely on the basis of seniority is no longer guaranteed. Since 1975 committee chairs and those who rank at the top in seniority on various committees have been more likely to vote with their party than other members. The removal of seniority as the sole criterion for selecting committee chairs has in a sense strengthened the party structure in Congress.

The Party Structure as a Centralizing Force

As a moderate counterforce to the decentralization in the committee system, the party structure and its leadership help shape and manage the committee system by setting committee size and party ratios in the committees. These kinds of decisions allow party leaders to affect the possible long-term compositions of committees (Smith and Deering 1984, 231). Leaders may attempt to centralize decision making by using the party machinery to improve interpersonal communication among members of the same party or with leaders of the other party.

The two parties organize other aspects of congressional life. Party organization often affects the social life of a member since informal social groupings of representatives seldom cross party divisions. Each political party has its own cloakroom and sits separately on the floor. The parties also provide members with separate clubs and meeting places.

Members of each political party meet to select their respective leaders, the Republicans in the Republican Conference and the Democrats in the Democratic Conference. The ratio of Republicans to Democrats on the committees is fixed by the majority party. The ratios are supposed to be set fairly and based on the proportion of Republicans in the Congress to Democrats in the Congress but as the procedure actually operates, the majority has the freedom to set any ratio they wish. For example, in 1981, disturbed by the Republican takeover in the Senate, House Democrats reacted by "overrepresenting" themselves on major committees including the Rules Committee, the Ways and Means Committee and the Budget Committee. Ratios on these prestigious committees were set as high as eleven Democrats to five Republicans despite the fact that the real ratio of Democrats to Republicans in the House was about five to four. Usually committee seats are divided between the two parties in a ratio that provides a slight advantage to the majority party.

The party structure in Congress performs the functions of formulating policy positions and building coalitions to pass necessary legislation. In the House of Representatives, the Speaker of the House is a member of the majority party and is elected to this powerful position. The Speaker's formal powers include presiding over the House, referring bills and resolutions to appropriate House committees, appointing members to select, joint and House-Senate conference committees, and deciding points of order. The Speaker is the most powerful leader in the House, although most Speakers rarely participate in floor debate or vote except in instances where a tie-breaking vote is needed (Peabody 1985, 258).

Second in the House command is the majority leader, who is elected by the majority party caucus. Responsibilities for majority leaders include scheduling bills, managing legislation on the floor and building party coalitions into majorities on upcoming votes. The efforts of the majority leader are supplemented by the majority and deputy whips who aid the leader in attaining head counts of party members for and against bills and try to coalesce support for the legislation favored by the party. The minority party has a separate set of leaders, including a minority leader and minority whips. The minority floor leader, the losing candidate for Speaker, has similar duties to those of the majority leader.

In the Senate the leader with the most influence is the majority leader. The Senate majority leader often affects legislative committee assignments, nominates members to party committees, schedules Senate floor business and is aided by the majority whips. The formal presiding officer of the Senate is the vice-president who rarely performs this task, but may cast a tie-breaking vote on critical bills. The president pro tempore is the ceremonial head of the majority party in the Senate and typically presides over the Senate although junior senators of the majority party are frequently tapped for this routine and tedious duty. Like the House, the Senate also has a minority leader and minority whips.

The ability of party leaders to form winning coalitions depends on the size and cohesiveness of both the majority party and the minority party. There is much evidence to substantiate the argument that party cohesion has declined. Many factors contribute to unpredictability in forming coalitions, including controversial issues that divide parties and overall intra-party ideological disagreements which become internal sources of unpredictability (Sinclair 1981, 215-220).

Factors external to the organization of Congress, such as the decline in partisanship in the electorate and the concomitant growth of personalistic campaigns, have weakened the party mechanisms for channeling the behavior of the members of Congress. Constituency concerns vary from representative to representative and may pressure members of Congress to defect from the party line on a variety of issues. In addition, the party structure is weakened by the increased tendency and capacity of incumbents to deliver nonpartisan services (Collie and Brady 1985, 282).

Sources of Executive-Congressional Tensions

Characteristic of the U.S. presidential system is the separation of powers among three branches. This often produces conflict, particularly between the president and the Congress. This separation of powers may also undermine the ability of the party structure to centralize and direct policy. Often the president, as party leader, takes policy stances in order to influence the members of his party to support him. Yet the president's success depends more frequently on his popularity and his ability to understand congressional processes and deal with Congress.

The inherent conflict between Congress and the presidency resides in their institutional differences. The system was designed by the framers to ensure that the separate branches would be captured by different interests and that compromise would have to occur if the system was to remain in operation. Even more conflict is likely when the presidency is occupied by one political party and the majority of Congress in both houses is composed primarily of another political party.

Institutional sources of conflict abound. The length of time the president and members of Congress serve in office affects their judgement on what is politically salient. For example, the president may feel a need to pass high-priority features of his program as quickly as possible, realizing that his time in office is limited. The president's length of service is fixed, allowing eight years at the most for an individual to accomplish his goals. Time is a precious resource, as the president often loses the opportunity to pursue his program during crises, before elections and in the lame duck phase.

Members of Congress are less constrained by time. Since they must frequently worry about their reelection chances and how votes on particular issues may affect their careers, time is viewed as more open-ended, as congressmen continually plan to extend their term of office. Conflict between presidential and congressional perceptions of time arise when the president asks congressional allies to assist him on an immediate goal and the congressmen are reluctant to expend power on his behalf due to concerns about accumulating political capital for future use (Polsby 1986, 194).

In addition to conflictual perceptions of time, there are more conflicting perceptions of constituencies. Members of Congress are more parochial than the president in their concerns as they seek to please the limited constituencies from which they are elected. Due to this orientation, legislators are prone to intercede in the president's behalf only in those instances where intervention would be noticeable to constituents. The president, on the other hand, tends to have a nationwide and governmentwide perspective. The president is accountable to the largest of constituencies—the nation—and may sacrifice local interests to achieve and maintain the general welfare (Sundquist 1977, 230).

Because the president and the Congress have different levels of information and expertise at their disposal, conflicts may arise. Despite recent increases in congressional staff and the expansion of information units such as the General Accounting Office, the Congressional Research Service, the Office of Technology Assessment and the

Congressional Budget Office, members of Congress still lack the quantity and quality of information accessible to the president. In the hiring of staff, members of Congress tend to hire generalists rather than specialists. Individual staff members may become experts in a particular area but in comparison to their counterparts in the executive branch they may be amateurish. Due to the differences in information and expertise available to the president and the Congress, they may come to view issues and solutions to problems from different perspectives (Edwards 1980, 46–47).

Executive-congressional tensions are sometimes exacerbated by the conflict between maintaining secrecy and the need for disclosure.In the past, Congress was sometimes not apprised of U.S. commitments or even troop actions until after the fact. The activities of the intelligence agencies, especially those such as the Central Intelligence Agency, which engages in covert operations abroad, have not been disclosed to Congress. Some key budgetary matters concerning new weapons systems as well as intelligence operations are revealed only to key officers in the executive branch and to members of Congress on committees with oversight responsibilities and a consequent need to know. Members of Congress may feel betrayed when the executive branch fails to inform them of matters affecting national security and interests abroad. Unilateral presidential action without consulting Congress, particularly in areas such as arms sales, committing military advisors and surprise attacks on foreign countries, may cause extreme tension and policy failure (Destler 1985, 346).

Besides unilateral presidential actions and secrecy in foreign affairs, executive privilege is a custom which occasionally contributes to executive tendencies toward secrecy, protection, and classification and which increases tension between the executive and legislative branches. Executive privilege allows presidents to classify information which might jeopardize national security if released to the press or to Congress. Executive privilege also allows the president to shield his closest advisors from testimony before Congress.

Emerging as a custom, and not directly supported by the Constitution, the logic of executive privilege is that presidents, as chief executives, need to be able to consult their advisors in privacy without the interference of news coverage. Because Congress has an implied power to investigate and because the president may, in the execution of his duties, withhold information, the two branches sometimes collide. Presidents have tended to broaden the scope of executive privilege across time.

During the Watergate scandal President Nixon tried to apply executive privilege to matters that were "intra-executive" in character. By claiming that executive privilege was applicable, Nixon attempted to suppress a subpoena requiring that he surrender certain tapes needed for a criminal trial involving indictments of some of his closest aides who were charged with conspiracy to obstruct justice and defraud the government. The grand jury also named the president as an unindicted coconspirator. The president, in a last ditch effort to clear himself of possible criminal charges, published an edited version of the disputed tapes—a politically damaging move. The Supreme Court in *United States v. Nixon* (1974) ruled that the president was obligated to comply with the judicial subpoena and narrowed presidential interpretations of executive privilege by rejecting the notion that the president, rather than judges, had the final word about what information to release and what to withhold.

The clash of prerogatives that occurs due to shared powers may heighten tension between Congress and the presidency. One such shared power is the president's power to veto and the power of Congress to override his veto. The president may veto a bill by returning it to the house in which it originated or he may use the pocket veto. Usually if the president does not sign or veto a bill within ten weekdays, the bill becomes law without the president's signature. However, if Congress adjourns within his ten-day period, the president may kill the bill by not signing it and thus "placing it in his pocket."

The pocket veto controversy that emerged in the Nixon administration highlighted the possibility of friction when two branches share similar prerogatives. When, in 1970, President Nixon pocket vetoed a bill while the Senate was absent for four days and the House for five days during Christmas, many congressional Democrats believed Nixon had misused his authority to pocket veto. The appellate court also decided that the pocket veto power had been abused by Nixon (Fisher 1981, 15). Although the checks and balances system often produces conflicts where overlapping authority leads to tension, there are still advantages to presidential government.

THE ADVANTAGES OF PRESIDENTIAL GOVERNMENT

In a presidential government as practiced in the United States, government occurs by design. The American governmental system was structured to reduce the possibility of error. As envisioned by the constitutional framers, it was intended to become the world's first truly rational government (Deutsch et al. 1981, 21). Madison, Jefferson, Hamilton and others attempted to establish a government based on reason. To channel the behavior of politicians and citizens in certain ways, institutional mechanisms were needed.

Separation of powers and checks and balances were two such mechanisms which are useful for preventing the rise of tyranny. These constitutional mechanisms of U.S. presidential government prevent the total power of the state from being concentrated in the hands of one interest or one branch of government. The goal, of course, is to preserve liberty by preventing government from becoming so effective and efficient that it abuses governmental power and approves unwise legislation. By providing numerous gates through which legislation must pass, these devices may reduce the amount of unwise legislation that might easily pass through a more centralized system.

Federalism forms another check on the centralization of power. Instead of one level of government, the United States has two constitutionally defined levels and, in practice, actually has three or more levels, each with its own focus and functions. Supporters argue that federalism promotes diversity, heterogeneity and responsiveness to local needs.

Single-member districts in the U.S. political system tend to support a two-party system, which some critics praise for preventing the emergence of extreme ideological parties and unmanageable factions. In most two-party systems, conflict amelioration is an intra-party function, allowing issues to be resolved somewhat removed from the glaring scrutiny of the public eye. Compared to multi-party systems, two-party systems tend to be more stable.

The U.S. political system has some disadvantages however. Because of the separation of powers, checks and balances, bicameralism, and federalism, the danger of stagnated government is always there—the "Deadlock of Democracy" as James MacGregor Burns has called it. The difficulty of getting prompt action from government has caused some to disparage the system as outdated and outmoded. Even the presidency has been called "no win" by Light (1983) and "impossible" by Barger (1984). This, combined with the stranglehold of the "iron triangle" and the proliferation of PACs and interest groups, has encouraged many critics to look to parliamentary systems for solutions.

THE STRUCTURE AND OPERATIONS OF PARLIAMENTARY LEGISLATURES

Parliamentary systems have exhibited several general characteristics, including the fusion of executive and legislative power, the dominance of parliament, and party discipline and accountability. In addition, some but not all parliamentary systems have proportional representation.

The Fusion of Executive and Legislative Power

Whereas the American presidential system is characterized by separation of powers, most parliamentary systems are distinguished by a fusion of powers. In the presidential system, members of Congress may not concurrently hold executive office. In contrast, the Cabinet under a parliamentary system consists of leaders of the majority party in the national legislature. This Cabinet, usually headed by a prime minister, has sole responsibility for formulating policy and initiating legislation.

The exact composition of the Cabinet and the executive branch varies among different countries, but most parliamentary systems have, in addition to a prime minister, ministers of treasury or finance, foreign affairs, education, labor, commerce and trade, and defense. Parliamentary systems typically have few bureaucratic political appointees beyond the Cabinet, with career civil service appointments beginning immediately below the position of minister.

In order to become a prime minister or Cabinet member, politicians must spend many years in the service of their party in Parliament (Putnam 1976). In 1980, the average length of service in the Parliament for British prime ministers prior to assuming that position was twenty-eight years. The result of long apprenticeships is that the leadership in parliamentary systems often has considerable experience at the national level. By contrast, more personalized and media-oriented campaigns in the U.S. sometimes catapult politicians with little national experience into national prominence.

Dominance of Parliament

Under many parliamentary systems, there are no legal limits on the powers of the national legislature. Judicial review as it is known in the U.S. system, which gives the courts the right to declare laws of Congress unconstitutional, does not exist in most parliamentary systems. Unlike the U.S. presidential system where elections are staggered (with presidential elections every four years, Senate elections every six years and congressional elections every two years), the dominance of parliaments in their own political systems is strengthened by indefinite terms of office. Irregularly scheduled elections may be interspersed with regularly scheduled elections—for example, in Great Britain the government must stand for reelection every five years.

Irregularly scheduled elections result from a "no confidence" vote which is called by the opposition party if the position of the majority party becomes untenable or scandalous. Passage of a no confidence vote, which in a majority government can only occur with defection of members of the majority party, forces the sitting government to resign and stand for reelection. The ruling majority party may also call for an irregularly scheduled election at any time if it feels it can strengthen its position in the country and in Parliament. Public opinion polls often determine the timing of these snap elections.

Party Strength and Discipline

According to supporters, parliamentary systems result in stronger political parties (Epstein 1980; Scarrow 1974; Drucker 1984). Parliamentary parties are said to exhibit more parliamentary discipline than U.S. political parties (Burns 1963; Lees and Kimber 1972). Political parties in parliamentary systems, unlike their U.S. counterparts, maintain rigorous party platforms. Citizens are typically aware of these platforms and vote accordingly. Once elected, the majority party in a parliamentary system uses its mandate from the public to develop and administer government policy.

Party members are expected to support the programs promised by the majority party and to enact legislation to fulfill those promises. If majority party members do not vote with the party on an important legislative issue, they risk the possibility of being purged permanently from the party or of forcing the government to lose a vote of confidence and stand for reelection. The party's refusal of support in the next election usually means defeat for an errant member of Parliament (M.P.). This is usually a sufficient threat to enforce party discipline.

Although majority parties in parliamentary systems can enact legislative programs on their own, minority parties can also have an impact on legislative agenda setting and development via their role as the loyal opposition. Occasionally they may influence majority party actions by criticizing policies and issues and pointing out deficiencies in proposed legislation. Recognizing that new elections may result in a shift of power between the majority and minority parties helps to ensure that criticisms by the minority party are thoughtful, substantive and serious rather than trivial or petty, since minority parties realize that they could become majority parties after a new vote.

Proportional Representation

Some but not all parliamentary systems, have proportional representation systems in at least one house. Under proportional representation, seats in the national legislature are allocated to each party based on the percentage of the popular vote that party receives. The major alternative electoral system comprises single-member districts where only one legislator is elected from a particular geographic district. In Great Britain and many countries previously under British rule, such as Canada, Australia, India and New Zealand, members of parliament are elected in at least one house through single-member districts. Other systems, such as those in West Germany, Israel, France, Japan and Italy, elect at least one house by proportional representation.

Proportional representation systems tend to result in multi-party systems, while single member districts result in two-party systems. Minority parties which can garner a small but consistent proportion of the popular vote under single-member districts will never secure the necessary fifty-one percent to win office, and therefore have little incentive to continue in the long run. By contrast, in proportional representation (PR) systems, minority parties secure seats in the national legislature in approximate proportion to their percentage of the popular vote. The fact that minority parties can win and secure some seats in PR systems provides them with the incentive to continue running in national elections.

Proportional representation systems also may result in coalition governments, an occurrence more rare under single-member districts. If many parties develop and run under a PR system, no party may gain enough popular support to win and absolute majority of the seats in the national legislature. Consequently, two or more parties may combine to form a coalition government, with compromises occurring across party lines rather than within the party, as most typically happens with a majority government. Because separate parties (often with separate goals, histories and leadership) must agree on common platforms in coalition governments, they tend to be less stable and result in greater turnover than majority governments. Frequently, however, some parties in the fallen coalition reappear in a reformed alliance which includes a different combination of parties constituting a new working majority.

THE ADVANTAGES OF PARLIAMENTARY SYSTEMS

Many students of national legislative structures, and U.S. scholars in particular, have long been enamored of the virtues of parliamentary governments. The reasons for their affection include the belief that parliamentary systems are more efficient, more accountable, and more adept at promoting the national interest.

Efficiency

Because parliamentary systems are less fragmented and more centralized than presidential systems, they are comparatively more efficient in passing major legislative programs. Supporters argue that within parliaments legislation is more easily shepherded through legislative and political hurdles than within presidential systems. By contrast, the numerous vetoes and other gate-like structures in the congressional system impede the ready passage of much national legislation which citizens desire (Schattsneider 1942).

Parliaments tend to have fewer standing committees than does Congress, and parliamentary committees rarely hold hearings or solicit expert testimony. In some systems the legislation to be addressed by a particular committee is not predetermined, but may vary depending upon assignments by the leadership. In essence, committees become task forces to facilitate the leadership's goal of approving major programs, rather than substantively oriented bodies created to probe a particular problem and develop a legislative solution.

Party Discipline and Citizen Accountability

Party discipline as a mechanism enforces accountability of party members to the voters for programs and policy stances promised by the majority party. Citizen awareness of party positions is assumed to be greater within parliamentary systems where party labels have greater ideological meaning than in congressional systems where heterogeneous ideologies masquerade under the same party name (Drucker 1979).

In parliamentary systems the executive and legislative branches have merged, unlike presidential systems where these two branches are constitutionally separated. The prime minister is the leader of the majority party in the Parliament and is not independently elected by citizens. The members of the executive Cabinet are also members of the parliament. Both executive and legislative power is concentrated in the Parliament. The absence of an independently elected president in parliamentary systems presumably facilitates efficiency and minimizes interbranch conflict (Groth 1970; Hardin 1974). Because the parliamentary system permits a greater concentration of power than the presidential system, proponents contend that parliamentary leadership is stronger and more effective than congressional leadership (Elliott 1935; Finletter 1945).

Parliamentary Dominance and National Interests

An additional advantage of parliamentary systems claimed by proponents is that parliamentary structures help prevent narrow minority interests from prevailing over the needs of the wider community or the "public interest" (Scarrow 1974). According to this argument, when power is concentrated in a single governing body such as the Cabinet, it is less likely that seemingly unfair concessions will be made to narrow interests because this might place the chances of party reelection in jeopardy.

Thus parliamentary systems fight possible pork-barrel legislation more effectively since the parliamentary system places the controlling party in the position of total victory or total defeat. Unlike a presidential system where a political party may capture one branch of government but not another, in a parliamentary system there is no chance, for example, of winning the presidency but not the Congress (Lepawsky 1977; Gregory 1980; Pennock 1962; Borthwick 1984). The fact that most of the work of legislative development and modification in a parliamentary system is conducted in the Cabinet rather than in standing committees provides fewer opportunities for special interest groups to intervene in the process to promote their own particular causes.

PARLIAMENTARY CHARACTERISTICS AND PROPOSED REFORMS

Despite their advantages of greater centralization, party strength and discipline, clarity of party platforms, citizen accountability and focus on national rather than specialized interests, parliamentary systems are not without weaknesses. Across the variants of parliamentary structure, a trade-off seems to exist between more narrowly defined political parties (which more cogently and closely represent the preferences of individual citizens) and party effectiveness and strength on the one hand, and overall system stability on the other.

Single-member district systems which generate two major parties often result in stable majority governments and responsible parties, but the parties must necessarily define their interests and positions more broadly than in a multi-party system where they can be more narrowly focused. In single-member district parliamentary systems, the voter is confronted with the same problem of being unable to disaggregate preferences for voting that currently confronts citizens in presidential systems. In these parliamentary systems, party platforms may be more visible and parties may have greater ability to deliver proposed programs, but voters must still choose between two alternatives, neither of which may come close to their own preference structure. Nor may voters disaggregate their votes electorally for different policies.

In the British version of the single-member-district parliamentary system, one of the major complaints made by back bench members is that their voice is stilled by the strict party discipline imposed by the Cabinet. Not only are they supposed to follow the party line largely set by the front benches, but their voice is seldom heard in the House of Commons debates. Theirs is an increasingly impotent role involving loss of individuality and self-esteem.

Another disadvantage of the British parliamentary model is that a change of party can mean radical rather than incremental changes in policies. A Labour victory can mean nationalization of major industries and services while a Conservative victory can bring denationalization and privatization. Policies toward the trade unions, the Common Market, the North Atlantic Treaty Organization (NATO) and South Africa can vary greatly with a change of parties. The resulting lurches in policy can cause major dislocations in British life.

The British model also puts a premium on collective leadership through the Cabinet. As Waltz (1967, 304) has pointed out in his seminal comparative study of British and U.S. foreign policy making:

Though Prime Ministers are assumed to be in a strong position, British policy moves forward only after careful preparation of the ground upon which members of the governing party will be expected to stand. The fusion of powers and the concentration of responsibility encourage governments to avoid problems while broad accommodations are sought.

This situation makes it difficult to develop the kind of vigorous, innovative leadership that U.S. presidents frequently exhibit. Needless to say, Margaret Thatcher never let this stand in her way while serving as prime minister.

Those systems which use proportional representation often have many and more narrowly focused parties but, in the absence of functional specialization, each party still typically covers the gamut of policy issues, albeit within a more narrow ideological range. An additional disadvantage is that multi-party systems often result in coalition governments which exhibit high turnover and instability.

Typically, reformers of the U.S. Constitution suggest structural changes which would more closely approximate some if not all of the features of parliamentary systems, including the strengthening of political parties. These reforms fall into one of three categories. Exemplary of suggested constitutional reforms to strengthen political parties, especially the governing political party, there are those which prohibit ticket splitting and advocate close sequencing of presidential and congressional elections so that presidential elections precede congressional elections by two weeks; creating bonus seats for the president elect's party in Congress; formulating a national ticket including major cabinet officers; and abolishing the prohibition of dual office holding in the executive and legislative branches (see table 7-1).

A second category of constitutional reforms designed to simulate features of parliamentary systems suggested by Sundquist (1986) would alter or lengthen terms for national office to allow national politicians to take a broader and more long-term perspective. Included in this type of reform are proposals to lengthen the term of office for congressmen, to abolish congressional mid-term elections and to repeal the Twenty-second Amendment limitation on the number of times a president can be elected. A third category of constitutional reforms would allow provisions for reconstituting a failed government including broadening the impeachment clause to cover "maladministration" as

Table 7-1
Proposed Constitutional Reforms to Approximate Parliamentary System Features

REFORMS TO STRENGTHEN POLITICAL PARTIES:

Prohibiting ticket splitting

Presidential elections preceding Congressional elections
by short time interval

Creating bonus seats in Congress for the President Elect's party

Formulating a national ticket including major cabinet officers

Abolishing the prohibition on dual office holding in
the executive and legislative branches

REFORMS TO ENCOURAGE A MORE NATIONAL AND LONG TERM PERSPECTIVE:

Lengthening terms for members of Congress

Abolishing Congressional midterm elections

Allowing Presidents to be elected for more than two terms
by repealing the Twenty-Second Amendment

REFORMS TO RECONSTITUTE A FAILED GOVERNMENT:

Making "maladministration" impeachable

Establishing provisions for special elections

well as treason, bribery, and other high crimes and misdemeanors; and making provisions for special elections.

These reforms advocating piecemeal adoption of portions of parliamentary government may improve some aspects of government functioning. None, however, force a merging of executive and legislative power, which is the central feature of parliamentary government, although the elimination of current constitutional prohibitions on dual office holding would allow, but not require, movement in that direction. None of these reforms, even those designed to strengthen political parties, gives the voter a chance to disaggregate policy preferences in a meaningful electoral expression, yet this inability remains a central cause of increasing voter apathy and alienation. Unless alienation and apathy are addressed, the weeds of corruption and the abuse of power may flourish while the plant of democracy will face a climate of drought.

REFERENCES

Barger, Harold. 1984. *The Impossible Presidency*. Glenview, Ill.: Scott, Foresman and Company.
Blondel, J. 1973. *Comparative Legislatures*. Englewood Cliffs, N. J.: Prentice-Hall, Inc.
Borthwick, R. L. 1984. "Parliament." In *British Politics in Perspective*. R. L. Borthwick and J.E. Spence, eds. New York: St. Martin's Press.
Burns, James MacGregor. 1963. *The Deadlock of Democracy: Four-Party Politics in America*. Englewood Cliffs, N. J.: Prentice-Hall, Inc.
Collie, Melissa P., and David W. Brady. 1985. "The Decline of Partisan Voting Coalitions in the House of Representatives." In *Congress Reconsidered*. 3rd ed. Lawrence C. Dodd and Bruce I. Oppenheimer, eds. Washington, D.C.: Congressional Quarterly Press.
Davidson, Roger H. 1981. "Subcommittee Government: New Channels for Policy Making." In *The New Congress*. Thomas E. Mann and Norman J. Ornstein, eds. Washington, D.C.: American Enterprise Institute for Public Policy Research.
Destler, I. M. 1985. "Executive-Congressional Conflict in Foreign Policy: Explaining It, Coping With It." In *Congress Reconsidered*. 3rd edition. Lawrence C. Dodd and Bruce I. Oppenheimer, eds. Washington, D.C.: Congressional Quarterly Press.
Deutsch, Karl W., Jorge Il Dominguez, and Hugh Heclo. 1981. *Comparative Government: Politics of Industrialized and Developing Nations*. Boston: Houghton Mifflin Co.
Drucker, H. M. 1984. "The Evolution of the Political Parties." *British Politics in Perspective*. R. L. Borthwick and J. E. Spence, eds. New York: St. Martin's Press.
———. 1979. "Two-Party Politics in Britain." *Multi-Party Britain*. H. M. Drucker, ed. New York: Praeger.
Dyson, James W., and John W. Soule. 1970. "Congressional Committee Behavior on Roll Call Votes: The U.S. House of Representatives, 1955–1964." *Midwest Journal of Political Science* 14:626–647.
Easton, David. 1966. *The Political System: An Inquiry into the State of Political Science*. New York: Alfred A. Knopf.
Edwards, George C., III. 1980. *Presidential Influence in Congress*. San Francisco: W. H. Freeman and Co.
Elliott, William Y. 1935. *The Need for Constitutional Reform*. New York: McGraw-Hill.
Epstein, Leon D. 1980. "What Happened to the British Party Model?" *American Political Science Review* 74:9–22.
Fenno, Richard. 1973. *Congressmen in Committees*. Boston: Little, Brown and Co.
Finletter, Thomas K. 1945. *Can Representative Government Do the Job?* New York: Reynal & Hitchcock.

Fisher, Louis. 1981. *The Politics of Shared Power: Congress and the Executive.* Washington, D.C.: Congressional Quarterly Press.

Gregory, Roy. 1980. "Executive Power and Constituency Representation in United Kingdom Politics." *Political Studies* 28:63–83.

Groth, Alexander J. 1970. "Britain and America: Some Requisites of Executive Leadership Compared." *Political Science Quarterly* 85:217–239.

Hardin, Charles M. 1974. *Presidential Power and Accountability: Toward a New Constitution.* Chicago: The University of Chicago Press.

Jewell, Malcolm E., and Samuel C. Patterson. 1986. *The Legislative Process in the United States.* 4th ed. New York: Random House.

Lees, John D., and Richard Kimber, eds. 1972. *Political Parties in Modern Britain: An Organizational and Functional Guide.* London: Routledge and Kegan Paul.

Lepawsky, Albert. 1977. "Reconstituted Presidency and Resurgent Congress." In *The Prospect for Presidential-Congressional Government.* Albert Lepawsky, ed. University of California, Berkeley: Institute of Governmental Studies.

Light, Paul C. 1983. *The President's Agenda.* Baltimore: The Johns Hopkins University Press.

Oleszek, Walter J. 1984. *Congressional Procedures and the Policy Process.* 2nd ed. Washington, D.C.: Congressional Quarterly Press.

Peabody, Robert L. 1985. "House Party Leadership: Stability and Change." In *Congress Reconsidered.* 3rd ed. Lawrence C. Dodd and Bruce I. Oppenheimer, eds. Washington, D.C.: Congressional Quarterly Press.

Pennock, J. Roland. 1962. "Agricultural Subsidies in England and the United States." *American Political Science Review* 56:621–633.

Polsby, Nelson W. 1986. *Congress and the Presidency.* 4th edition. Englewood Cliffs, N.J.: Prentice-Hall.

Putnam, Robert D. 1976. *The Comparative Study of Political Elites.* Englewood Cliffs, N.J.: Prentice-Hall.

Scarrow, Howard A. 1974. "Parliamentary and Presidential Government Compared." *Current History* 66:264–267, 272.

Schattsneider, E. E. 1942. *Party Government.* New York: Rinehart.

Sinclair, Barbara. 1981. "Coping With Uncertainty: Building Coalitions in the House and the Senate." In *The New Congress.* Thomas E. Mann and Norman J. Ornstein, eds. Washington, D.C.: American Enterprise Institute for Public Policy Research.

Smith, Steven S., and Christopher J. Deering. 1984. *Committees in Congress.* Washington, D.C.: Congressional Quarterly Press.

Sundquist, James L. 1977. "Congress and the President: Enemies or Partners?" In *Congress Reconsidered.* Lawrence C. Dodd and Bruce I. Oppenheimer, eds. New York: Praeger Publishers.

———. 1986. *Constitutional Reform and Effective Government.* Washington, D.C.: Brookings Institution.

Waltz, Kenneth N. 1967. *Foreign Policy and Democratic Politics.* Boston: Little, Brown and Company.

Chapter Eight

Policy Specialization:
A Time for Constitutional
Change?

How should constitutions and the governments they create be evaluated? How might the U.S. Constitution be modified to create a government which remains deliberative but is more representative, more responsive to citizen preferences and better able to handle the burdens of an increasingly technological society? Is there an option superior to the parliamentary system proposed by many reformers? This chapter explores one such proposal for structural change. It also develops criteria for a desirable legislature which can be used to evaluate the effectiveness of the existing one and compare it with an alternative structure.

CRITERIA FOR A DESIRABLE LEGISLATURE

National legislatures are among the most complex and paradoxical of social institutions. They are at once both collegial in their deliberations and debates, and hierarchical in their leadership structure. They are collective and assumed to be striving for the public good and national interest, yet they are fiercely individualistic and parochial. They are ponderously slow and deliberative, yet capable of lightning speed when threatened with a crisis. Presumably they are representative of the entire population and speak on its behalf, yet their composition is often elitist, male, affluent, well-educated, caucasian and nonrepresentative (Blondel 1973, 106–161). Due to their importance, criteria for evaluating legislatures are useful for distinguishing between idiosyncratic but relatively insignificant foibles and major shortcomings.

Criterion #1: A National View and the National Interest

One desirable criterion for national legislatures is the ability of both individual members and the institution to take a broad national view of problems and to act in the national interest. Legislative politics involves a reconciliation between the claims of competing interests at the sub-national level and the welfare of the nation as a whole. A small benefit for the nation as a whole, for example, should not necessarily be implemented if serious damage would accrue to a region of the nation. At the same time, a minor benefit for part of the nation should not be purchased at the cost of severe hardship to the nation as a whole (Pitkin 1967, 218).

A representative in a national legislature typically plays the dual role of special pleader and judge in an effort to be an agent for both a local unit and the national unit. In the process of playing this role, the goal of the national legislator should be to find the "final-objective-interest" of a nation. Since the interests of the parts may not always add up to the interest of the nation, finding the final-objective-interest is often a difficult (but not theoretically impossible) task (Wolin 1960, 63–66).

Criterion #2: Efficiency and Responsibility

Efficiency, as a desirable criterion for national legislatures, is concerned with three main values. One value associated with efficiency is financial—whether or not resources are being allocated in the most useful manner. The second value is effectiveness. Is the national legislature performing functions and fulfilling goals expeditiously and completely? Is the national legislature capable of planning for the long term and for possible problems that might arise? Finally, the third value concentrates on whether the national legislative institution coordinates and integrates its goals in a way that makes for minimal incompatibility and loss of motion (Griffith and Valeo 1975, 130). Efficiency, as defined by these three values, is a desirable trait and should be present in national legislatures.

The authoritative allocation of resources often occurs in national legislatures. This is a critical task and when performed poorly can result in waste. In some instances the resources being allocated are scarce. The waste of such resources may inflict harsh costs on a particular segment in a society or on the nation at large. The thoughtful allocation of resources in an efficient manner can make or break the welfare of a nation.

The ability of the national legislature to perform its functions expeditiously and to plan for the future is also a matter of great concern. In today's constantly changing, big government society, the populace is particularly dependent upon the lawmakers' abilities for fulfilling its objectives. The citizens of such nations rely on the efficient delivery of services and completion of goals.

In times of crisis it is especially imperative that the national legislature act quickly to remedy a possibly disruptive problem. A problem can worsen or proposed solutions can become obsolete if effective action is not taken. The ability to plan for the long term as well as short term is important: forward thinking is an essential ingredient for anticipating and preventing crises.

The national legislature should coordinate its activities in a manner that reduces duplication of goals and use of resources. It should avoid enacting laws that sponsor incompatible and competing goals. The ability of the national legislature to successfully integrate policies determines its level of perceived and actual overall effectiveness.

Criterion #3: The Approximation of Citizen Preferences

Another desirable criterion for national legislatures is the attempt by representatives to approximate citizen preferences. To be labeled a truly "representative" assembly, legislators should accurately reflect constituency opinion (Carpenter 1925, 53). This criterion, dubbed the delegate model of representation, may conflict with the trustee model where the representative is expected to act in the national interest.

The national legislature should represent a constituency different from that of the executive branch. Legislatures, from this standpoint, provide a check on presidential or executive power by reflecting district or state opinion rather than national opinion per se. This Madisonian model of representation ensures viable checks and balances by allowing interests not necessarily held by a national majority to be represented by particular legislators. This standard emphasizes the need for more accurate correspondence between constituent preferences and legislative lawmaking rather then the need for rapid decision making (Vogler 1983, 78).

For this criterion to be successfully met, a legislator's votes in the national legislature should agree with his or her own perceptions of the constituency and should not be determined by external influences. The legislator's perceptions of constituency opinion must also correspond to actual constituent opinion. For this kind of representation, it is necessary for constituents to be cognizant of the candidate's policy views when they vote (Miller and Stokes 1963, 45–56).

There are reasons why representatives may not understand the wishes of their constituents. For example, a representative may not receive a clear indication of how the majority of his constituents feel about a particular issue—opinion may be extremely divided. Certain less divisive issues may not be particularly salient to constituents. Other issues may be so complicated that constituents are unable to supply informed opinions. Despite these obstacles, the approximation of constituent preferences is still a desirable goal (Harris and Hain 1983, 18).

Criterion #4: Accountability

A fourth criterion is accountability. In every form of government power exists and is distributed among certain leaders. In a representative government, the ones entrusted with power should have to account for their actions (Ford 1924, 57). Likewise, members of national legislatures should be held accountable. The national legislature ought to be reviewed regularly by the citizenry. Legislators should feel anxious about their reelection chances and should feel insecure about possibly deteriorating home-base support from their constituents. This motivates members of the national legislature to devote more time and care to cultivating the voters (Davidson and Oleszek 1985, 136).

If the voters find their representatives lacking, they can "turn the rascals out." If the national legislature fails to act or makes poor policy choices, or if the electorate perceives that members are acting unethically by placing self-interest above the general public welfare, then the public should use the ballot box to elect wiser and more honest representatives. Accountability operates in a retrospective fashion. Unwise decision making may result in loss of power if the electorate decides that new representatives would use the powers of the office with more success. Consequently, legislators should feel compelled to constantly assess popular reaction, real or imagined, to their decisions (Rieselbach 1986, 12).

An accountable national legislature must necessarily be on public display. Interested citizens should have the opportunity to listen to representatives in committees and in the floor debate. This kind of openness to the public discourages representatives from making rash statements. As legislators attempt to avoid alienating blocs of voters, they will be cautious about assuming extreme stances on issues and will seek moderation. To the extent that accountability as a criterion discourages extremism and encourages moderation, it is a desirable standard to employ in evaluating national legislatures.

Criterion #5: The Encouragement of Citizen Participation

The encouragement of citizen participation by the bodies of government, especially the national legislature, has important implications for a representative democracy. Lack of citizen participation results in an apathetic society where political institutions go unobserved and unchecked. Representation of citizens' interests is most likely to happen when citizens are aware of the legislative activities corresponding to their various interests.

Voter ignorance often results from the failure of institutions and their members to educate voters about legislative process and activities. The consequences of voter ignorance are immeasurable. While the national legislature as an entity may receive low popular ratings, it is possible for individual legislators to receive undeserved high ratings from their states or districts. Many of these legislators are reelected and as incumbents appear to benefit from citizen ignorance. Apparently the electorate perceives that the problems with the national legislature are caused by representatives from districts or states other than their own, and legislators often reinforce this view (Vogler and Waldman 1985, 26).

Due to ignorance, citizens may not discern whether or not their representatives are good legislators who can mobilize support for their bills and pass legislation, thereby solving problems and implementing their objectives. Citizens may also have difficulty identifying merely symbolic action wherein legislators express an opinion but suggest no policy changes, or make statements of policy without sponsoring legislation to implement it. This may discourage citizen involvement in the political process (Mayhew 1974, 130–136).

Members may contribute to voter ignorance and apathy in a variety of ways. Legislators may stress voter access and identification with the constituents more than what is going on in the national legislature. Since voters are not made aware of legislative activities, they tend to settle for access to their representative with little real oversight of legislative activities.

The structure of the national legislature and the goal of reelection may provide disincentives for legislative members to better inform the citizens. The more educated the voters are, the more opportunities they may have to criticize their legislators. The more information they receive, the higher their expectations for their representatives. Legislators may fear that the legitimacy of the national legislature would erode if they communicated more frequently or more effectively with the citizenry (Fenno 1978, 240–241: Mansbridge 1983, 30). Citizen participation should be encouraged by the structure of the national legislature. Channeling the behavior of legislators in a way that gives them an incentive to inform the public and at the same time increases citizen interest in the legislative process as a desirable goal.

EVALUATING CONGRESS BY CRITERIA FOR A GOOD LEGISLATURE

National View

Congress is often accused of being parochial, reflecting narrowly based constituent interests rather than assuming a national view. This criticism has been levied particularly at the House of Representatives, where each member is elected from a relatively small and homogeneous geographic district. Senators are typically elected from larger and more heterogeneous areas but have been similarly accused of placing the interests of their states above the national interest.

Several factors have exacerbated the parochial orientation of Congress, including the internal congressional committee structure, the maintenance of the seniority system and the power of special interest groups in the national political process. Both houses of Congress have developed internal functional specialization by nurturing fairly elaborate committee and subcommittee structures. In the mid-1980s, the House had twenty-two standing committees and about 135 subcommittees, while the Senate had sixteen standing committees and about ninety subcommittees. Typically, members attempt to secure positions on committees of the greatest importance to their constituents, making committees a vehicle for the expression of particularized rather than generalized or national views. Congressional subcommittees and committees join with the bureaucratic agencies they authorize, oversee and fund. Along with the clients of the bureaucracies and congressionally funded programs, they form the classic "iron triangle" of special interests.

The seniority system in Congress (the means used to select committee and subcommittee chairs) contributes to the particularized and parochial rather than national and generalized views of Congress. Through the seniority system, members from noncompetitive and relatively homogeneous districts rise to power within Congress. Not only do the district characteristics of senior members often distinguish them from members from more competitive districts, but the seniority system itself diminishes leadership turnover, assuring the long-term and meaningful representation of some parochial interests at the expense of others.

One measure of parochialism in Congress is the delivery of pork barrel legislation to congressional districts and states. This may consist of special projects, new programs, or public works or buildings which benefit constituents in a particular geographic region and do not benefit other citizens. The conferment of such benefits is a constant feature of congressional policy making. Particularized benefits have two properties: they are usually given out to a specific individual group or geographic constituency and are usually distributed in an ad hoc fashion so that the member of Congress representing the benefited constituency can claim credit for the allocation. Representatives and Senators view pork barrel legislation as crucial to reelection, a perception which diminishes the incentive among current members to abolish or limit its use.

Because Congress has reflected parochial and particularized rather than national interests, the executive branch has gained preeminence in recent times. Elected by all the people, the president is assumed to reflect national views more than members of Congress who are elected by smaller constituencies. Growth of executive power has been accelerated by congressional difficulties in setting national priorities and allocating resources accordingly.

Efficiency and Responsibility

A criticism often leveled at the U.S. Congress is its inability to enact legislation concerned with pressing national problems without long, arduous delays. It is not unusual for Congress to adjourn after a long session without having dealt with some urgent matter before it. In past years it has failed, for example, to pass a fiscal year appropriations bill until months after the date when the actual fiscal year began.

This lack of action handicaps orderly administration. It is not uncommon for Congress to approve minor, nondivisive measures in every session; moreover, in crises it can act quickly. But often it is unable or unwilling to act on pressing problems unless they reach a crisis stage (Harris 1972, 19).

The speed with which legislation is passed, or more accurately, the lack of speed, is a major problem with congressional performance. In addition to the difficulty of obtaining rapid agreement in a pluralistic environment, structurally rooted phenomena have also contributed to delays in legislative outcomes. Internal specialization within each house of Congress has led to a lengthy sequential process, with hearings, investigations and debates occurring at the subcommittee, committee and full house levels. In the House of Representatives, the House Rules Committee which functions as a traffic regulator through which all committee-originated legislation must pass, serves as an additional level between full committee hearings and full debates. Spending measures must sometimes pass through authorizing subcommittees and committees as well as a network of appropriations subcommittees and committees in each house.

The bicameral structure of Congress lengthens the legislative process even further by requiring that legislation pass through a second subcommittee, a full committee and the full house. Differences between legislative output from each house must be ironed out in yet another committee, jointly appointed by each house, called the Conference Committee. Further reaffirmation of the Conference Committee-approved compromises must then be secured in each house. Given this number of legislative hurdles, important legislation is often sidetracked, permanently derailed or significantly modified by interest groups at any one of the various gates through which proposed statutes must pass. Interest groups have become well aware of the lengthy, sequential, internally specialized, bicameral legislative processes. They often manage to impede or alter bills at veto points along the process. The length of the process is not only ponderous, but in the Washington environment where the interest group legislative "hunting season" never closes, the long duration of the process increases bill vulnerability to special interest attacks.

If history is an indicator of how Congress will behave in the future, efficiency and responsibility will take a back seat to expediency and stalemate. During the Great Depression of the 1930s, Congress had the opportunity to take the initiative and propose a program of recovery. In the White House, President Hoover believed in the independence of the legislature and would not intervene except in extreme cases where action was definitely needed. As the years passed, Congress made only a few attempts to cope with the ever-deepening crisis. These pitiful efforts proved hopelessly inadequate in dealing with the depression. Would history repeat itself if the United States were to experience another depression or similar crisis? Is Congress only capable of incremental, piecemeal policy making? Due to such historical examples as the Great Depression and the concomitant inaction in Congress, many have concluded that Congress is ineffectual in times of crisis (Burns 1966, 120–121).

Congress may not only be slow to act in many crises but it also may allocate funds wastefully. For example, in 1965 President Lyndon Johnson suggested a bold solution to the problems of crime and poverty in inner-city slums. As the bill was originally drafted, about a dozen cities would have received large sums of money to be spent under federal supervision in order to promote racial integration and renovate the slums. Passage of this program in Congress became a study in compromise. Compromise, in itself, is not an undesirable value, but it can subvert the original purpose of legislation. Proponents of the "Demonstration Cities" legislation had to compromise extensively. They had to dismiss the goal of racial integration, loosen federal control over the administration of the program, and make more cities eligible to participate (approximately 150). What began as a noble attempt to renew decaying urban centers ended up as another pork barrel project that ineffectively divided funds among constituencies in Congress (Rieselbach 1986, 24–25).

Approximation of Citizen Preferences

In its infancy, government had few responsibilities. Today Congress legislates in almost every conceivable arena in the public domain. The expanded scope of federal intervention into all aspects of life in the United States results in more dissatisfaction with government, and the growth in scope simultaneously produces size and coordination problems which mitigate the possibilities of lowered or even constant dissatisfaction rates.

Several phenomena have contributed to an expansion of federal policy making. Historically, unprecedented post–World War II economic growth has allowed more resources to be diverted to public goods, since greater national wealth saturates demand for private goods in a relative fashion and allows previously neglected public concerns to be addressed. Keynesian philosophy was adopted in back-door fashion by the national government grappling with the ravages of the Great Depression. Keynesian philosophy indirectly supported federal policy expansion by providing an additional rationale for federal spending. The federal government also had no structural limitations on deficit spending, other than congressionally imposed debt ceilings which could be changed by the very body wishing to deficit spend.

Another contributing phenomenon to federal policy expansion has been public expectations. U.S. citizens have increasingly turned to government to solve problems as increased personal mobility and changing attitudes have weakened competing support institutions such as the extended family, the neighborhood and community ties. While the U.S. has lagged behind other industrialized democracies in creating social programs, concern for helping the poor and the elderly has also contributed to the growth in the federal role. Excessive fragmentation of subnational political jurisdictions often makes coordination and problem solving at the federal level desirable. National defense concerns have similarly contributed to this growth.

The expansion of the role of the federal government is congruent with cross-national findings that government expenditures are income-elastic. As the wealth and income of a nation increase, citizens desire more output and more public goods from their government. However, the expansion simultaneously creates problems for the expression of citizen preferences as to what those public goods should be. The problem of expression of citizen preferences is particularly acute when citizens must vote for representatives solely on the basis of geography.

Under the current congressional system, a single representative is supposed to reflect the views of the constituent in all policy areas. Since constituents are unable to electorally disaggregate their representative's policy stances (selecting some positions and omitting others) they must accept all the stances of their representative. Opposition candidates broaden the selection of policy packages available to citizens at the ballot box, but do not necessarily assure constituents of finding a policy package resembling their own preferences. Across the range of policy issues, the likelihood of a candidate reflecting the views of any particular constituent is very remote.

The constituent's dilemma is particularly acute when a single candidate assumes some policy positions which the constituent intensely prefers, while simultaneously assuming other policy positions the constituent intensely dislikes. The broadening of the scope of issue areas regarded by both Congress and the public as amenable to legislation has exacerbated the problem created by single member geographic districts in the current congressional system.

Another problem with the implementation of citizen preferences under the current congressional system is the internal committee specialization within Congress. Not only does such specialization lengthen the time frame for legislation, but it also serves to effectively disenfranchise most constituents from legislation initiation in most policy areas. Even constituents who are fortunate enough to have a congressional representative whose policy positions are similar to their own preferences on a particular issue are not guaranteed a meaningful legislative expression of those preferences. This is especially the case when constituency preferences involve initiating new legislation and developing policies which differ from the status quo.

Members of Congress are primarily limited to effectively initiating legislation in the policy areas covered by the subcommittees and committees on which they serve. Recognizing this political reality, most members of Congress strive to acquire memberships on committees dealing with legislation of particular salience to their own constituencies. The consequence of this functional specialization, (internal to each house of Congress) is that constituents cannot effectively initiate new policies in issue areas where their own legislative representative has no committee membership and therefore little clout.

While the internally specialized committee structure is the primary culprit in the inability of Congress to meet the criterion of approximating citizen preferences, the seniority system contributes to the flaw. Under the seniority system, the most important and desirable committee assignments have traditionally been acquired by older congressional members from noncompetitive districts whose views are frequently out of step with national sentiment and trends.

Accountability

Some scholars contend that popular indifference to Congress explains why the public does not hold it more accountable for its actions. Three conditions must exist for citizens to hold Congress accountable. First, the voters must be cognizant of legislative behavior. Second, citizens must have some policy views that they wish their legislators to attain, and third, if legislative voting patterns and citizen preferences do not correspond, citizens must have some mechanism to express dissatisfaction. Congressional observers in the fifties and sixties found these conditions poorly met (Rieselbach 1986, 31).

Congressional critics argue that citizens are generally not knowledgeable about major details of the legislative process, often failing to recognize the complexity of the process and its various decision points. Many voters are not aware of the most visible acts—roll call votes—or of how their own representatives perform on recorded votes. Nor are members of Congress supportive of the standard of accountability. To avoid accountability, members often exploit the decentralized nature of the institution, acting incongruently by denouncing a bill in committee and later supporting it in a roll call vote. Nor does the media facilitate citizen understanding of Congress as much as it might, since news coverage focuses predominantly on the president.

The expansion of the work load of Congress, especially in recent decades, has further undermined the accountability of representatives to citizens. The work of Congress has grown dramatically, but the number of representatives elected to do the work has not. Additionally, with the rise of the importance of the media in modern campaigns, members of Congress must spend more time campaigning and raising funds to retain their seats in reelection bids. The number of constituents served by each member has also increased with national population growth, increasing the demands for constituent service. Constituent service is especially a burden for senators from large, populous states. Indicative of the growing duties and demands placed on members of Congress are data on the average length of congressional sessions. When Congress was new in the early 1800s, the average session length was 290 days. By the 1860s the length had expanded to 410 days. Today, in the 1980s, the average congressional session lasts over 640 days (Vogler 1983, 47).

As the demands of being a member of Congress have increased to almost superhuman levels, members have been forced to rely more heavily on and delegate more responsibility to nonelected staff. The number of committee staff has gradually increased over this century from fewer than 300 in 1924 to 3,200 in 1980. Personal staff have increased dramatically from 3,800 in 1960 to almost 13,000 in 1980. In

1980, Congress was also aided by personnel in Congressional support agencies: 5,300 in the General Accounting Office; 5,400 in the Congressional Research Service; 210 in the Congressional Budget Office; and 150 in the Office of Technology Assessment (Smith and Deering 1984, 205, 221).

In many instances, key congressional staff have become kingpins and power brokers upon Capitol Hill. Michael Malbin identifies four rationales for increasing the dependence of Congress on staff: to reduce congressional dependence for information on the executive branch, to give members increased opportunities to have an impact on national issues, to provide members with resources to examine new issues and to help members manage the increased workload (1980, 6). Malbin argues, however, that the solution to the problem of burdensome work loads has actually exacerbated demands on members by creating new work through the identification of new legislative issues. While support staff can enhance the ability of Congress to respond to citizen preferences by providing members with the resources to address more issues, staff growth results in more decisions being made by nonelected officials who, unlike bureaucrats, are not selected by merit systems and who owe allegiance to no one but the members they serve.

Encouragement of Citizen Participation

The post–World War II era in the United States has been punctuated by increasing alienation and distrust of government. Government is doing more than ever before but most citizens seem to like it less. The status of politicians has deteriorated so much that national opinion polls rank members of the U.S. Congress and senators below business executives, doctors, accountants, professors, teachers and other professionals in public esteem. This disenchantment of citizens with politicians and particularly members of Congress contributes to declining turnout rates. Turnout for nonpresidential mid-term elections is even lower than for presidential elections, sometimes by as much as ten percent. As an example of midterm election voting behavior, average turnout in 1986 was 37.3 percent of the eligible voters.

Nor does the high cost of modern campaigns encourage citizens to run for national office themselves. The average cost of a campaign for the House of Representatives in the early 1980s was $200,000, with some campaigns approaching half a million dollars. In the Senate, the average campaign cost was $2 million, with some exceeding $7 million. Such costs prohibit average citizen involvement. Additionally, being a Congressman has become a full-time job, so that members must either have wealth before they take office or must be able to live on their congressional salaries—a difficult feat in the high-cost environment of

Table 8-1
Structural Features of the Current Congress

```
CURRENT CONGRESSIONAL STRUCTURE:

    (1) Limited number of representatives results in
        (a) higher constituent to representative ratios
        (b) unreasonable workloads for representatives

    (2) Selecting senators on the basis of states
        (a) violates the democratic critierion of one-
            person one-vote
        (b) malapportionment biases power against citizens
            from large states

    (3) Non-functionally specialized houses
        (a) leaves citizens unable to effectively disaggregate
            electorally their policy preferences
        (b) undercuts representative responsibility and
            accountability and leads to single issue voting

    (4) Bicameral passage of all legislation
        (a) results in lengthy delays in developing programs
        (b) creates multiple veto points where interest groups
            can wield disproportionate power

    (5) No hierarchical accountability between the Senate
        and the House of Representatives
        (a) undermines long term planning, national interests,
            and coordination
        (b) leads to internal committee specialization which
            disenfranchises voters from most policy initiation
```

Washington given the need to maintain a residence both in the nation's capital and in the home district or state (see table 8-1).

AN ALTERNATIVE STRUCTURE FOR CONGRESS

Various proposals have been made in the past to modify Congress so as to correct for some of its structural defects. Such proposals are often treated lightly. In light of the failure of current Congressional structure to meet many of the desirable criteria for national legislatures, serious attention should be directed to ideas concerning reform. Serious difficulties with the present structure imply a need for sweeping change.

Changes which modify the current congressional structure to facilitate meeting legislative criteria are desirable, although changes which improve one aspect of performance while simultaneously worsening another may not be worth the cost and effort. Only if reforms with negative repercussions create significant net gains in legislative performance would such changes be preferable.

Many of the problems with congressional performance relate to the efficiency and speed with which legislative matters are treated. Congress may have outgrown collegial organization as the scope of policy issues of congressional concern and the number of constituents demanding service has grown. Traditionally, collegial associations have functioned less efficiently than bureaucratic hierarchies. Bureaucracies delineate lines of authority clearly, specify accountability, separate work from personal responsibilities and promote merit. Reforms which emulate these optimal features of bureaucracy are desirable.

Many academicians and other elites assume that constituents do not know their own interests in most instances. In those circumstances where preferences are expressed, constituent intent is considered oppressive and reactionary. Consequently, elites tend to resist further democratization and downward delegation of power to constituents. An alternative view is that a nation founded upon the democratic principles of equality, liberty and freedom should continue to evolve to further implement those ideals.

Following is a description of an alternative Congress called REFORMS. REFORMS stands for Representational Efficient Functional Open Responsive Multi-cameral System. This system differs from previously proposed reforms as well as from the current Congress in several crucial ways, yet simultaneously retains some features of the current system. A discussion of each major structural feature of REFORMS follows (see tables 8-2 and 8-3).

Increased Number of Representatives

In order to enhance accountability, increased numbers of representatives would prevent distance between constituents and important decision-makers. In an extreme scenario, without an increase in the number of representatives, national policies would most likely be established more frequently by anonymous staffers who never appear on the ballot. A concomitant increase in the number of representatives would prevent this undercutting of democratic principles. Lines of accountability would be shorter and more obvious.

The number of representatives could be increased in either of two ways. Under one method, congressional districts could be made smaller with the number of districts increasing and the number of constituents served by a single representative diminishing. There is some evidence that the framers of the Constitution, particularly James Madison, envi-

Table 8-2
Structural Features of REFORMS—a Representational Efficient Functional Open Responsive Multicameral System

REFORMS STRUCTURE:

(1) Increased number of representatives to promote
    (a) a lower constituent to representative ratio
    (b) reasonable representative workloads

(2) Selecting senators on the basis of population
    (a) to promote the one-person one-vote principle
    (b) to restore power to citizens from large states

(3) Functionally specialized houses
    (a) to allow citizens to effectively express elect-
        orally their policy preferences
    (b) to enhance representative responsibility and
        accountability

(4) Shifting to single house passage of most legislation
    (a) to promote efficiency
    (b) to allow greater functional specialization and
        accountability

(5) Establishing hierarchical accountability between the
    Senate and the functionally specialized houses
    (a) to facilitate long term planning, national
        interests, and coordination
    (b) to allow all citizens a method of electorally
        expressing preferences for national priority
        setting, taxing, and spending policies

sioned an expansion of the number of representatives so that in the House of Representatives the ratio of representatives to constitutents would remain at one representative for very thirty thousand inhabitants. If this ratio had been maintained to the present day, the number of members of the House would total over seven thousand. This clearly illustrates the unwieldiness of this first method of increasing the number of representatives. The resulting legislative body would be too large for serious deliberations or meaningful debate.

A second method of increasing the number of representatives is the election of multiple representatives from current congressional districts. This approach is more desirable than the first for two reasons. First, multiple representatives from current districts make possible external functional specialization across a number of potential houses. Second, the larger the constituency to which a representative is elector-

Table 8-3
Powers of the Houses in REFORMS—a Representational Efficient
Functional Open Responsive Multicameral System

THE SUPER SENATE

MAJOR POWERS:

(1) Drafts and passes all revenue bills

(2) Establishes a binding national budget ceiling and binding subceiling targets for broad functional areas

(3) Manages overall fiscal policy of the economy

(4) Ratifies treaties

(5) Confirms presidential executive and judicial appointments

(6) Performs as binding mediator in cases of jurisdictional disputes between the functionally specialized houses

(7) Wields an internal legislative veto over substantive legislation passed by the functionally specialized houses

COMPOSITION:

Senators are selected on the basis of population from large districts for four year terms; one quarter of the Senate stands for reelection each year.

THE FUNCTIONALLY SPECIALIZED HOUSES

MAJOR POWERS:

(1) Each house is responsible for separate functional areas

(2) Within its functional areas, each house:
    (a) allocates monies within Senate specified budget ceilings
    (b) writes and passes all authorizing legislation
    (c) engages in oversight

COMPOSITION:

Representatives are elected from present congressional districts for four year terms; each district has one representative in each of four houses; one-fourth of each house stands for reelection each year; each congressional district has an annual election, but not necessarily for the same house as neighboring districts.

---

ally accountable, the more closely the member's policy stances will reflect the preferences of a national majority, all things being equal. In contrast to the first method of increasing the number of representatives, smaller congressional districts would increase the likelihood of homogeneous constituencies, thereby increasing the possibility of narrowly focused legislative positions by representatives as well as heightening the role of special interest groups.

Selecting Senators on the Basis of Population

The establishment of a one-person one-vote criterion for the U.S. Senate is critical for equalizing constituent voting power among citizens from states with different-sized populations. While small states will no doubt resist losing their electoral advantage, the one-person one-vote criterion is a basic underpinning of democratic principle. Equalizing constituent voting power in the Senate may be achieved in two ways.

One method is to continue to elect senators by states, but to weight the impact of the votes of the various senators by the populations of the states which they represent. This has the advantage of requiring less structural change since the weighting could occur internally. Such a system, however, would ultimately become convoluted and would still underrepresent constituents in big states in the sense that large numbers of voters would have their preferences aggregated and compressed into single senatorial votes, while voters from smaller states would not undergo aggregation and compression of the same magnitude. This distortion is not unlike that which occurs in the electoral college. While this system would weight all voter preferences equally, the probability that voters in a small state would have their preferences expressed by a single senator would still be greater than the probability of voter preferences being reflected by a single senator from a large state. The minority for whom the senator did not speak could conceivably be much larger in a populous state than in a less populous state. A greater number of citizens could thus fail to have their views expressed in a large state.

A second and preferred way to elect senators on the basis of population and fulfill the one-person one-vote criterion is to elect senators based on some geographic region other than the states. Some prespecified number of regions could be established based on population. Regions could be reapportioned every decade (as are congressional districts) to account for population shifts. Regions could serve as senatorial districts and would subsume several congressional districts. Senatorial districts could be either multi-member or single-member in nature. If single member districts were used and if the number of senators were to remain approximately the same as in the current Senate, each Senate district could consist of four congressional districts. Alternatively, larger regions from which multiple members could be selected on a proportional representation basis could be used. Although not favored by two-party advocates because proportional representation systems are correlated with multi-party systems, this latter method has the advantage of discriminating least against third and minority parties.

Creating Several Functionally Specialized Houses

There are two options for reforming the current House of Representatives. One option is to increase the size of the already unwieldly House. The second is to create additional houses, each with a functionally specialized area of legislative authority. The former is not desirable since the gargantuan size of such an expanded house would inhibit coordination and communication. In addition, such an augmentation would not alleviate voter inability to express policy preferences, since all preferences would still be compressed into one geographically based vote. Nor would it help voters to initiate policy preferences, since the current functional specialization that exists in the committee structure in Congress would remain internal to Congress and inaccessible to voters.

On the other hand, creating more houses would alleviate voter inability to effectively express policy preferences and to initiate policy changes. As the scope of government has grown, functional specialization among national legislators has become necessary. With the minor exception of the constitutional specification that revenue bills must originate in the House of Representatives and treaties and executive and judicial appointments must be confirmed by the Senate, most congressional functional specialization has been internal to each house of Congress. Internal functional specialization effectively disenfranchises voters from legislative initiation in policy areas where their representatives hold no committee appointment. External specialization across a number of functionally specialized houses would not disenfranchise voters in this manner.

Under REFORMS, each constituent would have four members of Congress in four different functionally specialized houses, instead of one member in a geographically based and nonfunctionally specialized single house as under the current system. Four houses are convenient and feasible, but the number four has been selected primarily for illustration. The actual number of houses could expand with growth in the scope of government. The crucial point is that a number of functionally specialized as well as geographically based houses be created.

Each of the four members of Congress from a single geographic district would sit in a different House of Representatives and would have legislative responsibility for a specific policy domain. The multiple, functionally specialized houses allow the voters to disaggregate the electoral expression of their preferences for different policies. Voters dissatisfied with defense policy, for example, could express that dissatisfaction directly through their votes for their representative for the house which deals with defense. Similarly, other voters anxious to improve the education system could also express that desire electorally through their votes for their representative in the house which deals with education.

How the whole universe of policy domains would be divided among the houses to give each house mutually exclusive jurisdiction over some policy areas and not over others is also arbitrary and secondary to the main point of multifunctionally specialized houses. Most crucial is the fact that the policy universe would be divided among several houses and that external functional specialization would occur. While jurisdictional fights between houses would no doubt occur under REFORMS, jurisdictional conflicts occur between committees under the current system of internal functional specialization as well and are resolved by the House leadership. Under REFORMS, jurisdictional disputes between the multiple Houses of Representatives might be resolved by the Senate.

Supporters of the current system might levy two criticisms at this multihouse feature of REFORMS. One criticism is that voters are apathetic about issues and do not have preferences to express on specific policy areas, voting instead on candidate appeal and personality. A valid counter-argument to this charge is that voters who are informed about issues in the current system have little or no method of expressing their preferences. Being informed is not cost-effective for voters without special political connections or personal links to politicians. Much like the proverbial chicken and egg dilemma, the causal link between citizen issue ignorance and structurally induced impotence of voters in expressing issue preference is unclear. Clearly the ignorance does not cause the impotence since the latter is structurally induced. A more plausible causal link is that structural impotence induces, creates, or at least perpetuates voter ignorance and apathy on issues. Removing the structurally induced impotence may remove the driving force behind voter apathy on issues.

A second criticism by supporters of the status quo is that modern voters who can select daily from a complex and varied array of consumer products will be cognitively unable to deal with the selection of four different representatives for the functionally specialized houses over a four year time period. This criticism is invalid for two reasons. First, it significantly underestimates the cognitive ability of the modern U.S. voters, over half of whom have graduated from high school and an increasing number of whom are college educated. Secondly, it underestimates the incentives voters will have to be informed under REFORMS, since their functionally disaggregated votes will more clearly express their individual preferences.

One method for handling the election of the four members of four different houses from the same congressional district is for each district to elect a single member to a different house each year. A congressional election would be held every year in every district. This sequencing of elections annually would prevent voter information overload in any year, since even average voters can be informed about one election per year. Further, at the house level, the number of seats up for reelection could be staggered across the four years so that every year, one fourth of each house would be standing for reelection. These staggered elections would continue the philosophy of the Founding Fathers of preventing a single minority interest from capturing the entire government apparatus or even any major part of the government apparatus at once. Furthermore, there would be elections for some seats in each house each year, so, every year, in at least some part of the country, an electoral forum would be provided for debating the current policy issues in that functional area.

Supporters of the status quo will charge that voters will become overloaded with so much electoral activity. However, politics is a continous activity today as reelection campaigns for Congress, especially the House of Representatives, begin almost immediately after the previous election. Under the current system, campaigns often focus on the personalities of the candidates and the horse race aspects of the electoral race rather than on meaningful policy debate. Under REFORMS, candidates would have stronger incentives to focus their campaign activities on policy issues.

Shift to Single-house Passage of Legislation

Political scientists have argued that parliamentary systems are more efficient and accountable because often legislation must pass through only one house. This is particularly true of single-member-district, British-based parliamentary systems where the major decision-making body is the House of Commons, and the House of Lords fulfills only an auxiliary research and delaying role. It is less true of some proportional representation systems such as in West Germany where two houses have meaningful input into national legislative decisions. In the U.S. system, bicameralism not only creates delays in the passage of legislation, but also may encourage one house to act less responsibly than the other. The first house to address an issue may spend or act extravagantly to win constituency and interest group support for electoral reasons, relying on the second house to rectify its profligacy. The subsequent discrepancy between the bills of the two houses further lengthens the legislative process by requiring a joint house conference committee and subsequent bicameral approval of the conference report.

Bicameralism does not necessarily increase democracy because it diminishes accountability and effectiveness by providing several more decision points at which powerful special interests may thwart legislation which actually reflects majority opinion. Bicameralism then serves the interests of powerful, often economically based minority factions, which can muster the money, knowledge and resources to engage in machinations in the halls of Congress. Bicameralism does nothing to serve the interests of minority interests which have traditionally been excluded from societal power structures, and often results in thwarting majority rule.

Some obstacles should be established to poorly conceived and hastily passed legislation. Under the current system, bicameralism provided one such obstacle. Under REFORMS, an internal legislative veto of the Senate over the functionally specialized houses would allow less controversial legislation to pass expeditiously while simultaneously creating an additional forum in the Senate for controversial legislation. The Senate would only consider legislation from each of the specialized houses that it wished to veto. A Senate veto would require an extraordinary two-thirds majority. Most legislation would presumably not be debated in the Senate but would go directly to the president for approval. Provisions for an internal legislative override of the Senate veto might be arranged, such as a three-fourths override vote in the originating, functionally specialized house.

Establishing Hierarchical Accountability between the Senate and the Functionally Specialized Houses

The presentation of REFORMS may conjur up images of a series of independent legislative houses, each fighting over jurisdictional turf and passing laws in blithe ignorance of each other's deliberations and actions. However, REFORMS actually uses the bureaucratic principles of coordination and accountability to prevent chaos. Under the current system, conflicts over committee jurisdictions and control of legislative agendas are handled internally by the leadership of each house. The drawback to this internal method is that congressional leaders have limited resources to enforce coordination or expedite deliberations since the reelection of members of Congress is controlled by their constituencies, not congressional leadership.

Currently budgetary allocations, tradeoffs and priority setting are handled by budget and appropriations subcommittees and committees, while taxes and revenues are handled by the House Ways and Means Committee and the Senate Finance Committee. These functions are extremely important, but voters currently suffer from their internal delegation since many voters do not have representatives or senators who sit on these important committees. The problem of effective voter

disenfranchisement from issue areas due to internal functional specialization under the current system becomes severe when the issues of
concern are as far-reaching as setting national agendas, deciding who
pays what public revenues and determining who receives what public
services. Under REFORMS, each person would be represented directly
in these important decisions.

One way to achieve universal voter representation in these important
agenda-setting, finance and spending decisions is to make the U.S. Senate a "super Senate" responsible for these functions. The Senate would
acquire major responsibilities that span substantive legislative areas, including settling jurisdictional disputes among the functionally differentiated houses, raising taxes and handling revenues, assuming the primary responsibility for overall economic stability and growth, and for
manipulating Keynesian economic control. The new "super Senate"
would also have responsibility for establishing a congressional budget
with total budget expenditures and binding expenditure ceilings for
each of the major legislative areas handled by the functionally specialized house, approving or disapproving treaties and approving or disapproving executive and judicial branch appointments.

In turn, each of the fuctionally differentiated houses would pass legislation in their specified areas, oversee bureaucracies and spend monies within the Senate-established ceilings in their own respective policy
domains. In this fashion, hierarchical coordination and accountability
would be maintained, yet democratic principles would be further implemented, and voter control would be enhanced, since each voter would
have representatives directly accountable for all major areas, including
the crucial areas of taxing, spending, and setting national priorities.

EVALUATING THE ALTERNATIVE CONGRESSIONAL STRUCTURE

Just as the current congressional structure may be evaluated by the
desirable criteria for a national legislature, the Representational Efficient Functional Open Responsive Multi-cameral System, REFORMS,
may also be evaluated by the same criteria.

Promotes a National View and National Interests

REFORMS supports national interests and a national view in several
ways. The Senate becomes a "super Senate" in a hierarchical ordering,
in contrast with the functionally specialized houses. Since senators would
be selected from either larger senatorial districts or regions, they would
presumably be less narrowly focused and less parochial than representatives selected from smaller geographic regions. The vantage point of

senators would be particularly broadened if large regions were the basis for Senate representation. Nor would members of the various houses necessarily be as parochial as current members of the House of Representatives. Members of the functionally specialized houses would have particular policy concerns which would span local geographic differences. In other words, functional specialization would diminish some parochialism engendered by geographic representation alone.

Under REFORMS, the Senate could assume more of a national view since its primary duties would be national agenda setting and managing the overall economy and government spending and taxing levels. Unlike the present situation, the Senate would not be burdened by the need to examine every issue addressed by Congress, but rather could select those controversial issues with implications for the whole nation. This specialization by the Senate would allow it the time and resources to focus more attention on national priority setting, something often neglected in the current system.

Promotes Efficiency and Responsibility

One of the great strengths of REFORMS is that it would promote efficiency and responsibility. The ability to plan for the future is enhanced, since functional specialization frees members of the specialized houses from being so burdened that there is little time for planning. Since most substantive legislation must pass through only one house—the functionally specialized house in which it originates—the efficiency and speed with which proposed statutes are handled would be increased. Functional specialization allows members to build up policy expertise in substantive areas to an even greater extent than is possible in the current system, thereby promoting further efficiency. Greater policy expertise would also allow members of the functionally specialized houses to better anticipate problems and engage in planning. The fact that ill-conceived policies could clearly be identified with the house in which they originated would provide a strong incentive for members of the functionally specialized houses to act responsibly.

Approximates Citizen Preferences

Citizens could disaggregate their policy votes across functional areas under REFORMS, a preference expression now denied them under the current Congressional structure. With more representatives to provide constituent service for the same number of constituents, representatives could devote more time to examining and implementing citizen preferences through legislation. Since there could be as few as four functionally specialized houses, citizens would still have to compress some preferences into a single vote for a representative from their Congressional district. However, the ability of citizens to express substantive policy preferences would be at least four times as great as under the status quo. Furthermore, by voting for their senators, all citizens could clearly express satisfaction or dissatisfaction with overall national priorities and taxing and spending levels, an expression also denied most voters under the current system.

Promotes Accountability

REFORMS enhances accountability for both the institution and the individual legislator. Since one fourth of each functionally specialized house, as well as one fourth of the Senate, would be standing for reelection every year, each house would have a forum for debating new legislative issues on the national agenda within its policy domain. Since citizens could effectively express their preferences electorally, they would be provided with a mechanism to hold representatives to a higher level of accountability than currently exists. Under the current system single-issue voting is an anathema since voters must aggregate all preferences in one geographically based vote. The implications of single-issue voting under the current system are that legislators are not held accountable for issues where citizen preferences are less intense, but rather are accountable only for that issue where citizen preferences are greater.

Creating a "super Senate" which deals with major issues of taxing and spending gives citizens more direct control over mounting federal deficits. Citizens who are concerned with rising national debt and ballooning annual deficits could vote for senators who campaign on a platform of curbing deficits. The designation of these functions to the Senate gives citizens a clearer sense of who is to be held accountable for fiscal policies.

Under REFORMS, functionally specialized representatives would be held accountable across the array of policy issues. REFORMS also undercuts the confusion in which legislators often intentionally or unintentionally engage in the current decentralized, nonfunctionally specialized institution. With functionally specialized houses and a smaller issue domain, representatives would be more clearly identified in voters' minds with specific issue positions, and would be less able to avoid accountability.

Encourages Citizen Participation

Citizens would have more incentive to be informed about public issues under REFORMS than under the current congressional structure, since their votes for senators and members of the functionally specialized houses could be used to express policy preferences directly. Previous political studies have clearly shown a link between issue awareness and education levels on the one hand and citizen participation on the other. The number of positions in the national legislature would increase by a factor of at least four, so more citizens would be encouraged to participate directly in politics by running for elected office. Citizen education would become a more important function for members of the multiple houses than it currently is for members of the House and Senate, since under REFORMS, the total amount of resources available for citizen education, both in terms of numbers of representatives and congressional staff, would be likely to increase. Furthermore, representatives would be expected to be knowledgeable on the policy areas covered by their houses and would be under some electoral pressure to demonstrate this expertise.

CONCLUSIONS

Although REFORMS is a radical departure in some ways from the current congressional system (in other ways it is like the application of Keynesian fiscal intervention to free enterprise), like Keynesian economics, REFORMS is a conservative revolution designed to bolster and save the constitutional system it proposes to change. In many ways, REFORMS is less radical than the often discussed proposals to move toward a parliamentary government. REFORMS retains many structural features and principles created by the Founding Fathers. Unlike a shift to a parliamentary system, REFORMS retains the presidential form of government, since the structure and office of the presidency remain unchanged. By contrast, a shift to a parliamentary system would abolish the presidency and merge executive and legislative power in the office of the prime minister.

REFORMS also retains the principles of checks and balances, separation of powers, and federalism. One major check on both the executive and legislative branches, the independent power of the judiciary, would also remain unchanged. The judiciary could continue to function as a defender of minority rights much as it does under the current system. The three branches of government created in the 1787 Constitution would remain. The primary intent of REFORMS is not to alter relationships between branches or levels of government but rather to restructure the national legislative branch to restore some of its lost power and make Congress simultaneously more efficient and more responsive to the people.

Under REFORMS, decentralized state and local government would remain intact. These reforms would not abolish states nor change their current constitutionally defined functions. Rather, states, with their great variations in population, would no longer be the basis for selecting U.S. senators. The process of changing the basis for selecting U.S. senators from one of malapportionment and violation of the democratic principle of one-person one-vote to one of equal apportionment and implementation of one-person one-vote would not handicap or significantly change the national powers of Congress. Rather, this process would be similar in impact to the court-ordered reapportionment of state legislatures in the 1960s to conform with the principle of one-person one-vote. That reapportionment did not significantly alter state legislative power vis-à-vis other branches of state government or the federal government.

Unless proportional representation is adopted for the Senate, single-member districts in both the Senate and the fuctionally specialized houses will continue to support the maintenance of the current two-party system. Political party organizations will continue to flourish at both the national and state levels. At the national level, REFORMS will provide strong incentives for political parties to become more responsible, since citizens can disaggregate their votes on major policy issues. Due to the enhanced ability of citizens to electorally express their policy preferences, party platforms will become more specific. Failure to fulfill promises included in party platforms may more readily become a political issue in subsequent campaigns.

What is the possibility of enacting REFORMS? REFORMS would require a major Constitutional amendment to Article I which specifies the current bicameral structure of Congress. REFORMS would also require the amending of Article V, a part of which holds that there must be equal state representation in the Senate. Critics of REFORMS might charge that Congress would lose its ability to determine its own organizational structure. Supporters would counter that currently, certain organizational features of Congress are not within congressional control but are set in the Constitution, such as the number of houses, the most rudimentary features of specialization between the houses and the necessity of legislative approval by both the House and the Senate. REFORMS would set no more structural features of Congress in constitutional concrete than are set under the current structure. The Senate and the functionally specialized houses would still have latitude to determine the rules of their own proceedings, to develop internal committee structures and to specify the criteria for leadership and committee chair selections.

To pass through the constitutional amendment process of congressional initiation by two-thirds of the House and the Senate and ratification by three-fourths of the state legislatures, would require considerable consensus that the structural features contained in REFORMS are beneficial for the nation as a whole and for the immediately affected political representatives. While such a consensus would be difficult to obtain, Congress has undergone major internal reforms in the past. As Congress becomes less and less able to deal with major national crises, the conservative revolution incorporated in REFORMS may become a desirable alternative to stagnation, lack of long-term planning, crisis development of public policy and increasing citizen alienation. Such revisions in our rarely amended two hundred-year-old Constitution may create the flexibility and resilience that it needs not just to survive, but to thrive into the twenty-first century. The twenty-first century will most likely be an era of even more rapid technological change and greater tension over scarce world resources than ever. The U.S. Constitution is under pressure. The time to change and meet those pressures is now.

REFERENCES

Blondel, J. 1973. *Comparative Legislatures.* Englewood Cliffs, N.J.: Prentice-Hall, Inc.
Burns, James MacGregor. 1966. *Congress On Trial: The Legislative Process and the Administrative State.* New York: Gordian Press, Inc.
Carpenter, William Seal. 1925. *Democracy and Representation.* Princeton, N.J.: Princeton University Press.
Davidson, Roger H., and Walter J. Oleszek. 1985. *Congress and Its Members.* 2nd ed. Washington, D.C.: Congressional Quarterly, Inc.
Fenno, Richard F. 1978. *Home Style: House Members and Their Districts.* Boston: Little, Brown, and Co.
Ford, Henry J. 1924. *Representative Government.* New York: Henry Holt and Co.
Griffith, Ernest S., and Francis R. Valeo. 1975. *Congress: Its Contemporary Role.* 5th ed. New York: New York University Press.
Harris, Fred R., and Paul L. Hain. 1983. *America's Legislative Processes: Congress and the States.* Glenview, Ill.: Scott, Foresman and Co.
Harris, Joseph P. 1972. *Congress and the Legislative Process.* New York: McGraw-Hill Co.
Malbin, Michael J. 1980. *Unelected Representatives: Congressional Staff and the Future of Representative Government.* New York: Basic Books.
Mansbridge, Jane J. 1983. *Beyond Adversary Democracy.* Chicago: University of Chicago Press.
Mayhew, David. 1974. *Congress: The Electoral Connection.* New Haven: Yale University Press.
Miller, Warren, and Donald Stokes. 1963. "Constituency Influence in Congress." *American Political Science Review* 57:45–56.
Pitkin, Hanna Fenichel. 1967. *The Concept of Representation.* Berkeley, Calif.: University of California Press.
Rieselbach, Leroy N. 1986. *Congressional Reform.* Washington, D.C.: Congressional Quarterly Press, Inc.

Smith, Steven S., and Christopher J. Deering. 1984. *Committees in Congress.* Washington, D.C.: Congressional Quarterly, Inc.

Vogler, David J. 1983. *The Politics of Congress.* 4th ed. Boston: Allyn and Bacon, Inc.

Vogler, David J., and Sidney R. Waldman. 1985. *Congress and Democracy.* Washington, D.C.: Congressional Quarterly Press.

Wolin, Sheldon S. 1960. *Politics and Vision.* Boston: Little, Brown, and Co.

Bibliography

Abraham, Henry J. 1983. *The Judiciary: The Supreme Court and the Governmental Process.* 6th ed. Boston: Allyn and Bacon, Inc.

———. 1980. *The Judicial Process.* 4th ed. New York: Oxford University Press.

Almond, Gabriel A., and Sidney Verba. 1963. *The Civic Culture.* Princeton, N.J.: Princeton University Press.

Bailey, Thomas A., and David M. Kennedy. 1983. *The American Pageant.* 7th ed. Lexington, Mass.: D. C. Heath and Co.

Baker, Gordon E. 1955. *Rural Versus Urban Political Power: The Nature and Consequences of Unbalanced Representation.* Garden City, N.Y.: Doubleday and Co., Inc.

Baradat, Leon P. 1979. *Political Ideologies.* Englewood Cliffs, N.J.: Prentice-Hall, Inc.

Barber, Sotirios A. 1984. *On What the Constitution Means.* Baltimore: Johns Hopkins University Press.

Barger, Harold. 1984. *The Impossible Presidency.* Glenview, Ill.: Scott, Foresman and Company.

Bartholowmew, Paul C. 1978. *American Consitutional Law (Volume II): Limitations on Government.* 2nd ed. Totowa, N.J.: Littlefield, Adams and Co.

Baum, Lawrence, 1981. *The Supreme Court.* Washington, D.C.: Congressional Quarterly Press.

Beard, Charles. 1913. *An Economic Interpretation of the Constitution of the United States.* New York: Macmillan.

Beck, James. M. 1924. *The Constitution of the United States: Yesterday, Today—and Tomorrow?* New York: George H. Doran Co.

Beer, Samuel H., Edward M. Kennedy, Helen F. Ladd, Norman Y. Mineta, Charles Royer, and Lester M. Salamon. 1982. *Federalism: Making the System Work.* Washington, D.C.: Center for National Policy.

Berelson, B. R., P. F. Lazarsfeld, and W. N. McPhee. 1956. *Voting.* Chicago: University of Chicago Press.

Blondel, J. 1973. *Comparative Legislatures.* Englewood Cliffs, N.J.: Prentice-Hall, Inc.

Borthwick, R. L. 1984. "Parliament." *British Politics in Perspective.* R. L. Borthwick and J. E. Spence, eds. New York: St. Martin's Press.

Bowers, Robert T. 1973. *Television and the Public.* New York: Holt, Rinehart and Winston, Inc.

Bowman, Ann O'M., and Richard C. Kearney. 1986. *The Resurgence of the States.* Englewood Cliffs, N.J.: Prentice-Hall, Inc.

Broder, David. 1971. *The Party's Over.* New York: Harper and Row.

Brown, Everett S. 1935. "The Ratification of the Twenty-First Amendment." *American Political Science Review* 29:1008–1009.

Brown, Robert E. 1956. *Charles Beard and the Constitution: A Critical Analysis of an Economic Interpretation of the Constitution.* Princeton, N.J.: Princeton University Press.

Burke, Edmund. 1949. *Burke's Politics.* Ross J. S. Hoffman and Paul Levack, eds. New York: Alfred A. Knopf, Inc.

Burns, James MacGregor. 1963. *The Deadlock of Democracy: Four-Party Politics in America.* Englewood Cliffs, N.J.: Prentice-Hall, Inc.

Burns, James MacGregor. 1966. *Congress On Trial: The Legislative Process and the Administrative State.* New York: Gordian Press, Inc.

———. 1982. *The Vineyard of Liberty: The American Experiment.* New York: Alfred A. Knopf.

Burns, James MacGregor, J. W. Peltason, and Thomas E. Cronin. 1985. *Government by the People.* 12th alt. ed. Englewood Cliffs, N.J.: Prentice-Hall Inc.

Carpenter, William Seal. 1925. *Democracy and Representation.* Princeton, N.J.: Princeton University Press.

Carr, Robert K. 1970. *The Supreme Court and Judicial Review.* Westport, Conn.: Greenwood Press.

Champagne, Antony, and Stuart S. Nagel. 1982. "The Advocates of Restraint: Holmes, Brandeis, Stone, and Frankfurter." In *Supreme Court Activism and Restraint.* Stephen C. Halpern and Charles M. Lamb, eds. Lexington, Mass.: D.C. Heath and Co.

Chelf, Carl P. 1977. *Congress in the American System.* Chicago: Nelson-Hall, Inc.

Colella, Cynthia Cates. 1986. "The United States Supreme Court and and Intergovernmental Relations." *American Intergovernmental Relations Today: Perspectives and Controversies.* Robert Jay Dilger, ed. Englewood Cliffs, N.J.: Prentice-Hall, Inc.

Collie, Melissa P., and David W. Brady. 1985. "The Decline of Partisan Voting Coalitions in the House of Representatives." In *Congress Reconsidered.* 3rd ed. Lawrence C. Dodd and Bruce I. Oppenheimer, eds. Washington, D.C.: Congressional Quarterly Press.

Comstock, George. 1980. *Television in America.* Beverly Hills, Calif.: Sage Publications.

Crotty, William. 1985. *The Party Game.* New York: W. H. Freeman and Co.

Dahl, Robert. 1956. *A Preface to Democratic Theory.* Chicago: University of Chicago Press.

Davidson, Roger H. 1981. "Subcommittee Government: New Channels for Policy Making." In *The New Congress.* Thomas E. Mann and Norman J. Ornstein, eds. Washington, D.C.: American Enterprise Institute for Public Policy Research.

Davidson, Roger H., and Walter J. Oleszek. 1985. *Congress and Its Members.* 2nd ed. Washington, D.C.: Congressional Quarterly, Inc.

Dawson, Richard E., and James A Robinson. 1963. "Inter-Party Competition, Economic Variables, and Welfare Policies in the American States." *Journal of Politics* 25:265–289.

Dellinger, Walter. 1986. "The Process of Constitutional Amendment: Law, History, and Politics." *News for Teachers of Political Science* 49:16–19.

Destler, I. M. 1985. "Executive-Congressional Conflict in Foreign Policy: Explaining It, Coping With It." In *Congress Reconsidered.* 3rd edition. Lawrence C. Dodd and Bruce I. Oppenheimer, eds. Washington, D.C.: Congressional Quarterly Press.

Deutsch, Karl W., Jorge Il Dominguez and Hugh Heclo. 1981. *Comparative Government: Politics of Industrialized and Developing Nations.* Boston: Houghton Mifflin Co.

Dilger, Robert Jay, ed. 1986. *American Intergovernmental Relations Today: Perspectives and Controversies.* Englewood Cliffs, N.J.: Prentice-Hall, Inc.

Downs, Anthony. 1957. *An Economic Theory of Democracy.* New York: Harper and Row.

Drucker, H. M. 1984. "The Evolution of the Political Parties." *British Politics in Perspective.* R. L. Borthwick and J. E. Spence, eds. New York: St. Martin's Press.

———. 1979. "Two-Party Politics in Britain." *Multi-Party Britain.* H. M. Drucker, ed. New York: Praeger.

Dye, Thomas. 1966. *Politics, Economics, and the Public: Policy Outcomes in the American States.* Chicago: Rand McNally.

Dyson, James W., and John W. Soule. 1970. "Congressional Committee Behavior on Roll Call Votes: The U.S. House of Representatives, 1955–1964." *Midwest Journal of Political Science* 14:626–647.

Earle, Valerie A. 1984. "The Federal Structure." In *Founding Principles of American Government: Two Hundred Years of Democracy on Trial.* George J. Graham, Jr. and Scarlett G. Graham, eds. Chatham, N.J.: Chatham House Publishers.

Easton, David. 1966. *The Political System: An Inquiry into the State of Political Science.* New York: Alfred A. Knopf.

Edel, Wilbur. 1981. *A Constitutional Convention: Threat or Challenge?* New York: Praeger Publishers.

Edelman, Murray. 1964. *The Symbolic Uses of Politics.* Urbana, Ill.: University of Illinois Press.

Edwards, George C., III. 1980. *Presidential Influence in Congress.* San Francisco: W. H. Freeman and Co.

Eidelberg, Paul. 1968. *The Philosophy of the American Constitution: A Reinterpretation of the Intentions of the Founding Fathers.* New York: Free Press.

Elazar, Daniel J. 1984. *American Federalism: A View from the States.* 3rd ed. New York: Harper and Row.

Elliott, William Y. 1935. *The Need for Constitutional Reform.* New York: McGraw-Hill.

Ely, John Hart. 1980. *Democracy and Distrust: A Theory of Judicial Review.* Cambridge, Mass.: Harvard University Press.

Epstein, Leon D. 1980. "What Happened to the British Party Model?" *American Political Science Review* 74:9–22.

Fallon, Richard H. Jr., and Paul C. Weiler. 1984. "*Firefighters v. Stotts:* Conflicting Models of Racial Justice." In *1984: The Supreme Court Review.* Philip B. Kurland, Gerhard Casper, and Dennis J. Hutchinson, eds. Chicago: University of Chicago Press.

Fenno, Richard. 1973. *Congressmen in Committees.* Boston: Little, Brown and Co.

———. 1978. *Home Style: House Members and Their Districts.* Boston: Little, Brown and Co.

Finletter, Thomas K. 1945. *Can Representative Government Do the Job?* New York: Reynal & Hitchcock.

Fiorina, Morris P. 1977. *Congress: Keystone of the Washington Establishment.* New Haven: Yale University Press.

Fisher, Louis. 1981. *The Politics of Shared Power: Congress and the Executive.* Washington, D.C.: Congressional Quarterly Press.

Flanigan, William H., and Nancy H. Zingale. 1983. *Political Behavior of the American Electorate.* 5th ed. Boston: Allyn and Bacon, Inc.

Ford, Henry J. 1924. *Representative Government.* New York: Henry Holt and Co.

Friedman, Milton. 1962. *Capitalism and Freedom.* Chicago: University of Chicago Press.

Friedman, Milton, and Rose Friedman. 1980. *Free to Choose.* New York: Harcourt Brace Jovanovich.

Friedrich, Carl J. 1950. *Constitutional Government and Democracy.* Boston: Ginn and Co.

Friendly, Fred W., and Martha J. H. Elliott. 1984. *The Constitution: That Delicate Balance.* New York: Random House.

Fry, Brian R., and Richard F. Winters. 1970. "The Politics of Redistribution." *American Political Science Review* 64:508–522.

Galbraith, John Kenneth. 1958. *The Affluent Society.* New York: The New American Library.

———. 1956. *American Capitalism: The Concept of Countervailing Power.* Boston: Houghton Mifflin.

Glendening, Parris, and Mavis Mann Reeves. 1977. *Pragmatic Federalism: An Intergovernmental View of American Government.* Pacific Palisades, Calif.: Palisades Publishers.

Graglia, Lina A. 1982. "In Defense of Judicial Restraint." In *Supreme Court Activism and Restraint.* Stephen C. Halpern and Charles M. Lamb, eds. Lexington, Mass.: D.C. Heath and Co.

Graham, George J., Jr., and Scarlett G. Graham. 1984. *Founding Principles of American Government: Two Hundred Years of Democracy on Trial.* Chatham, N.J.: Chatham House Publishers, Inc.

Gregory, Roy. 1980. "Executive Power and Constituency Representation in United Kingdom Politics." *Political Studies* 28:63–83.

Griffith, Ernest S., and Francis R. Valeo. 1975. *Congress: Its Contemporary Role.* 5th ed. New York: New York University Press.

Groth, Alexander J. 1970. "Britain and America: Some Requisites of Executive Leadership Compared." *Political Science Quarterly* 85:217–239.

Hagopian, Mark N. 1985. *Ideals and Ideologies of Modern Politics.* New York: Longman, Inc.

Hamilton, Alexander, James Madison, and John Jay. 1961. *The Federalist Papers.* Introduced by Clinton Rossiter. New York: The New American Library.

Hardin, Charles M. 1974. *Presidential Power and Accountability: Toward a New Constitution.* Chicago: The University of Chicago Press.

Hardy, Leroy, Alan Heslop, and Stuart Anderson. 1981. *Reapportionment Politics: The History of Redistricting in the 50 States.* Beverly Hills, Calif.: Sage Publications.

Harris, Fred R., and Paul L. Hain. 1983. *America's Legislative Processes: Congress and the States.* Glenview, Ill.: Scott, Foresman and Co.

Harris, Joseph P. 1972. *Congress and the Legislative Process.* New York: McGraw-Hill Co.

Hawkins, Robert B., Jr., ed. 1982. *American Federalism: A New Partnership for the Republic.* San Francisco: Institute for Contemporary Studies.

Herson, Lawrence J. R. 1984. *The Politics of Ideas: Political Theory and American Public Policy.* Homewood, Ill.: Dorsey Press.

Hirschfield, Robert S. 1962. *The Constitution and the Court: The Development of the Basic Law Through Judicial Interpretation.* New York: Random House.

Hofferbert, Richard. 1968. "Socio-economic Dimensions of the American States: 1890–1980." *Midwest Journal of Political Science* 12:401–418.

Hofstadter, Richard, William Miller, and Daniel Aaron. 1967. *The United States: The History of a Republic.* Englewood Cliffs, N.J.: Prentice-Hall, Inc.

Holcombe, Arthur N. 1950. *Our More Perfect Union: From Eighteenth Century Principles to Twentieth Century Practice.* Cambridge, Mass.: Harvard University Press.

Hyneman, Charles S. 1963. *The Supreme Court on Trial.* New York: Atherton Press.

Jacobson, Gary C. 1983. *The Politics of Congressional Elections.* Boston: Little, Brown and Co.

Jeffreys-Jones, Rhodri, and Bruce Collins. 1983. *The Growth of Federal Power in American History.* Edinburgh: Scottish Academic Press.

Jennings, Edward T. 1979. "Competition, Constituencies, and Welfare Policies." *American Political Science Review* 73:414–429.

Jewell, Malcolm E., ed. 1962. *The Politics of Reapportionment.* New York: Atherton Press.

Jewell, Malcolm E., and Samuel C. Patterson. 1986. *The Legislative Process in the United States.* 4th ed. New York: Random House.

Johnson, Charles A., and Bradley C. Canon. 1984. *Judicial Policies: Implementation and Impact.* Washington, D.C.: Congressional Quarterly Press.

Jones, Charles O., and Robert D. Thomas, eds. 1976. *Public Policy Making in a Federal System.* Beverly Hills, Calif.: Sage Publications.

Kelly, Alfred H., and Winfred A. Harbison. 1976. *The American Constitution: Its Origin and Development.* 5th ed. New York: W. W. Norton and Co.

Key, V. O., Jr. 1949. *Southern Politics in State and Nation.* New York: Random House.

Kilpatrick, James J. 1986. "One More Political Thicket." *The State.* Columbia, S.C. July 6.

Kincaid, John, ed. 1982. *Political Culture, Public Policy, and the American States.* Philadelphia: Institute for the Study of Human Issues.

Kreml, William P. 1985. *A Model of Politics.* New York: Macmillan Publishing Co.

Kurland, Philip B. 1971. *Mr. Justice Frankfurter and the Supreme Court.* Chicago: University of Chicago Press.

Lee, Eugene C. 1978. "California." *Referendums: A Comparative Study of Practice and Theory.* David Butler and Austin Ranney, eds. Washington, D.C.: American Enterprise Institute for Public Policy Research.

Lees, John D., and Richard Kimber, eds. 1972. *Political Parties in Modern Britain: An Organizational and Functional Guide.* London: Routledge and Kegan Paul.

Lepawsky, Albert. 1977. "Reconstituted Presidency and Resurgent Congress." In *The Prospect for Presidental-Congressional Government.* Albert Lepawsky, ed. University of California, Berkeley: Institute of Governmental Studies.

Light, Paul C. 1983. *The President's Agenda.* Baltimore: The Johns Hopkins University Press.

Livingston, William S. 1956. *Federalism and Constitutional Change.* Oxford; Clarendon Press.

Lowi, Theodore J. 1979. *The End of Liberalism: The Second Republic of the United States.* 2nd ed. New York: W. W. Norton and Co.

Lundberg, Ferdinand. 1980. *Cracks in the Constitution.* Secaucus, N.J.: Lyle Stuart, Inc.

McCoy, Charles Allan. 1982. *Contempory ISMs: A Political Economy Perspective.* New York: Franklin Watts.

McDonald, Forrest. 1958. *We the People: The Economic Origins of the Constitution.* Chicago: University of Chicago Press.

McKay, Robert B. 1965. *Reapportionment: The Law and Politics of Equal Representation.* New York: The Twentieth Century Fund.

McLaughlin, Andrew C. 1935. *A Constitutional History of the United States.* New York: Appleton-Century-Crofts Inc.

Macridis, Roy C. 1983. *Contemporary Political Ideologies: Movements and Regimes.* 2nd ed. Boston: Little, Brown & Co.

Magleby, David B. 1984. *Direct Legislation: Voting on Ballot Propositions in the United States.* Baltimore: Johns Hopkins University Press.

Malbin, Michael J. 1980. *Unelected Representatives: Congressional Staff and the Future of Representative Government.* New York: Basic Books.

Mansbridge, Jane J. 1983. *Beyond Adversary Democracy.* Chicago: University of Chicago Press.

Mayhew, David R. 1974. *Congress: The Electoral Connection.* New Haven: Yale University Press.

Medcalf, Linda J., and Kenneth M. Dolbeae. 1985. *Neopolitics: American Political Ideas in the 1980s*. New York: Random House.

Meier, Hugo A. 1981. "Thomas Jefferson and a Democratic Technology." *Technology in America: A History of Individuals and Ideas*. Carroll W. Pursell, Jr, ed. Cambridge, Mass.: MIT Press.

Mendelson, Wallace. 1966. *The Constitution and the Supreme Court*. 2nd ed. New York: Dodd, Mead, and Co.

Miller, Arthur Selwyn. 1981. *Democratic Dictatorship: The Emergent Constitution of Control*. Westport, Conn.: Greenwood Press.

———. 1982. "In Defense of Judicial Activism." In *Supreme Court Activism and Restraint*. Stephen C. Halpern and Charles M. Lamb, eds. Lexington, Mass.: D.C. Heath and Co.

Miller, Warren, and Donald Stokes. 1963. "Constituency Influence in Congress." *American Political Science Review* 57:45–56.

Monroe, Alan D. 1975. *Public Opinion in America*. New York: Dodd, Mead and Co.

Morris, Richard B., William Greenleaf, and Robert H. Ferrell. 1971. *America: A History of the People*. Chicago: Rand McNally & Co.

Murphy, Paul L. 1972. *The Constitution in Crisis Times 1918–1969*. New York: Harper & Row, Publishers.

Murphy, Walter F., and C. Herman Pritchett. 1986. *Courts, Judges and Politics*. 4th ed. New York: Random House.

Musgrave, Richard B., and Peggy B. Musgrave. 1984. *Public Finance in Theory and Practice*. 4th ed. New York: McGraw-Hill.

Neustadt, Richard E. 1976. *Presidential Power: The Politics of Leadership With Reflections on Johnson and Nixon*. 2nd ed. New York: Wiley.

Ogburn, William F. 1950. *Social Change with Respect to Culture and Original Nature*. Rev. ed. New York: Viking Press.

Oleszek, Walter J. 1984. *Congressional Procedures and the Policy Process*. 2nd ed. Washington, D.C.: Congressional Quarterly Press.

Oliver, John W. 1956. *History of American Technology*. New York: The Ronald Press Co.

Olson, David M. 1980. *The Legislative Process: A Comparative Approach*. New York: Harper and Row, Publishers.

Page, Benjamin I. 1978. *Choices and Echoes in Presidential Elections: Rational Man and Electoral Democracy*. Chicago: University of Chicago.

Parenti, Michael. 1980. "The Constitution as an Elitist Document." In *How Democratic Is the Constitution?* Robert A. Goldwin and William A. Schambra, eds. Washington, D.C.: American Enterprise Institute.

Peabody, Robert L. 1985. "House Party Leadership: Stability and Change." In *Congress Reconsidered*. 3rd ed. Lawrence C. Dodd and Bruce I. Oppenheimer, eds. Washington, D.C.: Congressional Quarterly Press.

Pechman, Joseph A. 1977. *Federal Tax Policy*. 3rd ed. Washington, D.C.: Brookings Institution.

Pennock, J. Roland. 1962. "Agricultural Subsidies in England and the United States." *American Political Science Review* 56:621–633.

Pennock, J. Rolland. 1979. "Another Legislative Typology." *Journal of Politics* 41:1206–1213.

Pitkin, Hanna Fenichel. 1967. *The Concept of Representation*. Berkeley, Calif.: University of California Press.

Polsby, Nelson W. 1986. *Congress and the Presidency*. 4th edition. Englewood Cliffs, N.J.: Prentice-Hall.

Pomper, Gerald M., with Susan S. Lederman. 1980. *Elections in America: Control and Influence in Democratic Politics*. 2nd ed. New York: Longman.

Pritchett, C. Herman. 1971. *The American Constitutional System*. 3rd ed. New York: McGraw-Hill.

———. 1984. *Constitutional Civil Liberties*. Englewood Cliffs, N.J.: Prentice-Hall, Inc.

Putnam, Robert D. 1976. *The Comparative Study of Political Elites*. Englewood Cliffs, N.J.: Prentice-Hall.

———. 1982. *Governing*. 3rd ed. New York: Holt, Rinehart and Winston.

Ranney, Austin. 1978. "The United States of America." *Referendums: A Comparative Study of Practice and Theory*. David Butler and Austin Ranney, eds. Washington, D.C.: American Enterprise Institute for Public Policy Research.

Richter, Albert J. 1986. "The President and Intergovernmental Relations." *American Intergovernmental Relations Today: Perspectives and Controversies*. Robert Jay Dilger, ed. Englewood Cliffs, N.J.: Prentice-Hall, Inc.

Rieselbach, Leroy N. 1986. *Congressional Reform*. Washington, D.C.: Congressional Quarterly Press, Inc.

Rosenstone, Steven J., Roy L. Behr, and Edward H. Lazarus. 1984. *Third Parties in America: Citizen Response to Major Party Failure*. Princeton: Princeton University Press.

Rossiter, Clinton. 1968. *1787: The Grand Convention*. New York: Signet Classics.

Rottschaeffer, Henry. 1948. *The Constitution and Socio-Economic Change*. Ann Arbor, Mich.: University of Michigan Law School.

Rousseau, J. J. 1948. *The Social Contract*. London, England: Oxford University Press.

Rutland, Robert Allen. 1983. *The Ordeal of the Constitution: The Anti-Federalists and the Ratification Struggle of 1787–1788*. Boston: Northeastern University Press.

Sabato, Larry J. 1985. *PAC Power: Inside the World of Political Action Committees*. New York: W. W. Norton & Co.

San Miguel, Guadaloupe. 1982. "Mexican American Organizations and the Changing Politics of School Desegregation in Texas." *Social Science Quarterly* 63:701–715.

Sayre, Wallace S., and Judith H. Parris. 1970. *Voting for President: The Electoral College and the American Political System*. Washington, D.C.: The Brookings Institution.

Scarrow, Howard A. 1974. "Parliamentary and Presidential Government Compared." *Current History* 66:264–267; 272.

Schattsneider, E. E. 1942. *Party Government*. New York: Rinehart.

Schechter, Stephen L., ed. 1983. *Publius: Annual Review of American Federalism: 1981*. Lanham Md.: University Press of America.

Schick, Marvin. 1982. "Judicial Activism on the Supreme Court." In *Supreme*

Court Activism and Restraint. Stephen C. Halpern and Charles M. Lamb, eds. Lexington, Mass.: D.C. Heath and Co.

Schlesinger, Arthur M., Jr., ed. 1983. *The Almanac of American History.* New York: G. P. Putnam's Sons.

Schmidhauser, John R., ed. 1963. *Constitutional Law in the Political Process.* Chicago: Rand McNally & Company.

Sederberg, Peter C. 1977. *Interpreting Politics: An Introduction to Political Science.* San Francisco, Calif.: Chandler and Sharp.

Settel, Irving, and William Laas. 1969. *A Pictorial History of Television.* New York: Grosset and Dunlap, Inc.

Sinclair, Barbara. 1981. "Coping With Uncertainty: Building Coalitions in the House and the Senate." In *The New Congress.* Thomas E. Mann and Norman J. Ornstein, eds. Washington, D.C.: American Enterprise Institute for Public Policy Research.

Smith, Adam. 1952. *An Inquiry into the Nature and Causes of the Wealth of Nations.* Chicago, Ill.: Encyclopaedia Britannica, Inc.

Smith, Steven S., and Christopher J. Deering. 1984. *Committees in Congress.* Washington, D.C.: Congressional Quarterly, Inc.

Smithsonian Institution. 1978. *The Smithsonian Book of Invention.* New York: W. W. Norton and Co.

Sorauf, Frank J. 1984. *Party Politics in America.* 5th ed. Boston: Little, Brown and Co.

Southerland, Arthur E. 1965. *Constitutionalism in America: Origin and Evolution of Its Fundamental Ideas.* New York: Blaisdell Publishing Co.

Stone, Allan, and Richard P. Barke. 1985. *Governing The American Republic: Economics, Law, and Policies.* New York: St. Martin's Press.

Strong, C. F. 1963. *A History of Modern Political Constitutions.* New York: Capricorn Books.

Sundquist, James L. 1977. "Congress and the President: Enemies or Partners?" In *Congress Reconsidered.* Lawrence C. Dodd and Bruce I. Oppenheimer, eds. New York: Praeger Publishers.

———. 1986. *Constitutional Reform and Effective Government.* Washington, D.C.: Brookings Institution.

Swisher, Carl Brent. 1954. *American Constitutional Development.* 2nd ed. Cambridge, Mass.: Houghton-Mifflin Co.

Tamm, Edward A., and Paul C. Reardon. 1985. "The Office of the Chief Justice" In *Views From the Bench.* Mark A. Cannon and David M. O'Brien, eds. 1985. Chatham, N.J.: Chatham House Publishers Inc.

Tatalovich, Raymond, and Bryon W. Daynes. 1981. "From Abortion Reformed to Abortion Repealed: The Trauma of Abortion Politics." *Commonweal* 108:644–649.

Tinder, Glenn. 1979. *Political Thinking: The Perennial Questions.* 3rd ed. Boston: Little, Brown & Co.

Tugwell, Rexford G. 1976. *The Compromising of the Constitution (Early Departures).* Notre Dame, Ind.: University of Notre Dame Press.

Van Doren, Carl. 1948. *The Great Rehearsal: The Story of the Making and Ratifying of the Constitution of the United States.* New York: Viking Press.

Vogler, David J. 1983. *The Politics of Congress*. 4th ed. Boston: Allyn and Bacon, Inc.

Vogler, David J., and Sidney R. Waldman. 1985. *Congress and Democracy*. Washington, D.C.: Congressional Quarterly Press.

Vose, Clement E. 1972. *Constitutional Change: Amendment Politics and Supreme Court Litigation Since 1900*. Lexington, Mass.: D. C. Heath and Company.

Walker, David B. 1981. *Toward a Functioning of Federalism*. Cambridge, Mass.: Winthrop Publishers, Inc.

Waltz, Kenneth N. 1967. *Foreign Policy and Democratic Politics*. Boston: Little, Brown and Company.

Wasby, Stephen L. 1978. *The Supreme Court in the Federal Judicial System*. New York: Holt, Rinehart, and Winston.

Wheare, K.C. 1966. *Modern Constitutions*. London: Oxford University Press.

Wildavsky, Aaron, ed. 1967. *American Federalism in Perspective*. Boston: Little, Brown and Co.

Wills, Gary. 1982. *Explaining America: The Federalist*. New York: Penguin Books.

Winters, Richard. 1976. "Party Control and Policy Change." *American Journal of Political Science* 20:597–636.

Wolin, Sheldon S. 1960. *Politics and Vision*. Boston: Little, Brown, and Co.

Wright, Deil S. 1982. *Understanding Intergovernmental Relations*. 2nd ed. Monterey, Calif.: Brooks-Cole Publishing Co.

Index

About the Authors

MARCIA L. WHICKER is Professor of Public Administration at Virginia Commonwealth University, Richmond, Virginia. Until 1986 she was an Associate Professor in the Department of Government and International Studies at the University of South Carolina. Dr. Whicker has published widely in the fields of public administration and U.S. government. Her coauthored books include *U.S. Health Policy, Sex Role Changes* and *Perspectives on Taxing and Spending Limitations in the United States.*

RUTH ANN STRICKLAND is a Ph.D. candidate in Political Science at the University of South Carolina. Ms. Strickland has published two articles in the field of U.S. government and has contributed a chapter to a book on South Carolina state government.

RAYMOND A. MOORE is Professor of Government and International Studies at the University of South Carolina, Columbia. Dr. Moore has published widely in the field of U.S. foreign policy and international relations. He is the author of *National Building and the Pakistan Army,* the editor of *The United Nations Reconsidered* and has contributed to *The Carter Years, Peace and War in the Modern Age* and numerous journals.